Directory of Scotland's Organisations

compiled by
W.W. Baird and K.H.Whittles

Whittles Publishing

Typeset by
Whittles Publishing Services

Published by
Whittles Publishing,
Roseleigh House,
Latheronwheel,
Caithness, KW5 6DW,
Scotland, UK

ISBN 1-870325-27-3

Contents

Preface

At a time when Scotland is about to experience major changes in its structure of government, this book emphasises the strength and distinctiveness of Scottish life. Although first and foremost a reference book cataloguing organisations, associations and institutions which operate across Scotland, it gives a fascinating insight into the diversity of Scottish society.

Omitting only those organisations of a purely local nature, we have tried to be as thorough as possible but inevitably such a volume, particularly in its first edition, cannot be truly exhaustive. Nevertheless, with almost 2000 entries, this book goes a very long way in its coverage of Scotland's organisations and it is anticipated that it will prove useful to many people in different sectors of industry and commerce, finance, leisure and social activities, and not only in Scotland.

Each organisation has been invited to check its own entry and every effort has been made to ensure the accuracy of the data (an asterisk indicates that the organisation in question replied). Even so, it is possible that inaccuracies may have crept in to the entries and we hope that these will be brought to our attention for future editions. In addition, we would invite any organisation not represented here, who consider themselves suitable for inclusion in a future edition of the Directory, to photocopy the blank form near the index and send in their details.

We feel sure the Directory will be a valuable tool for many people in diverse occupations whether a single address or a list of organisations is sought.

W.W.B. & K.H.W.

From the Minister for Home Affairs, Devolution and Local Government   St. Andrew's House
Henry McLeish MP   Regent Road
                                                                        Edinburgh EH1 3DG

Telephone: 0131-244 4012
Fax: 0131-244 2756

I was pleased to be given the opportunity to provide a short foreword for this new publication 'The Directory of Scotland's Organisations' which brings together in one volume details of almost 2,000 organisations operating across Scotland.

The publication of this book occurs at a time of particular historic importance for Scotland as we move even closer towards the creation of the first Scottish Parliament for almost 300 years. The establishment of the Parliament recognises the strength of Scotland's national identity and the distinctive nature of many aspects of Scottish life. This is clearly reflected in the range and diversity of the organisations operating in Scotland whose details are contained in this book.

Publications such as this provide an important resource for businesses, the public sector and personal users enabling them to quickly identify and access the organisations they wish to contact. I believe that the accessibility of information from a wide variety of sources is important for the people of Scotland. Indeed, our aim through the creation of a Scottish Parliament and the other constitutional reforms that are being undertaken is to make Government more open, more accessible and more accountable to the people whom we serve.

HENRY McLEISH

AAA (Action Against Allergy) Scotland Branch

55 Manor Place,
Edinburgh, EH3 7EG
Tel: 0131-225-7503   Fax: 0131-225-7503

Mrs. Fabienne Smith, *Scottish Representative*

To give allergy information and advice by letter or telephone. *

ACTAC Scotland (Association of Community Technical Aid Centres Scotland Ltd)

20 St. Andrew's Street,
Glasgow, G1 5PD
Tel: 0141-552-6721

ASH: Action on Smoking and Health (Scotland)

8 Frederick Street,
Edinburgh, EH2 2HB
Tel: 0131-225-4725   Fax: 0131-220-6604

The Information Officer

ASLIB, Scottish Branch

SPUR, K/1,
Saughton House,
Broomhouse Drive,
Edinburgh, EH11 3XD
Tel: 0131-244-8164

Mr. Graham Cummins, *Secretary*

ASSIST (Scotland)

Norton Park,
Albion Road,
Edinburgh, EH7 5QY
Tel: 0131-475-2325   Fax: 0131-475-2326

Mr. Alun Evans

Develop and assist networks of advice, information, support and training for users, carers or professionals in advocacy, community mediation, empowerment or self-assessment. *

Abbeyfield Society for Scotland Limited

15 West Maitland Street,
Edinburgh, EH12 5EA
Tel: 0131-225-7801   Fax: 0131-225-7606

Mr. A.B. Fairweather

The provision of accommodation for elderly people in their own rooms in family-sized houses through the medium of voluntary local Abbeyfield Societies. *

Aberdeen Angus Cattle Society

6 King's Place,
Perth, PH2 8AD
Tel: 01738-622477   Fax: 01738-636436

Mr. R. Anderson, *Secretary* *

Aberlour Child Care Trust

36 Park Terrace,
Stirling, FK8 2JR
Tel: 01786-450335   Fax: 01786-473238

Mr. William Grieve, M.A., *Director*

*A Scottish charity caring for children, young
people and families throughout Scotland.* *

Accountant in Bankruptcy

George House,
126 George Street,
Edinburgh, EH2 4HH
Tel: 0131-473-4600

Mr. G. Leslie Kerr

*The Accountant in Bankruptcy is responsible for
the administration of personal bankruptcies
in Scotland; he acts as trustee on sequestrated
estates and supervises the actings of insolvency
practitioners elected or apppointed as trustees.
He maintains a register of all sequestrations
awarded in the Scottish courts and of
protected trust deeds.* *

Accounts Commission for Scotland

18 George Street,
Edinburgh, EH2 2QU
Tel: 0131-477-1234   Fax: 0131-477-4567

Mr. W.F. Magee, *Secretary*

*The Commission arranges for the independent
external audit of all health service and local
government bodies as well as police and fire
authorities. The Commission also identifies
and reports on good management practice
and value for money. The Commission
arranges for the annual publication of
performance information about councils.* *

Across Scotland

52 Westermains Avenue,
Kirkintilloch,
Glasgow, G66 1EH
Tel: 0141-777-6931   Fax: 0141-777-6931

Mr. Ken Stark

*Provides holidays and pilgrimages across
Europe for severely chronically sick persons.
Volunteer doctors, nurses and helpers are
always needed. Transport for disabled
persons can be arranged throughout the UK.* *

Action for ME in Scotland

PO Box 45,
Edinburgh

Mr. Neil Conn

Action for Sick Children - National Association for the Welfare of Children in Hospital (Scotland)

15 Smith's Place,
Edinburgh, EH6 8NT
Tel: 0131-553-6553   Fax: 0131-553-6553

Mr. George L. Allen, *Co-ordinator and
Company Secretary*

*NAWCH (National Association for the Welfare
of Children in Hospital) supports sick
children and their families and works to
ensure that high quality health services are
planned for them at home, in hospital and in
the community.* *

Action of Churches Together in Scotland (ACTS)

Scottish Churches House,
Kirk Street, Dunblane,
Perthshire, FK15 0AJ
Tel: 01786-823588 Fax: 01786-825844

Rev. Maxwell Craig, *General Secretary*

ACTS (Action of Churches Together in Scotland) is ten Scottish churches uniting in commitment to work together in the cause of Christ's kingdom. *

Action on Child Exploitation

53 Windsor Place,
Edinburgh, EH15 2AF
Tel: 0131-468-0087 Fax: 0131-468-0087

Dr. David Colvin, C.B.E., *Scottish Representative*

An organisation committed to campaigning against the exploitation of children in the UK and abroad particularly with regard to child pornography, sexual exploitation abroad by British paedophiles and for general improvement in child protection systems. *

Actionaid (Scotland)

Office 7, 3rd Floor,
Channel House,
Channel Street,
Galashiels, TD1 1BA
Tel: 01896-51231

Action Research Scotland

49 Marywood Square,
Glasgow, G41 2BN
Tel: 0141-422 2940 Fax: 0141-422 2940

Advice Service Capability Scotland (ASCS)

11 Ellersly Road,
Edinburgh, EH12 6HY
Tel: 0131-313-5510 Fax: 0131-346-1681

The Advice Workers

ASCS is a confidential, free enquiry service on all aspects of living with cerebral palsy. Our website is http://www.capability-scotland.org.uk. *

Advocates for Animals (AFA)

10 Queensferry Street,
Edinburgh, EH2 4PG
Tel: 0131-225-6039 Fax: 0131-220-6377

Mr. Les Ward, *Director*

AFA's objects are the protection of animals from cruelty, the prevention of the infliction of suffering and the abolition of vivisection. *

Advocates' Business Law Group

Parliament House,
Edinburgh, EH1 1RF
Tel: 0131-226-5071 Fax: 0131-225-3692

Afghan Hound Club of Scotland

Balmuir House,
Bridgecastle,
Bathgate,
West Lothian, EH48 3BD
Tel: 01501-732286

Mrs. Dorothy Hunter

*Promoting the breeding, rearing, showing and
general wellbeig of Afghan hounds. To
encourage the showing of Afghans and to help
newcomers to the breed.* *

Africa Centre Scotland

45 Blackfriars Street,
Edinburgh, EH1 1NB
Tel: 0131-557-4591

Dr. Sarah Sieley

Age Concern Scotland

113 Rose Street,
Edinburgh, EH2 3DT
Tel: 0131-220-3345   Fax: 0131-220-2779

Ms. Maureen O'Neill, *Director*

*Age Concern Scotland is a national voluntary
organisation with the primary aim of
improving the quality of life for older people
in Scotland. There are over 250 local groups
providing daycare, lunch clubs and information and advice.* *

Aged Christian Friend Society of Scotland

Brodies W.S.
Atholl Crescent,
Edinburgh, EH3 8HA
Tel: 0131-228-3777   Fax: 0131-228-3878

Mr. J.G. Clark, *Partner*

Agricultural Education Association

Scottish Agricultural College,
Oakbank Road,
Perth, PH1 1HF
Tel: 01738-36611

Agricultural Training Board

Rural Centre,
West Mains,
Ingliston, EH28 8NZ
Tel: 0131-335-3830

Air Training Corps

25 Learmouth Terrace,
Edinburgh, EH12 0AG

Airedale Terrier Club of Scotland

East Lodge,
Coodham,
Symington,
Ayrshire, KA1 5PH
Tel: 0141-553 3456

Mr. I. Thomson

Alcoholics Anonymous (Scotland)

50 Wellington Street,
Glasgow, G2 6HJ
Tel: 0141-226-2214

Mr. Ian Whyte, *Scottish Secretary*

Alexandra Rose Day – Scottish Office

45 Cumberland Street,
Edinburgh, EH3 6RA
Tel: 0131-557-4545   Fax: 0131-556-7758

Mrs. Jenny Cochrane

Founded in 1912 by Queen Alexandra, A.R.D. was Britain's first flag day. It helps organisations caring for the sick, aged, disabled and young people to take part in street or house-to-house collections annually. 80% of the amount collected is retained by the participating organisation. *

Alzheimer Scotland - Action on Dementia

22 Drumsheugh Gardens,
Edinburgh, EH3 7RN
Tel: 0131-243-1453   Fax: 0131-243-1450

Ms. Kate Fearnley

We help people with dementia and their carers and campaign to improve public policies. Services include 46 service provision projects, carer education and a 24 hour dementia helpline (0800 317 817). *

Amalgamated Engineering & Electrical Union

145/165 West Regent Street,
Glasgow, G2 4RZ
Tel: 0141-248-7131   Fax: 0141-221-4613

Mr. D. Carrigan, *Regional Secretary* *

Amnesty International

11 Jeffrey Street,
Edinburgh, EH1 1DR
Tel: 0131-557-2957   Fax: 0131-557-8501

Ms. Louise Carlin, *Scottish Development Officer*

Amnesty International works worldwide for the release of prisoners of conscience, fair trials for political prisoners and an end to torture, extra-judicial executions, 'disappearances' and the death penalty. *

An Comunn Gaidhealach

109 Church Street,
Inverness, IV1 1SY
Tel: 01463-231226   Fax: 01463-715557

Ancient Monuments Board for Scotland

Longmore House,
Salisbury Place,
Edinburgh, EH9 1SH
Tel: 0131-668-8764   Fax: 0131-668 8765

R.A.J. Dalziel, *Secretary*

Advises the Secretary of State for Scotland on the exercise of his functions, under the Ancient Monuments and Archaeological Areas Act 1979, of providing protection for monuments of national importance. *

Animal Concern

62 Old Dumbarton Road,
Glasgow, G3 8RE
Tel: 0141-334-6014   Fax: 0141-445-6470

John Robins, *Organising Secretary*

Incorporating the Scottish Anti-Vivisection Society (founded 1876), this is Scotland's oldest pressure group for animals. It runs various campaigns and 24-hour information line. *

Anthony Nolan Bone Marrow Trust

86 Main Street,
Callander,
Perthshire, FK17 8DU
Tel: 01877-331374   Fax: 01877-330212

Mrs. Anne Parish

Apex Trust Scotland

9 Great Stuart Street,
Edinburgh, EH3 7TP
Tel: 0131-220-0130   Fax: 0131-220-6796

Mr. Martin Currie, *Assistant Director*

Apex Scotland is the training and guidance organisation for offenders, ex-offenders and young people at risk helping them to move into employment and training. Apex also offers consultancy and training to employers and trainers on their recruitment policy and practice. *

Apostleship of the Sea (Scotland)

937 Dumbarton Road,
Glasgow, G14 9UF
Tel: 0141-339-6657   Fax: 0141-334-3463

Mr. Leo Gilbert *

Architectural Heritage Society of Scotland

The Glasite Meeting House,
33 Barony Street,
Edinburgh, EH3 6NX
Tel: 0131-557-0019   Fax: 0131-557-0049

Ms. Susan Brown, *Administrator*

The Society organises visits and tours to castles, country houses, towns, villages and archaeological, industrial and other sites. There are also talks, lectures, conferences and social events with an annual journal, Architectural Heritage. *

Army Benevolent Fund Scotland

The Castle,
Edinburgh, EH1 2YT
Tel: 0131-310-5132   Fax: 0131-310-5075

Lieutenant Colonel I. Shepherd, *Scottish Organiser*

Registered charity no. 211645. *

Army Cadet Force Association (Scotland)

Army Headquarters Scotland,
Craigiehall,
South Queensferry,
West Lothian, EH30 9TN
Tel: 0131-337-7672   Fax: 0131-337-7672

Lt Col A. Rose

*The Army Cadet Force is a national voluntary
youth organisation sponsored by the Army
and provides challenging military, adventurous and community activities.* *

Art In Partnership (Scotland) Limited

233 Cowgate,
Edinburgh, EH1 1JQ
Tel: 0131-225-4463   Fax: 0131-225-6879

Mr. Robert Breen, *Executive Director*

*Art In Partnership, Scotland's leading public
art commissions agency, works to promote the
role artists and contemporary art can play in
developing the urban/rural environment.* *

Arthritis Care

68 Woodvale Avenue,
Bearsden,
Glasgow, G61 2NZ
Tel: 0141-942-2322   Fax: 0141-942-2322

Pat Wallace, *Arthritis Care Manager–Scotland*

*Provides information, self-help groups, support,
training courses and volunteering opportunities for people with arthritis of all ages.
Includes Young Arthritis Care for those under
45.* *

Arthritis Research Campaign (Scotland)

140 High Street,
Lochee,
Dundee, DD2 3BZ
Tel: 01382-400911   Fax: 01382-400933

Miss Patricia Reynolds, *Events Organiser*

*ARC Scotland is currently committed to a £2
million research and education programme in
Scottish hospitals and universities, dedicated
to providing a better understanding and
treatment of the disease.* *

Arthrogryposis Group

166 Wallacewell Road,
Balornock,
Glasgow, G21 3NX
Tel: 0141-557-1120

Joanne & Lawrence Coll

*We offer contact and support for children and
adults with this condition. We have
information on hand and a vast wealth of
knowledge to pass on.* *

Arts Management Training Initiative (Scotland)

Moray House Institute of Education,
Holyrood Road,
Edinburgh, EH8 8AQ
Tel: 0131-556-8455   Fax: 0131-557-3458

Brian Martin, *Director*

Associated Society of Locomotive Engineers & Firemen

1 Coxton Place,
Glasgow, G33 4EW
Tel: 0141-774-7395   **Fax:** 0141-774-7227

Mr. P. O'Connor, *Secretary*

Association for Applied Arts

Allander House,
141 Leith Walk,
Edinburgh, EH6 8NQ
Tel: 0131-553-5566   **Fax:** 0131-555-2354

Mandy Lee, *Administrator*

Association for Business Sponsorship of the Arts

Room 294,
102 West Port,
Edinburgh, EH3 9HS
Tel: 0131-228-4262   **Fax:** 0131-229-9008

Peggy McLeod, *Director*

Association for Children with Heart Disorders – Bravehearts Young Adults (YA)

26 Fernbank,
Ladywell,
Livingston, EH54 6DT
Tel: 01506-496628

Mr. Alan Kennedy

Association for Conductive Education for Scotland

Redcroft,
Bents,
Stoneyburn,
West Lothian, EH47 8EQ
Tel: 01501-763027

Association for Continence Advice

Allander House,
141 Leith Walk,
Edinburgh, EH6 8NP
Tel: 0131-467-8567   **Fax:** 0131-467-8566

Ms. Linda Morrow, *Chairperson Scotland*

Association for Fair Play for Children in Scotland

Unit 29,
Six Harmony Row,
Govan,
Glasgow, G51 3BA
Tel: 0141-425-1140   **Fax:** 0141-425-1140

Ms. Anne Keegan

A registered charity supporting the provision of play opportunities for 5–15 year olds. *

Association for Improvements in the Maternity Service (AIMS)

40 Leamington Terrace,
Edinburgh, EH10 4JL
Tel: 0131-229-6259   Fax: 0131-229-6259

Ms. Nadine Edwards

AIMS offers information and support to parents on many aspects of their maternity care. It has detailed information on the choices and options open to women and produces a quarterly journal plus other publications. Send SAE to above address for free publications list. *

Association for Management Education & Training in Scotland

Cottrell Building,
University of Stirling,
Stirling, FK9 4LA
Tel: 01786-450906   Fax: 01786-465070

Penny Neish

Association for Person-Centred Therapy

40 Kelvingrove Street,
Glasgow, G3 7RZ
Tel: 0141-332-6888

Association for Professionals in Services for Adolescents

13 Bonaly Drive,
Edinburgh, EH13 0EJ
Tel: 0131-441-1049

David Duff, *Honorary Treasurer*

Association for Scottish Literary Studies

c/o Department of Scottish History,
University of Glasgow,
9 University Gardens,
Glasgow, G12 8QH
Tel: 0141-330-5309

Catherine McInerney, *General Manager*

ASLS exisits to promote the study, teaching and writing of Scottish literature and to further the study of the languages of Scotland. *

Association for Veterinary Clinical Pharmacology & Therapeutics

Department of Veterinary Pharmacology,
University of Glasgow Veterinary School,
Bearsden Road,
Glasgow, G61 1QH
Tel: 0141-330-5700   Fax: 0141-330-4739

Dr. Andrea Nolan, *Secretary*

The Association acts to advance the study and practice of veterinary clinical pharmacology and therapeutics by encouraging exchange of knowledge and production of relevant meeting proceedings. *

Association for the Protection of Rural Scotland (APRS)

Gladstone's Land,
3rd floor,
483 Lawnmarket,
Edinburgh, EH1 2NT
Tel: 0131-225-7012/3   Fax: 0131-225-6592

Mrs. Elizabeth J. Garland, *Manager*

APRS seeks to protect Scotland's countryside and promotes ideas for its care and improvement via constructive proposals, research and active involvement in the maintenance of landscape features. *

Association in Scotland to Research into Astronautics Ltd (ASTRA)

Flat 65, Dalriada House,
56 Blythswood Court,
Anderston,
Glasgow, G2 7PE
Tel: 0141-221-7658   Fax: 0141-221-7658

Mr. Duncan Lunan

An educational society covering all aspects of spaceflight and astronomy (runs Airdrie Public Astronomy). There are lectures, talks, exhibitions and technical projects, etc. *

Association of Basic Science Teachers in Dentistry

c/o Oral Biochemistry Unit,
University of Glasgow Dental School,
378 Sauchiehall Street,
Glasgow, G2 3JZ
Tel: 0141-211-9755   Fax: 0141-353-1593

Dr. Josie A. Beeley, *Honorary Secretary*

This Association is dedicated to basic science in dental education. It includes members from all dental schools in the UK and Ireland and has an increasing membership from dental schools in other European countries. *

Association of British Insurers (Scottish Branch)

30 Gordon Street,
Glasgow, G1 3PU
Tel: 0141-226-3905   Fax: 0141-221-4516

Miss L Hamilton, *Regional Public Relations Officer*

Association of British Mountain Guides (Scotland)

11 Dean Park Crescent,
Edinburgh,
EH4 1EE
Tel: 0131-332-3468

Association of British Solid Fuel Appliance Manufacturers

11th Floor, Savoy Tower,
77 Renfrew Street,
Glasgow, G2 3BZ
Tel: 0141-332-0826   Fax: 0141-332-5788

Association of Chartered Certified Accountants, Scottish Branch

1 Woodside Place,
Glasgow, G3 7QF
Tel: 0141-309-4097   Fax: 0141-309-4090

Lindsay Taylor, *Regional Services Adviser*

ACCA is the fastest-growing UK-based accountancy body with nearly 200,000 members and students. For further information on the ACCA qualification contact Lindsay Taylor. *

Association of Chief Architects of Scottish Local Authorities

Property & Technical Services,
Inverclyde Council,
Cathcart House,
6 Cathcart Square,
Greenock, PA1 1LS
Tel: 01475-724400   Fax: 01475-882468

Alan Gilchrist

Association of Chief Police Officers (Scotland)

Police Headquarters,
Fettes Avenue,
Edinburgh, EH4 1RB
Tel: 0131-311-3051   Fax: 0131-311 3052

Sir William Sutherland, *Honorary Secretary*

Association of Consulting Engineers, Scottish Group

Scott Wilson Kirkpatrick,
6 Park Circus,
Glasgow, G3 6AX
Tel: 0141-332-2258

J.P. McCafferty, *Secretary*

Association of Deer Management Groups

Dalhousie Estates Office,
Brechin,
Angus, DD9 6SG
Tel: 01356-624566   Fax: 01356-623725

R.M.J. Cooke, *Secretary*

ADMG represents the majority of deer management groups in Scotland which are committed to the welfare of deer and their habitat through sustainable management practices. Also to protect employment and rural communities where deer management is a major economic land use. *

Association of Directors of Education in Scotland

Floor 8,
Tayside House,
28 Crichton Street,
Dundee, DD1 3RJ
Tel: 01382-433088   Fax: 01382-433080

Mrs. Anne Wilson, *General Secretary*

The Association of Directors of Education in Scotland (ADES) represents managers in local authority education departments. It promotes their professional interests and development and makes national representation on issues affecting the education service. *

Association of Directors of Social Work

Department of Social Work,
Borders Regional Council,
Regional HQ,
Newton St. Boswells,
Melrose, TD6 0SA
Tel: 01835-23301   Fax: 01835-23366

A. Cameron, *Secretary*

Association of Educational Advisers in Scotland

Dean Education Centre,
Belford Road,
Edinburgh, EH4 3DS
Tel: 0131-343-1931

George Cox, *Honorary Secretary*

Association of Head Teachers in Scotland

Room B34,
Northern College of Education,
Gardyne Road,
Dundee, DD5 1NY
Tel: 01382-458802

General Secretary

Professional Association. *

Association of Independent Forest Managers

Perth Agricultural Centre,
East Huntingtower,
Perth, PH1 3JJ
Tel: 01738-27655   Fax: 01738-29390

D.E. Carter, *Chairman*

Association of Installers & Unvented Hot Water Systems (Scotland & Ireland)

2 Walker Street,
Edinburgh, EH3 7LB
Tel: 0131-225-2255   Fax: 0131-226-7638

A. Wilson

*This Association was set up by the Scottish and
Northern Ireland Plumbing Employers'
Federation in January, 1986 for firms in
Scotland and Northern Ireland who wished
to become involved in the installation, repair
and maintenance of unvented hot water
supply systems. The Association operates as a
subsidiary association of SNIPEF.* *

Association of Jute Spinners & Manufacturers

c/o Sidlaw Textiles Limited,
Manhattan Works,
Dundonald Street,
Dundee, DD3 7PY
Tel: 01382-450645   Fax: 01382-462903

A.G. Scott, *Chairman*

Association of Local Television Operators

13 Bellevue Place,
Edinburgh, EH7 4BS
Tel: 0131-557-8610   Fax: 0131-557-8608

Lyndsay A. Bowditch, *Secretary*

Association of Managers in General Practice

see The Association of Managers in General Practice

Association of Model Railway Societies in Scotland

PO Box 177,
Glasgow, G1 2LY

Exhibition Manager

*The AMRSS mission is to further the model railway hobby in general and promote our annual model railway exhibition at the SECC – Model Rail Scotland. ***

Association of Multiple Sclerosis Therapy Centres (Scotland)

Stonefield,
Torvaig, Portree,
Isle of Skye, IV51 9HU
Tel: 01478-612066

Mr. Iain Smart

Association of Paediatric Anaesthetists of GB & Ireland

Department of Anaesthesia,
Royal Hospital for Sick Children,
Yorkhill,
Glasgow, G3 8SJ
Tel: 0141-339-8888   Fax: 0141-334-0972

Dr. D.S. Arthur

Association of Parents & Friends of Spastics

7 Queen's Crescent,
Glasgow, G4 9BW
Tel: 0141-332-2674

Association of Pension Lawyers – Scottish Group

Scottish Equitable plc,
Edinburgh Park,
Edinburgh, EH12 9SE
Tel: 0131-549-3735   Fax: 0131-549-4299

Stan Cook, *Secretary*

*The Group aims to promote interest and information on all types of pension. We run seminars and foster links between all those interested in pensions. ***

Association of Planning Supervisors Limited

16 Rutland Square,
Edinburgh, EH1 2BE
Tel: 0131-221-9959   Fax: 0131-222-0061

Mr. Brian B. Law, *Chief Executive*

*A multi-disciplinary, pan-industry, advisory and representative body for those acting as planning supervisors developing guidance and best practice for members, and providing a central source of information for clients seeking planning supervisors. ***

Association of Public Analysts of Scotland

Glasgow Scientific Services,
64 Everard Drive, Springburn,
Glasgow, G21 1XG
Tel: 0141-562-2203   Fax: 0141-563-5129

Dr. C. McDonald, *Honorary Secretary*

Association of Registrars of Scotland

7 East Fergus Place,
Kirkcaldy, KY1 1XT
Tel: 01592-412121

Mr. Eston A. Kilgor, *Honorary Secretary*

Association of Scotland's Self-Caterers

Dalreoch,
Dunning,
Perth, PH2 0QJ
Tel: 01764-684100   Fax: 01764-684633

Mrs. W.W. Marshall, *Secretary*

ASSC is a trade organisation of owners of self-catering property whose aim is to promote high standards and a professional approach in the tourism business in Scotland. *

Association of Scottish Bacon Curers

Spicer Watson and Company,
65 Renfield Street,
Glasgow, G2 1NS
Tel: 0141-331-1501

Association of Scottish Colleges

Argyll Court,
Castle Business Park,
Stirling, FK9 4TY
Tel: 01786-892103

Association of Scottish Community Councils (ASCC)

21 Grosvenor Street,
Edinburgh, EH12 5ED
Tel: 0131-225-4033   Fax: 0131-225-4033

The Secretary *

Association of Scottish District Salmon Fishery Boards

The Stables,
Cargill,
Perth, PH2 6DS
Tel: 01250-883365   Fax: 01250-883342

Lt Col. G.D.B. Keelan, *Director*

Association of Scottish Dowsers

Hinds Cottage,
Great Whittington,
Newcastle-upon-Tyne
Tel: 01434-672413

Association of Scottish Genealogists and Record Agents

P.O. Box 174,
Edinburgh, EH3 5QZ

Association of Scottish Life (Insurance) Offices

40 Thistle Street,
Edinburgh, EH2 1EN
Tel: 0131-220-4555   Fax: 0131-220-2280

W. W. Mair, *Secretary*

Association of Scottish Local Health Councils

21 Torphichen Street,
Edinburgh, EH3 8HX
Tel: 0131-229-2344

Penny Richardson, *Director*

Association of Scottish Philatelic Societies

36 Anson Avenue,
Falkirk, FK1 5BJ
Tel: 01324-625610

Mr. Alan Watson, *Secretary*

The Association co-ordinates 45 philatelic, postal history and postcard societies through-out Scotland. A congress and trade fair at Falkirk is organised annually in March. *

Association of Scottish Police Superintendents

see The Association of Scottish Police Superintendents

Association of Scottish Shellfish Growers

Mountview,
Ardvasar,
Isle of Skye, IV45 8RU
Tel: 01471-844324   Fax: 01471-844324

Mr. Doug McLeod, *Chairman*

Trade association representing the interests of the shellfish cultivation sector to Government, statutory bodies and commercial interests on issues ranging from environmental, water quality, legislation, implementation of EU directives to promoting its products at exhibitions and conferences. *

Association of Scottish Visitor Attractions

Suite 6, Admiral House,
29/30 Maritime Street,
Leith,
Edinburgh, EH6 6SE
Tel: 0131-555-2551   Fax: 0131-555-2552

Lena S. Gaw

A membership organisation aiming to improve the quality and viability of visitor attractions in Scotland. We offer networking and benchmarking, development advice and represent the industry on national commit-tees. *

Association of Ski Schools in Great Britain

BASI, Glenmore,
Aviemore,
Inverness-shire, PH22 1QU
Tel: 01479-861717   Fax: 01479-861718

R. Kinnaird, *Secretary*

*To promote and encourage greater knowledge,
understanding and practice of safe skiing; to
aim for a high standard of instruction, and
to administer ski tests at all levels.* *

Association of Speakers Clubs

28 High Street,
Auchterarder, PH3 1DF
Tel: 01764-662457   Fax: 01252-333901

Don Williams

Association of University Teachers (Scotland)

6 Castle Street,
Edinburgh, EH2 3AT
Tel: 0131-226-6694   Fax: 0131-226-2066

David Bleiman, *Regional Secretary*

Association of Veterinary Anaesthetists of GB & Ireland

Department of Veterinary Surgery,
University of Glasgow Veterinary School,
Bearsden Road, Bearsden,
Glasgow, G61 1QH
Tel: 0141-330-5700   Fax: 0141-942-7415

Dr. J. Reid, *Secretary*

Association of W.R.N.S.

47 Forrest Road,
Edinburgh, EH1 2QR
Tel: 0131-225-1454

Automatic Vending Association of Britain

Scottish Region,
Granada Vending Services Limited,
Unit 3d,
Monklands Industrial Estate,
Kirkshaws,
Coatbridge, ML5 4RP
Tel: 01236-424402

D. Webb

Automobile Association

Fanum House,
Erskine Harbour,
Erskine,
Renfrewshire, PA8 6AT
Tel: 0141-812-0144

Avenel Trust

1 Midmar Gardens,
Edinburgh, EH10 6DY
Tel: 0131-447-6805

Ayrshire Cattle Society of Great Britain & Ireland

1 Racecourse Road,
Ayr, KA7 2DE
Tel: 01292-267123   Fax: 01293-611973

Mr. Stuart Thomson, *Chief Executive*

*Promoting genetics, milk and dairy products
  from the world renowned Ayrshire dairy cow,
  whilst producing pedigrees and breeding
  information on a modern computer system.* *

BAFTA Scotland

74 Victoria Crescent Road,
Glasgow, G12 9JN
Tel: 0141-357-4317   Fax: 0141-337-1432

Ms. Alison Forsyth, *Director*

*The British Academy of Film and Television
Arts, rewarding excellence and achievement
in these major Scottish industries. Membership is within the industries and related
work.* *

BASPCAN, Scottish Branch

Medical Centre,
St. Andrew Street,
Dalkeith,
Midlothian, EH22 1AP

Dr. Michael Wilson

BBC Children in Need Appeal

Broadcasting House,
5 Queen Street,
Edinburgh, EH2 1JF
Tel: 0131-469-4225   Fax: 0131-469-4220

BECTU (Broadcasting, Entertainment, Cinematograph and Theatre Union)

114 Union Street,
Glasgow, G1 3QQ
Tel: 0141-248-9558

Bank of England

25 St. Vincent Place,
Glasgow, G1 2EB

Mr. David Shilson, *Agent for Scotland*

Banking, Insurance & Finance Union

146 Argyle Street,
Glasgow, G2 8BL
Tel: 0141-221-6475/6   Fax: 0141-204-3315

Mr. S. Boyle, *Deputy General Secretary*

Baptist Union of Scotland

Baptist Church House,
14 Aytoun Road,
Glasgow, G41 5RT
Tel: 0141-423-6169

Rev. Ian Mundie

Barnardo's Scotland

235 Corstorphine Road,
Edinburgh, EH12 7AR
Tel: 0131-334-9893   Fax: 0131-316-4008

Mr. Martin Crewe

*A varied range of child care initiatives includ-
ing families with young children; young
people with disabilities; community development; children needing families; disadvantaged young people.* *

Barnardo's: Scottish Adoption Advice Service

16 Sandyford Place,
Glasgow, G3 7NB
Tel: 0141-339-0772   Fax: 0141-248-8032

Ms. Ros MacMillan

SAAS offers advice, counselling and groupwork services to those affected by adoption. We offer training and consultancy to professionals and work with subscribing authorities. *

Basset Hound Club of Scotland

Four Winds,
Greenloaning,
Braco,
Dunblane, FK15 0LX
Tel: 01786-880259

Mr. D.T.C. Sharpe

Bearded Collie Club of Scotland

73 New Street,
Stonehouse,
Lanarkshire, ML9 3LT
Tel: 01698-792834

Mr. H.L. Griffiths

Bee Farmers Association

Arresgill Farm,
Langholm,
Dumfriesshire, DG1 3OR
Tel: 01387-380056

Brian Stenhouse, *Secretary*

Benevolent Fund for Nurses in Scotland

30 Biggar Road,
Edinburgh, EH10 7BH

Mrs. G.Donaldson, C.A., *Secretary*

Benevolent Society of the Licensed Trade of Scotland

79 West Regent Street,
Glasgow, G2 2AW
Tel: 0141-353-3596   Fax: 0141-353-3597

Mr. George McCulloch, C.A., *Secretary*

Persons in necessitous or distressed circum-stances who are or have been connected with the licensed trade in Scotland. *

Bernese Mountain Dog Club of Scotland

Bethshean,
Logie,
Montrose, DD10 9LD
Tel: 01674-830407

Mrs. M. Sutherland

Biological Recording in Scotland Campaign (BRISC)

Cramond House,
Kirk Cramond,
Cramond Glebe Road,
Edinburgh, EH4 6NS
Tel: 0131-312-7765   Fax: 0131-312-8705

Mr. Robert Bryson, *Co-ordinator*

Biomathematics and Statistics Scotland

University of Edinburgh,
Kings Buildings,
Mayfield Road,
Edinburgh, EH9 3JZ
Tel: 0131-650-4900   Fax: 0131-650-4901

E.M. Heyburn

BioSS is a UK leader with an international reputation in the field of mathematics and statistics applied in the biological sciences. *

Birth Centre

40 Leamington Terrace,
Edinburgh, EH10 4JL
Tel: 0131-229-6259

Ms. Nadine Edwards/Ms. Andrea McLaughlin

The Birth Centre provides a resource for women and their partners before and after childbirth. A range of services designed to help parents meet the challenges of birth and parenthood are provided. *

Birthlink Adoption Counselling Centre

21 Castle Street,
Edinburgh, EH2 3DN
Tel: 0131-225-6441   Fax: 0131-225-6441

Ms. Linda Paterson, *Director of National Services*

Birthlink Adoption Counselling Centre is a national and international service which operates Scotland's Adoption Contact Register, and a post-adoption service which includes tracing. *

Blackface Sheep Breeders' Association

Royal British House,
Leonard Street,
Perth, PH2 8HA
Tel: 01738-449430   Fax: 01738-449431

Miss Audrey M. Fenton, *Secretary*

A breed society promoting sheep. *

Blisslink Scotland

19 Victoria Park Gardens South,
Glasgow, G11 7BX
Tel: 0141-339-9836

Ms. Fiona Arthur

Blissymbol Communication UK

New Trinity Centre,
7a Loaning Road,
Edinburgh, EH7 6JE
Tel: 0131-661-1212   Fax: 0131-661-8643

Mrs. Alison MacDonald

A commnication system for those unable to speak. Suitable for people with spelling difficulties but who require a system that provides more flexibility than picture symbols. *

Bluefaced Leicester Sheep Breeders' Association

Kirkbeck,
Clarencefield,
Dumfries, DG1 4NY
Tel: 01387-870671   Fax: 01387-870337

Mrs. Fiona E. Sloan, *Secretary*

A UK National Association Breed Association. *

Bobath Scotland

2028 Great Western Road,
Knightswood,
Glasgow, G13 2HA
Tel: 0141-950-2922   Fax: 0141-950-2933

Ms. Susan Horsburgh, *Therapist in Charge*

Bobath Scotland offers children with cerebral palsy improved quality of life. The centre offers treatment, resources for therapists and helpers, mutual support for parents of the children and a venue for seminars and workshops to train therapists in the Bobath approach. *

Boiler and Radiator Manufacturers' Association Limited

77 Renfrew Street,
Glasgow, G2 3BZ
Tel: 0141-332-0826   Fax: 0141-332-5788

R.C. Robertson, *Secretary*

Book Publishers' Representatives' Association – Scottish Branch

'Rossnowlagh',
2 St. Clement Avenue,
Dunblane,
Perthshire, FK15 9DG
Tel: 01786-823294

Mr. Bill Baird, *Secretary*

An organisation open to all sales representatives in the book trade, providing a focus for social and professional activities for its members. *

Booksellers Association: Scottish Branch

Milngavie Bookshop,
37 Douglas Street,
Milngavie,
Glasgow, G62 6PE
Tel: 0141-956-4752   Fax: 0141-956-4819

Mr. Robin Lane, *Honorary Secretary*

Boston Terrier Club of Scotland

Lismore,
Foveran Newburgh,
Aberdeen, AB41 0AX

Ms. A. Strachan-Abel

Botanical Society of Scotland

c/o Royal Botanic Garden,
Inverleith Row,
Edinburgh, EH3 5LR
Tel: 0131-552 7171

Robert Galt, *Honorary Secretary*

Founded in 1836 as the Botanical Society of Edinburgh, the Society exists to promote the study of plants and to exchange botanical information between members. *

Boys' Brigade (BB)

see The Boys' Brigade

Boys' and Girls' Clubs of Scotland

88 Giles Street,
Edinburgh, EH6 6BZ
Tel: 0131-555-1729   Fax: 0131-555-5921

Mr. Les Beaton, *Secretary*

Boys' and Girls' Clubs of Scotland exists to assist clubs in their development for the benefit of our youngsters and to advise our volunteers. Within the organisation experience, resources, expertise and information is readily available to help clubs in all areas of their work. *

Breast Cancer Care

46 Gordon Street,
Glasgow, G1 3PU
Tel: 0141-221-2233   Fax: 0141-221-9499

Mrs. Frances R. McDowall, *Scottish Services Manager*

Provides a nationwide freeline (0500-245-345), information, prosthesis fitting service and emotional support for all those concerned about breast cancer and breast related issues. *

Brewers' Association of Scotland

6 St. Colme Street,
Edinburgh, EH3 6AD
Tel: 0131-225-4681

Bridges (Building the Awareness of Infertility)

62 Grampian Road,
Rosyth, KY11 2ES
Tel: 01383-412277   Fax: 01383-412277

Mrs. Christine Devlin

British & International Golf Greenkeepers Association

Scottish Region,
10 Meadowburn Avenue,
Newton Mearns,
Glasgow, G77 6TA
Tel: 0141-616-3440   Fax: 0141-616-3440

Mr. Peter Boyd, *Scottish Region Administrator.* *

British & International Sailors Society

Ground floor,
Mercantile Chambers,
53 Bothwell Street,
Glasgow, G2 6HT
Tel: 0141-221-8212   Fax: 0141-221-8212

Mrs. Janet Ferguson

*The BISS is a charity for seafarers. We provide welfare care and facilities with centres and chaplains. The society provides two retirement homes. **

British Actors' Equity Association

114 Union Street,
Glasgow, G1 3QQ
Tel: 0141-248-2472   Fax: 0141-248-2473

Mr. L. Boswell, *Secretary – Scotland*

*Trade union. **

British Agencies for Adoption and Fostering (BAAF)

40 Shandwick Place,
Edinburgh, EH2 4RT
Tel: 0131-225-9285   Fax: 0131-226-3778

Donal Giltinan, *Scottish Centre Manager*

British Association for Early Childhood Education

Kelso Nursery School,
170 Hawick Street,
Glasgow, G13 4HG
Tel: 0141-952-2502

Miss Anne Lannigan

*The Association is committed to the promotion of good practice in work with children 0–9 years. It provides publications and organises conferences to support this aim. **

British Association for Shooting and Conservation (BASC)

BASC Scotland,
Trochry,
Dunkeld,
Tayside, PH8 0DY
Tel: 01350-723226   Fax: 01350-723227

Mr. Alastair MacGugan, *Conservation & Training Officer*

*Since 1908 the BASC has promoted and protected sporting shooting. The strength and breadth of BASC's political representation is widely acknowledged and today BASC is the country's most powerful all-party lobby for shooting and conservation. **

British Association of Academic Phoneticians (BAAP)

Department of English Language,
The University,
Glasgow, G12 8QQ
Tel: 0141-330-4596   Fax: 0141-330-3531

Prof. M.K.C. MacMahon, *Honorary Secretary and Archivist*

BAAP acts as a forum for academic phoneticians and as a source of information for the wider public on phonetic matters. Regular colloquia are held. *

British Association of Clinical Anatomists

Department of Anatomy,
The University,
Glasgow, G12 8QQ
Tel: 0141-339-8855

Dr. Stuart W. McDonald

British Association of Prosthetists and Orthotists (BAPO)

Sir James Clark Building,
Abbey Mill Business Centre,
Paisley, PA1 1TJ
Tel: 0141-561-7217   Fax: 0141-561-7218

The Secretary

The British Association of Prosthetists and Orthotists exists to represent and protect the prosthetic and orthotic profession with regard to its status and interests. *

British Association of Ski Instructors

Glenmore,
Aviemore,
Inverness-shire, PH22 1QU
Tel: 01479-861717   Fax: 01479-861718

Robert Kinnaird, *Chief Executive*

BASI is the national training agency for ski instructors. The organisation currently has 2,200 members. Courses are run in six different countries with over 900 participants. *

British Association of Social Workers (Scotland)

28 North Bridge,
Edinburgh, EH1 1QG
Tel: 0131-225-4549   Fax: 0131-220-0636

Mr. David Colvin, *Scottish Secretary*

British Association of Teachers of Dancing

23 Marywood Square,
Glasgow, G41 2BP
Tel: 0141-423-4029

Mrs. Katrina Allen

British Association of Teachers of the Deaf (Scottish Region)

Earnock High School,
Wellhall Road,
Hamilton, ML3 9UE

Ms. Sylvia Gordon *

British Association of Women Entrepreneurs

Scottish Branch,
TBDA (Scotland) Limited,
112 John Player Building,
Stirling, FK7 7RP
Tel: 01786-446004   Fax: 01786-446005

Tanya Hine

The organisational mandate is to provide an environment for women to grow and develop in their business. The organisation encourages women to support each other and aims to enhance recognition of the achievements of women in business. *

British Broadcasting Corporation

Broadcasting House,
Queen Margaret Drive,
Glasgow, G12 8DG
Tel: 0141-338-2000   Fax: 0141-337-1674

Mr. John McCormick, *Controller (Scotland)*

Scotland's national broadcaster serving audiences with radio and television programmes for Scottish and UK audiences. *

British Colostomy Association

5 Cairnbank Road,
Penicuik,
Midlothian, EH26 9EB
Tel: 01968-672785

Mr. J. McLeod

British Deaf Association Scotland

100 Norfolk Street,
Glasgow, G5 9EJ
Tel: 0141-420-1759   Fax: 0141-420-1960

Mr. John A. Hay, *Community Services Officer*

British Deer Society – Scottish Office (BDS)

Trian House,
Comrie,
Perthshire, PH6 2HZ
Tel: 01764-670062   Fax: 01764-670062

Hugh Rose, *Scottish Secretary*

The British Deer Society is a national charity, no. 228659, concerned with promoting public knowledge of and research into deer, humane deer management and welfare. *

British Dental Association (Scottish Office)

19 Hay Street,
Perth, PH1 5HS
Tel: 01738-441040

British Diabetic Association

34 West George Street (4th floor),
Glasgow, G2 1DA
Tel: 0141-332-2700   Fax: 0141-332-4880

Ms. Delia Henry/Ms. Ann Travers

British Disabled Water Ski Association

9 Roseneath Street,
Edinburgh, EH9 1JH
Tel: 0131-228-2634   Fax: 0131-228-2634

Miss Lesley Baxter, *Chairperson*

The BDWSA aims to introduce newcomers to waterskiing no matter their disability. We cater for everyone from beginners to those who want to compete. *

British Educational Research Association

c/o SCRE,
15 St. John Street,
Edinburgh, EH8 8JR
Tel: 0131-557-2944   Fax: 0131-556-9454

Dr. Michael Bassey, *Executive Secretary*

BERA aims to encourage the pursuit of educational research and its aplications for the improvement of educational practice and the general benefit of the community. *

British Electrophoresis Society

c/o Dr. Philip Cash,
Department of Medical Microbiology,
University of Aberdeen,
Foresterhill,
Aberdeen, AB9 2ZD
Tel: 01224-681818   Fax: 01224-685604

British Executive Service Overseas

13 Bank Street,
Edinburgh, EH1 2LN
Tel: 0131-220-0012   Fax: 0131-220-1771

British Federation of Young Choirs

38 Swanston Avenue,
Edinburgh
Tel: 0131-445-3114

John Robertson, *Secretary*

British Field Sports Society (BFSS)

Green Burns,
Coupar Angus,
Blairgowrie,
Perthshire, PH13 9HA
Tel: 01828-628664   Fax: 01828-628664

Jamie Hepburn-White, *Director*

British Geological Survey – Scottish Office (BGS)

Murchison House,
West Mains Road,
Edinburgh, EH9 3LA
Tel: 0131-667-1000   Fax: 0131-668-2683

Dr. Chris W.A. Browitt, *Asst. Director/Head of Station*

BGS, Edinburgh is the centre for geological surveying on land and offshore in northern Britain, for petroleum geology, the monitoring of earthquakes and the Earth's magnetic field throughout the UK. *

British Geriatrics Society

The Royal Infirmary,
84 Castle Street,
Glasgow, G4 0SF
Tel: 0141-211-4926   Fax: 0141-211-1121

Dr. Paul Knight, *Clinical Director*

British Heart Foundation

45a Moray Place,
Edinburgh, EH3 6BQ
Tel: 0131-226-3705   Fax: 0131-225-3258

Mr. Iain Lowis, *Regional Director*

The British Heart Foundation is a national
charity which plays a leading role in the fight
against heart disease, Scotland's biggest
killer. *

British Holiday & Home Parks Association

50 Grange Loan,
Edinburgh, EH9 2EP
Tel: 0131-667-1229

British Horse Society – Scotland

Boreland,
Fearnan,
Aberfeldy,
Perthshire, PH15 2PG
Tel: 01887-830606   Fax: 01887-830606

I.M. Menzies, *Scottish Development Officer*

The leading equine charity in all matters
relating to the welfare of the horse and the
training, safety and access for horse and
rider. *

British Hospitality Association (Scotland)

Macroberts, Solicitors,
27 Melville Street,
Edinburgh, EH3 7JF
Tel: 0131-226-2552

John London, *Secretary*

The Scottish Office of BHA is the trade
association which represents all sections of the
industry including hoteliers, restaurateurs,
contract caterers and suppliers of every size. *

British Infection Society

Department of Microbiology,
Aberdeen Royal Infirmary,
Foresterhill,
Aberdeen, AB25 2ZN
Tel: 01224-840688   Fax: 01224-840632

Dr. I.M. Gould, *Honorary Treasurer* *

British International Studies Association

International Office,
Glasgow Caledonian University,
70 Cowcaddens Road,
Glasgow, G4 0LH
Tel: 0141-331-3165

Roger Carey, *Secretary*

British Ladder Manufacturers' Association

W.J. Clow Limited,
183–7 Broad Street,
Glasgow, G40 2QR
Tel: 0141-554-6272   Fax: 0141-551-0813

Douglas Clow, *Secretary*

British Limbless Ex-Servicemen's Association (BLESMA)

24 Dundas Street,
Edinburgh, EH3 6JN
Tel: 0131-536-6828

British Lung Foundation

Royal College of Physicians and Surgeons,
234–242 St. Vincent Street,
Glasgow, G2 5RJ
Tel: 0141-204-4110   Fax: 0141-204-4110

Ms. Jill Macrae

The only UK charity funding research into all lung diseases and providing self-help 'breathe easy' groups for people living with a lung complaint. *

British Marine Industries Federation Scotland

Westgate,
Toward,
Dunoon,
Argyll, PA23 7VA
Tel: 01369-870251   Fax: 01369-870251

M. Balmforth, *Administrator*

BMIF Scotland represents the interests of marine leisure companies in Scotland, and provides training, promotional and other services to members. *

British Maternity Trust

40 Leamington Terrace,
Edinburgh, EH10 4JL
Tel: 0131-229-6259

British Medical Association (Scottish Office)

3 Hill Place,
Edinburgh, EH8 9EQ
Tel: 0131-662-4820   Fax: 0131-667-6933

Dr. Brian T. Potter, *Scottish Secretary*

The BMA is a voluntary professional associa-tion of doctors representing and providing services to its members. *

British Metals Federation (Scottish Office)

112 West George Street,
Glasgow, G2 1QF
Tel: 0141-332-7484

British Nuclear Test Veterans Association

12 Walpole Place,
Johnstone,
Renfrewshire, PA5 0RE
Tel: 01505-704936

Ken McGinley, *Secretary*

British Numismatic Society

c/o Hunterian Museum,
Glasgow University,
Glasgow, G12 8QQ
Tel: 0141-330-4221   Fax: 0141-307-8059

J.D. Bateson

British Photobiology Society

Photobiology Unit,
Ninewells Hospital & Medical School,
Dundee, DD1 9SY
Tel: 01382-60111   Fax: 01382-646047

Dr. Brian E. Johnson, *Honorary Secretary*

British Photodermatology Group

Photobiology Unit,
Ninewells Hospital & Medical School,
Dundee, DD1 9SY
Tel: 01382-60111   Fax: 01382-646047

Neil K. Gibbs, *Secretary*

British Polyolefin Textiles Association

Newfordpark,
Glamis Road,
Forfar, DD8 1US
Tel: 01307-468659   Fax: 01307-468942

R.H.B. Learoyd, *Secretary* *

British Pregnancy Advisory Service (BPAS)

1st floor left,
245 North Street,
Glasgow, G3 7DL
Tel: 0141-204-1832   Fax: 0141-248-9370

Ms. Jacqueline Houston, *Branch Co-ordinator*

British Red Cross Society (Headquarters, Scotland)

Alexandra House,
204 Bath Street,
Glasgow, G2 4HL
Tel: 0141-332-9591   Fax: 0141-332-8493

Mr. David Whyte, *Director, Scotland*

The British Red Cross cares for people in crisis everywhere – meeting the needs of vulnerable people in times of emergency. *

British Romagnola Cattle Society

26 York Place,
Perth, PH2 8EH
Tel: 01738-23780

Miss Audrey M. Fenton, *Secretary*

British Show Jumping Association (Scottish Branch)

'Glenauld',
Hamilton Road,
Strathaven, ML10 6SX
Tel: 01357-522853   Fax: 01357-520022

Mrs. J. Mair, *Administrator* *

British Ski and Snowboard Federation

258 Main Street,
East Calder,
Edinburgh, EH53 0EE
Tel: 01506-884343   Fax: 01506-882952

Mike Jardine, *Chief Executive**

British Society for Medical & Dental Hypnosis, Scotland

P.O. Box 1007,
Glasgow, G31 2LE
Tel: 0141-556-1606   Fax: 0141-551-9104

The Secretary

*To encourage and promote excellence in the use of hypnosis by registered medical and dental practitioners; to advance scientific research, education and standards of practice in hypnosis; and to advise others about the value, application and ethical use of hypnosis.**

British Society for the History of Pharmacy

c/o Royal Pharmaceutical Society,
(Scottish Department),
36 York Place,
Edinburgh, EH1 3HU
Tel: 0131-556-4386

Dr. L.C. Howden, *Secretary*

British Society of Animal Science

P.O. Box 3,
Penicuik,
Edinburgh, EH26 0RZ
Tel: 0131-445-4508   Fax: 0131-445-5636

M.A. Steele, *Secretary*

*To enhance the understanding of animal sciences and their integration into animal production by organising conferences for those interested in meeting and exchanging information and ideas.**

British Society of Audiology (Scottish Branch)

St. Giles' Centre,
Broomhouse Crescent,
Edinburgh, EH11 3JB
Tel: 0131-443-0304   Fax: 0131-444-2351

Ms. Nancy Newton

British Society of Hearing Therapists

Audiology Department,
Royal Infirmary of Edinburgh,
Edinburgh, EH3 9YW
Tel: 0131-536-3681   Fax: 0131-536-3417

Ms. Judith Christie, *Hearing Therapist*

*A hearing therapist advises, supports and counsels anybody who experiences difficulty in communicating effectively because of a hearing problem and teaches lipreading.**

British Sub Aqua Club (Scottish Federation)

1 Henderson Place,
Edinburgh, EH3 5PJ

Ms. Ellie Iannetta

British Trust for Myelin Project

4 Cammo Walk,
Barnton,
Edinburgh, EH4 8AN
Tel: 0131-339-1316 Fax: 0131-317-1606

Mrs. Diana McGovern

British Union of Social Work Employees (Scottish Office)

P.O. Box 1543,
Dumfries, DG2 8CL
Tel: 01387-850435

British Veterinary Association (Scottish Branch)

Animal Health Office,
Scottish Agriculture and Fisheries Dept,
Thainstone Court,
Inverurie,
Aberdeenshire, AB51 5YA
Tel: 01467-626300 Fax: 01467-626321

Mr. F.O. Sless *

British Victims of Abortion

5 St. Vincent Place,
Glasgow, G1 2DH
Tel: 0141-226-5407 Fax: 0141-248-2105

Mrs. Linda Porter, *Administrator*

Supports anyone suffering from post-abortion trauma with free, confidential, one-to-one, telephone counselling. Additionally, a Helpline operates 7.00 pm–10.00 pm, 0845-6038501 (every evening). *

British Waterways

Canal House,
1 Applecross Street,
Glasgow, G4 9SP
Tel: 0141-332-6936 Fax: 0141-331-1688

Countryside Rangers

British Wheel of Yoga

Viewpark,
Luncarty,
Perth, PH1 3JB
Tel: 01738-583224

Mrs. Marjorie Grant, *Scottish Representative*

The British Wheel of Yoga, which has been recognized by the Sports Council as the governing body for yoga in Great Britain, is a non-profit-making charity run by voluntary support, to encourage, maintain and improve the standard of yoga teaching and practice. *

British Wind Energy Association, Scottish Branch

c/o Energy Unlimited,
Cloney,
Kippen,
Stirling, FK8 3EZ
Tel: 01786-870770   Fax: 01786-870828

Mr. Robert Forrest, *Press & PR Officer, SBWEA*

BWEA is the organisation that represents the UK wind energy industry. Contact us for a range of publications and policy documents. *

Brittle Bone Society (BBS)

30 Guthrie Street,
Strathmartine,
Dundee, DD1 5BS
Tel: 01382-204446/7   Fax: 01382-206771

Miss Morna Wilson, *Administrator*

The Society seeks to promote research into the causes, inheritance and treatment of osteogenesis imperfecta and similar disorders. It also provides advice, encouragement and practical help for patients and their relatives facing the difficulties of living with brittle bones. *

Broadcasting for Scotland Campaign

Victoria Crescent Road,
Glasgow, G12 9DD

Nigel R Smith, *Chairman*

Broadcasting, Entertainment, Cinematograph & Theatre Union (BECTU) (Scottish Office)

114 Union Street,
Glasgow, G1 3QQ
Tel: 0141-248-9558   Fax: 0141-248-9588

Mr. P. McManus, *Scottish Field Officer*

Building Research Establishment - Scottish Laboratory

Kelvin Road,
East Kilbride,
Glasgow, G75 0RZ
Tel: 01355-576200   Fax: 01355-576210

Mrs. Heather Cuckow, *Head of Scottish Laboratory*

Building Societies Association - Committee for Scotland

Nationwide Building Society,
71 George Street,
Edinburgh, EH2 3EH
Tel: 0131-456-0200   Fax: 0131-456-0236

John Urquhart, *Chairman*

B

Buildings of Scotland Trust

9 Palmerston Road,
Edinburgh, EH9 1TL
Tel: 0131-667-3692

Mr. David Connelly, *Secretary*

*The Buildings of Scotland Trust is a registered
charity which finances and manages the
research programme for the Penguin books
series* The Buildings of Scotland. *

Bulldog Club of Scotland

Burnside,
Thurstonfield,
Carlisle,
Cumbria, CA5 6HG
Tel: 01228-576424

Mrs. S. Rowe

Bullmastiff Society of Scotland

3 Moorfoot Path,
Moorfoot,
Paisley, PA2 8AU
Tel: 0141-884-7735

Mr. R. Taylor

Burns Federation

Dick Institute,
Elmbank Avenue,
Kilmarnock, KA1 3BV
Tel: 01563-26401

Allister Anderson, *Honorary Secretary*

Business Aircraft Users' Association Limited

Crossmount House,
Kinloch Rannoch,
Perthshire, PH16 5QF
Tel: 01882-632252   Fax: 01882-632454

D.C. Leggett, *Chief Executive*

Business Archives Council of Scotland

c/o The Archives,
University of Glasgow,
Glasgow, G12 8QQ
Tel: 0141-339 8855

Ms. Lesley Richmond, *Journal Editor*

Business Enterprise Scotland

National Association of Enterprise Trusts,
Media House,
Dunnswood Road,
Wardpark South,
Cumbernauld, G67 3ET
Tel: 01236-452777   Fax: 01236-452888

Mr. Robin Miller, *Chief Executive*

*Business Enterprise Scotland was founded in
1995 by the Enterprise Trusts who required a
lead body to guide, shape, promote and
represent their network. **

Business Women's Forum

12 Kelvinside Gardens,
Glasgow, G20 6BB
Tel: 0141-946-5062

Colette McCloskey, *Chairwoman*

Business for Scotland

P.O. Box 23087,
Edinburgh, EH2 4YT
Tel: 0131-225-9134   Fax: 0131-226-3009

Ms. Samantha Barber, *Director*

*A self-financing organisation providing a forum
for the Scottish business community to debate
and analyse the challenges and opportunities
presented by devolution and independence.* *

Business in the Arts Scotland

100 Wellington Street,
Glasgow, G2 6PB
Tel: 0141-204-3864   Fax: 0141-204-3897

Ms. Alison Hogg

*Business in the Arts Scotland aims to provide
business support for the arts management
sector by encouraging businessmen and
women to share their management skills and
experience with the arts management through
advice and training.* *

C

CARE

8 Roxburgh Drive,
Bearsden,
Glasgow, G61 3LH
Tel: 0141-563-7080

Mrs. Eileen Mackenzie, *Chairperson*

Registered charity which supports couples during and after a termination of pregnancy for foetal abnormality. Support given through telephone counselling. *

CARE for Scotland (Christian Action, Research and Education)

Challenge House,
Canal Street,
Glasgow, G4 0AD
Tel: 0141-332-7212   Fax: 0141-332-8500

Gordon Murray, *Manager*

CHARM (Amateur Chamber Musicians Register)

1 Burnbrae,
Edinburgh, EH12 8UB
Tel: 0131-339-8141

Dr. P.D. Welsby

A register of enthusiastic amateur chamber musicians who contact each other to organise gatherings. General meetings are held three or four times each year. *

CHARM: Children with Hand or Arm Deficiencies

22 Auchauan Gardens,
Finglassie,
Glenrothes,
Fife, KY7 4TU
Tel: 01592-631227

Mrs. C. Forrester

COSHEP (Committee of Scottish Higher Education Principals)

St. Andrew House,
141 West Nile Street,
Glasgow, G1 2RN
Tel: 0141-353-1880   Fax: 0141-353-1881

Dr. Ronald Crawford

COSHEP is the representative body for all institutions of higher education in Scotland. It exists in order to promote the common voice of higher education in a Scottish context. *

COSLA (Convention of Scottish Local Authorities)

Rosebery House,
9 Haymarket Terrace,
Edinburgh, EH12 5XZ
Tel: 0131-474-9200   Fax: 0131-474-9292

Ms. Maureen Ferrier

COSLA is the representative voice of Scotland's 32 local authorities. *

CREW 2000

32 Cockburn Street,
Edinburgh, EH1 1PB
Tel: 0131-220-3404   Fax: 0131-220-4446

Ms. Liz Skelton

CRISP Scotland (Chromosome Rarities Information & Support for Parents)

112 Broughton Road,
Edinburgh, EH7 4JL
Tel: 0131-556-1283

Ms. Joan Bryce

CRUSE – Bereavement Care Scotland

33-35 Boswall Parkway,
Edinburgh, EH5 2BR
Tel: 0131-551-1511   Fax: 0131-551-5234

Mrs. Ruth Hampton

Cruse Bereavement Care offers counselling to all those bereaved; training and education to those who work with death and the dying; and social support and advice. *

CSV Scotland (Community Service Volunteers Scotland)

236 Clyde Street,
Glasgow, G1 4JH
Tel: 0141-204-1681   Fax: 0141-204-0668

Ms. Aileen Robb, *Information Officer*

Caledonian Bulldog Club

2 Muttonhall Cottages,
Chapel Level,
Kirkcaldy,
Fife, KY2 6HG
Tel: 01592-261017

Mr. S.M. Wyse

Club and dog show for bulldogs from 6 months old to veteran (any age). Open show. *

Caledonian Dandie Dinmont Terrier Club

45 Springhill Brae,
Crossgates,
Fife, KY4 8BQ
Tel: 01383-510036

Mrs. D.J. McLeod

Caledonian Foundation

9 Lynedoch Crescent,
Glasgow, G3 6EQ
Tel: 0141-332-5668   Fax: 0141-332-5678

A non-sectarian non-political charitable trust that raises funds around the world, to help the work of charities in Scotland.

Caledonian Railway Association

45 Sycamore Drive,
Hamilton,
South Lanarkshire, ML3 7HF
Tel: 01698-457777

F.A. Landery, *Secretary*

Formed in 1983 to study the former Caledonian Railway Company in all its forms and activities. An illustrated journal The True Line *is published four times per year.**

Camanachd Association

Algarve, Badabrie,
Banavie,
Fort William, PH33 7LX
Tel: 01397-772461   Fax: 01397-772255

Mr. Alastair MacIntyre, *Executive Officer*

The governing body of the sport of shinty, the roots of which go back to Gaelic Scotland and the even earlier heritage of the Celtic race.*

Campaigners (Scotland)

Scottish Headquarters,
28 Manor Drive,
Airdrie,
Lanarkshire, ML6 0JH
Tel: 01236-763660   Fax: 01236-763660

Mr. Sam Bell, *Executive Development Officer*

Camping and Caravanning Club (Scottish Region)

70 Douglas Road,
Longniddry,
East Lothian, EH32 0LJ
Tel: 01875-853292

Mr. A. Strachan, *Secretary*

Cancer Research Campaign Scotland

Thain House,
226 Queensferry Road,
Edinburgh, EH4 2BP
Tel: 0131-343-1344   Fax: 0131-343-6812

Mr. Bill McKinlay, *Regional Director*

Cancer Research Campaign Scotland funds 65% of all cancer research in Scotland. Annually we spend almost £9 million on projects and programmes in hospitals, universities and research institutes throughout Scotland.*

CancerBACUP Scotland – British Association of Cancer United Patients

2/2, 30 Bell Street,
Glasgow, G1 1LG
Tel: 0141-553-1553   Fax: 0141-553-2686

Ms. Jenny Whelan, *Manager*

CancerBACUP is the leading national charity giving information, counselling and support to people with cancer, their families and friends.*

Canine Concern Scotland Trust (incorporating Therapet)

Minard House,
Machrihanish, by Campbeltown,
Argyll, PA28 6PZ
Tel: 01586-810314   Fax: 01586-810333

Mrs. Marjorie J. Henley Price, *Administrator*

Aims to improve the image of dogs by promotion of responsible dog ownership and to show benefits with THERAPET pet-facilitated therapy programme. Scottish charity no. 014924. e-mail: ccstwper@globalnet.co.uk. *

Capability Scotland

Central Office,
22 Corstorphine Road,
Edinburgh, EH12 6HP
Tel: 0131-337-9876   Fax: 0131-346-7864

Mr. Ian McBain, *Director*

Cardiac Risk in the Young (Scottish Branch)

Joseph Scott Gardens,
Broxburn,
West Lothian, EH52 5RU

Mrs. Lynne Lewis

Carers' National Association (Scotland)

3rd floor, 162 Buchanan Street,
Glasgow, G1 2LL
Tel: 0141-333-9494   Fax: 0141-353-3505

Mr. Alex Murphy, *Information Officer*

Caring Operations Joint Action Council (COJAC)

39 Arnprior Road,
Castlemilk,
Glasgow, G45 9EX
Tel: 0141-634-1002   Fax: 0141-634-0666

Ms. Marie Duncan

Catholic Aids Link Ministry (CALM)

P.O. Box 852,
Glasgow, G20 0PW
Tel: 0141-945-5305

Rev. Brian Donnelly

Catholic Education Commission, Scotland

43 Greenhill Road,
Rutherglen,
Glasgow, G73 2SW
Tel: 0141-647-2113

Mr. James McGrath, *Education Officer*

Catholic Marriage Advisory Council

13 North Bank Street,
Edinburgh, EH1 2LP
Tel: 0131-204-1239

Catholic Nurses, Midwives & Health Visitors Guild of Scotland

The Whinnocks,
11 Grieve Road,
Greenock, PA16 7LE
Tel: 01475-33777

Mrs. Jane C. Harkin

Celtic Congress Scotland

7 Teal Avenue,
Inverness, IV2 3TB
Tel: 01463-235351

Ms. Margaret MacIver, *Secretary*

Celtic Film & Television Association

The Library,
Farraline Park,
Inverness, IV1 1LS
Tel: 01463-226189   **Fax:** 01463-237001

Duncan MacLeod, *General Secretary*

Central Bureau for Educational Visits and Exchanges

3 Bruntsfield Crescent,
Edinburgh, EH10 4HD
Tel: 0131-447-8024   **Fax:** 0131-452-8569

Central Council for Education & Training in Social Work

78–80 George Street,
Edinburgh, EH2 3BU
Tel: 0131-220-0093   **Fax:** 0131-220-6717

Ms. Michelle Keenan

*CCETSW is responsible for promoting and
developing education and training in social
work and social care.* *

Central Office of Industrial Tribunals

St. Andrew's House,
141 West Nile Street,
Glasgow, G1 3RU
Tel: 0141-332-1601   **Fax:** 0141-332-3316

Centre for Eating Disorders (Scotland)

3 Sciennes Road,
Edinburgh, EH9 1LE
Tel: 0131-668-3051   **Fax:** 0131-667-9708

Ms. Mary Hart, *Psychotherapist*

*We offer psychotherapy on an individual basis
to those with anorexia and bulimia nervosa
and related conditions. We also work with
the weight disorders: overweight and obesity.
e-mail: MaryHMHart@aol.com. The Centre
is also at 10 Carment Drive, Glasgow, G41,
3PP, tel: 0141-632 6663 (Mrs Grace
Coia).* *

Centre for Education for Racial Equality in Scotland

Charteris, 2/5,
Moray House Institute of Education,
Holyrood Road,
Edinburgh, EH8 8AQ
Tel: 0131-558-6371   Fax: 0131-558-6511

Ms. Rowena Arshad, *Director*

*CERES is a Scottish Office funded project
promoting education for racial equality
within education services in Scotland.
Working in partnership with parents,
authorities and non-governmental organisations.* *

Centre for Environment and Business in Scotland

63 Northumberland Street,
Edinburgh, EH3 6JQ
Tel: 0131-558-8810   Fax: 0131-558-8820

Ms. Anne-Caroline Peckham

*The Centre for Environment and Business in
Scotland (CEBIS), is Scotland's leading co-
ordinating body for environment and business
issues affecting industry and economic
development in Scotland.* *

Centre for Human Ecology

P.O. Box 1972,
Edinburgh, EH1 1YP
Tel: 0131-624-1972   Fax: 0131-624-1973

Osbert Lancaster

*The CHE is an independent academic network
of excellence in teaching, research and
outreach. Working with individuals,
communities and institutions supporting
positive action towards sustainability.* *

Centre for Rural Buildings (formerly Scottish Farm Buildings Investigation Unit)

Craibstone,
Bucksburn,
Aberdeen, AB2 9TR
Tel: 01224-713622

Centre for Scottish Cultural Studies

University of Strathclyde,
Livingstone Tower,
26 Richmond Street,
Glasgow, G1 1XH
Tel: 0141-548-3518   Fax: 0141-552-3493

Dr. K.G. Simpson, *Director*

*The Centre for Scottish Cultural Studies serves
as a forum for creative activity and critical
debate across a broad spectrum of the arts in
Scotland.* *

Centre for Scottish Public Policy

20 Forth Street,
Edinburgh, EH1 3LH
Tel: 0131-477-8219   Fax: 0131-477-8220

The Director

*The Centre aims to provide a focus for imagina-
tive and innovative policy debate on the key
issues facing Scotland and a Scottish
Parliament. Website:
http://www.TheTron.org.uk/JWC.html.* *

Centre for Scottish Studies

Centre for Continuing Education,
University of Aberdeen,
Regent Walk,
Old Aberdeen,
AB9 1FX
Tel: 01224-272448

Cerebral Palsy Action

106 High Street,
Invergordon,
Ross-shire, IV18 0DR
Tel: 01349-854390   Fax: 01349-854390

Ms. Allyson Brannen, *National Liaison Officer*

Certification Office for Trade Unions and Employers' Association

58 Frederick Street,
Edinburgh, EH2 1LN
Tel: 0131-226-3224   Fax: 0131-469-2525

Mr. James L.J. Craig, *Asst. Certification Officer*

Certified Accountants' Benevolent Association, Scottish Office

1 Woodside Place,
Glasgow, G3 7QF
Tel: 0141-309-4053   Fax: 0141-309-4120

Benevolent Association for the ACCA. *

Challenger Children's Fund

ECAS, Cunningham Unit,
Astley Ainslie Hospital,
133 Grange Loan,
Edinburgh, EH9 2HL
Tel: 0131-537-9093   Fax: 0131-537-9095

Ms. Wendy Dunn

Chart and Nautical Instrument Trade Association

Dalmore House,
310 St. Vincent Street,
Glasgow, G2 5QR
Tel: 0141-228-8000   Fax: 0141-228-8310 *

Chartered Institute of Arbitrators (Arbiters), Scottish Branch

see The Chartered Institute of Arbitrators (Arbiters), Scottish Branch.

Chartered Institute of Bankers in Scotland

Drumsheugh House,
Drumsheugh Gardens,
Edinburgh, EH3 7SW
Tel: 0131-473-7777   Fax: 0131-473-7788 *

Chartered Institute of Housing in Scotland

6 Palmerston Place,
Edinburgh, EH12 5AA
Tel: 0131-225-4544   Fax: 0131-225-4566

Mr. Alan Ferguson, *Director*

Chartered Institute of Marketing

29 St. Vincent Place,
Glasgow, G1 2DT
Tel: 0141-221-7700   Fax: 0141-221-7766

Regional Director

The CIM is the leading marketing and sales management group in Europe. Services include membership, training, professional qualifications, library/information, consultancy and conference facilities. *

Chartered Institute of Public Finance and Accountancy

CIPFA Scottish Office,
8 North West Circus Place,
Edinburgh, EH3 6ST
Tel: 0131-220-4316   Fax: 0131-220-4305

Mr. Ian P. Doig, *Secretary*

Chartered Institute of Transport

Scottish Section,
40 Keal Avenue,
South Blairdardie,
Glasgow, G15 6NH

J.G. Fender, *Honorary Secretary*

Chartered Institution of Water and Environmental Management (Scottish Branch)

c/o Scottish Environment Protection
   Agency,
Erskine Court,
Castle Business Park,
Stirling, FK9 4TR
Tel: 01786-457700   Fax: 01786-446885

Mr. R.J. Sargent

Professional body promoting good practice in water and environmental management with approx 1000 members in Scotland. *

Chartered Society of Designers, Scottish Branch

Randall Design,
90 Mitchell Street,
Glasgow, G1 3NQ
Tel: 0141-221-2142

Lin Gibbon, *Chairman*

Chest, Heart and Stroke Scotland (CHSS)

65 North Castle Street,
Edinburgh, EH2 3LT
Tel: 0131-225-6963   Fax: 0131-220-6313

Ms. Lesley Munro

Chest, Heart and Stroke Scotland (CHSS) aims to improve the quality of life for people in Scotland affected by chest, heart and stroke illness, through programmes of medical research, health promotion and the provision of services. Adviceline: 0345–720720, Monday–Friday, 9.30–4.00. *

Chihuahua Club of Scotland

154 Halbeath Road,
Dunfermline,
Fife, KY11 4LB
Tel: 01383-724368

Mr. G.A.W. Baxter

Child Psychotherapy Trust in Scotland

see The Child Psychotherapy Trust in Scotland.

Child Support Commissioners

Edinburgh, EH3 7PW
Tel: 0131-225-2201   Fax: 0131-220-6782

R. Lindsay, *Secretary*

Child and Family Trust

Fleming House,
134 Renfrew Street,
Glasgow, G3 6ST
Tel: 0141-353-2424   Fax: 0141-353-2424

Ms. Heather Molloy

Fulton Mackay Nurse Projects – dealing with sexual abuse, suicide and overdose and also emotional/behavioural problems. There is a publication available for parents, How to cope when your child has been sexually abused. *

ChildLine Scotland

18 Albion Street,
Glasgow, G1 1LH
Tel: 0141-552-1123   Fax: 0141-552-3089

Administration Manager

*ChildLine is the free 24 hour national telephone counselling service for any child or young person with any problem. Telephone no. 0800-1111. *

Childlessness Overcome Through Surrogacy (COTS)

Loandhu Cottage,
Gruids,
Lairg,
Sutherland, IV27 4EF
Tel: 01549-402777   Fax: 01549-402777

Ms. Gena Dodd

*We are a voluntary organisation that helps and supports both couples and surrogates through all aspects of surrogacy. We also have information for students.
e-mail: cotsuk@enterprise.net.
Information line: 01549-402401.
Website: http.www.surrogacy.org.uk. *

Children 1st

Royal Scottish Society for Prevention of
   Cruelty to Children
Melville House,
41 Polwarth Terrace,
Edinburgh, EH11 1NU
Tel: 0131-337-8539   Fax: 0131-346-8284

Mr. A.M.M. Wood, *Chief Executive/General
   Secretary*

*For 114 years Children 1st, The Royal Scottish
   Society for Prevention of Cruelty to Children,
   has continued to protect children from harm,
   to provide support and help to children and
   young people who have suffered violence,
   exploitation and all kinds of abuse and
   neglect.* *

Children in Scotland

Princes House,
5 Shandwick Place,
Edinburgh, EH2 4RG
Tel: 0131-228-8484   Fax: 0131-228-8585

Ms. Annie Gunner

*Children in Scotland is the united voice of over
   300 voluntary, statutory and professional
   organisations and individuals working with
   children and families throughout Scotland.* *

Children's Heart Disease Trust

Cardiology Department,
Royal Hospital for Sick Children,
Sciennes Road,
Edinburgh, EH9 1LF
Tel: 0131-536-0621

Children's Hospice Association Scotland (CHAS)

18 Hanover Street,
Edinburgh, EH2 2EN
Tel: 0131-226-4933   Fax: 0131-220-1626

Ms. Heather Dillon, *Office Manager*

Children's Music Foundation in Scotland

537 Sauchiehall Street,
Glasgow, G3 7PQ
Tel: 0141-248-1611   Fax: 0141-248-1989

Louise Naftalin or Lizanne McKerrell

Chow Chow Club of Scotland

30 Toch Hill Road,
Fourdon,
Laurencekirk,
Near Aberdeen
Tel: 01561-320506

Mrs. I. Robertson

*A breed club to better the breed and its welfare;
   run shows and provide information on the
   breed. We also run a breed rescue service.* *

Christian Aid Scotland

41 George IV Bridge,
Edinburgh, EH1 1EL
Tel: 0131-220-1254   Fax: 0131-225-8861

Rev. John N. Wylie, *National Secretary*

In its fundraising, education and campaigning work, Christian Aid supports people's own organisations in 60 countries worldwide to overcome the causes and effects of poverty. *

Christian Centre Ministries Scotland

Olympia Arcade,
West End High Street,
Kirkcaldy,
Fife, KY1 1QF
Tel: 01592-206061

Rev. Peter Hadden

Christian Fellowship of Healing (Scotland)

6 Morningside Road,
Edinburgh, EH10 4DD
Tel: 0131-228-6553

Rev. Jenny Williams, *Chaplain*

A ministry of listening and prayer, weekdays and two evenings. We support churches interested in the healing ministry and encourage links with the medical profession. *

Church of Scotland – Hospital Chaplains

Department of National Mission (Hospitals),
121 George Street,
Edinburgh, EH2 4YN
Tel: 0131-225-5722   Fax: 0131-220-3113

Chaplaincies Administrator

Responsible for the encouragement, development, support and review of chaplaincies in hospitals and for the appointment of part-time and full-time chaplains. *

Church of Scotland Guild

see The Church of Scotland Guild.

Church of Scotland Total Abstainers' Association

McOmish Hart & Company,
5 St Vincent Place,
Glasgow, G1 2HT
Tel: 0141-248-6820

Mr. R.J.M. Hart, *Honorary Treasurer*

Churches' Agency for Inter-Faith Relations in Scotland

36 Queen's Drive,
Glasgow, G42 8DD
Tel: 0141-423-2971

Father Gordian Marshall, *Convenor*

Citizens Advice Scotland

26 George Square,
Edinburgh, EH8 9LD
Tel: 0131-667-0156   Fax: 0131-668-5349

Professor Martyn Evans

City Farms Scotland

244 Wilton Street,
Glasgow, G20 6BL
Tel: 0141-221-9855

Civil & Public Services Association

Room 321–323,
Baltic Chambers,
50 Wellington Street,
Glasgow, G2 6HJ
Tel: 0141-248-6978   Fax: 0141-248-6959

Mr. M. McCann

Clan Ranald Trust for Scotland

189 Canongate,
Royal Mile,
Edinburgh, EH8 8BN
Tel: 0131-558-9191   Fax: 0131-558-9191

Chick Allan, *Chief Executive*

To further promote the culture and heritage of Scotland by producing projects of interaction for the public and the tourism industry, e.g. mediaeval fort/village. *

Clinical Theology Association

86 Gordon Street,
Aberdeen, AB1 2EW

Mr. John Anthony

Clydesdale Horse Society of Great Britain & Ireland

24 Beresford Terrace,
Ayr, KA7 2EG
Tel: 01292-281650

Robert S. Gilmour

Coal Industry Social Welfare Organisation

2nd floor,
50 Hopetoun Street,
Bathgate,
West Lothian, EH48 4EU
Tel: 01506-635550   Fax: 01506-631555

Mr. Ian McAlpine, *Operations Manager (Scotland)*

The objects of the charity are the promotion of health, the relief of poverty and hardship and the advancement of education. Also, any other charitable purpose for the benefit of employees and former employees of the coal mining industry in the United Kingdom and their necessitous relatives, dependants and the communities in which they live. *

Cocker Spaniel Club of Scotland

140 Silvertonhill Avenue,
Hamilton,
Lanarkshire, ML3 7PA
Tel: 01698-428764

Mrs. A. Barnett

For information regarding the Club's activities, membership and purchasing a puppy, contact the Secretary as detailed above. *

College of Holistic Medicine

4 Craigpark,
Glasgow, G31 2NA
Tel: 0141-554-5808   Fax: 0141-554-9035

Ms. Judith Bolton/Elaine Johnston

College of Speech & Language Therapists

Dept. of Speech & Language Therapy,
Coylton Health Clinic,
11 Hole Road,
Coylton, KA6 6JL
Tel: 01292-571236   Fax: 01292-570624

Mrs. Jane Kerr, *Manager*

Colliery Officials & Staff Area NUM

7 Eastercraig Gardens,
Saline,
Dunfermline,
Fife, KY12 9TH
Tel: 01383-852526   Fax: 01383-850224

Mr. A. Kenney

Comhairle nan Leabhraichean/The Gaelic Books Council

22 Mansfield Street,
Glasgow, G11 5QP
Tel: 0141-337-6211   Fax: 0141-341-0515

Mr. Ian MacDonald, *Director*

Provides grants for Gaelic publishers and writers. Its shop stocks all Gaelic and Gaelic-related books in print, and a complete catalogue of these is available. *

Comhairle nan Sgoiltean Araich (CNSA), the Gaelic pre-school council

53 Church Street,
Inverness, IV1 1DR
Tel: 01463-225469   Fax: 01463-716943

Mr. Fionnlagh MacLeoid, *Chief Executive*

Promotion, development and provision of Gaelic pre-school facilities throughout Scotland, catering both for children and parents. Remit includes pre-school staff training. *

Commission for Racial Equality

45 Hanover Street,
Edinburgh, EH2 2PJ
Tel: 0131-226-5186   Fax: 0131-226-5243

Najimee Parveen

The Commission works towards the elimination of discrimination, promotes equal opportunities and good relations between people from different racial groups and keeps the Race Relations Act under review. *

Commissioner for Local Administration in Scotland (The Ombudsman)

23 Walker Street,
Edinburgh, EH3 7HX
Tel: 0131-225-5300   Fax: 0131-225-9495

Mr. Frederick C. Marks, O.B.E., *Commissioner*

The Local Government Ombudsman deals with complaints of injustice caused by maladministration by local authorities and Scottish Homes as landlord. The service is free, independent and impartial. *

Committee for the Promotion of Angling for the Disabled

Lomondside Cottage,
The Loan,
Falkland,
Fife, KY15 7BD
Tel: 01337-857519   Fax: 01592-415710

Mr. Mike Tudor, *Chairman*

CPAD run national and international competitions. We advise fisheries and clubs with their own water what facilities are needed for disabled anglers and give general advice and information. *

Committee of Scottish Clearing Banks

19 Rutland Square,
Edinburgh, EH1 2DD
Tel: 0131-229-1326   Fax: 0131-229-1852

Alan Scott, *Secretary*

Trade association of the Scottish clearing banks. *

Common Services Agency

Trinity Park House,
South Trinity Road,
Edinburgh, EH5 3SE
Tel: 0131-552-6255   Fax: 0131-552-6255

Mr. F.F. Gibb, *General Manager*

To be the preferred supplier of professional support services to the healthcare bodies of the National Health Service in Scotland. *

CommonWeal

41 George IV Bridge,
Edinburgh, EH1 1EL
Tel: 0131-225-1772

Executive Secretary

CommonWeal is a small membership organisation resourcing the Scottish churches and allied organisations on issues of justice and peace. A quarterly newsletter is produced. *

Commonwealth Games Council for Scotland

1 Craiglockhart Crescent,
Edinburgh, EH14 1EZ
Tel: 0131-443-2533   Fax: 0131-315-2918

G.A. Hunter, *Honorary Secretary*

To organise, equip and send a Scottish team to the Commonwealth Games every four years. *

Commonwealth Institute (Scotland)

8 Rutland Square,
Edinburgh, EH1 2AS
Tel: 0131-229-6668   Fax: 0131-229-6041

Communication Workers' Union

102 Lochend Road,
Edinburgh, EH6 8BU

Mr. T. McGee, *Secretary*

Communist Party of Scotland

2 Merkland Street,
Glasgow, G11 6DB
Tel: 0141-339 3889

Community Development Foundation (Scotland)

Suite 327,
Baltic Chambers,
50 Wellingon Street,
Glasgow, G2 6HJ
Tel: 0141-248-1925   Fax: 0141-248-4938

Community Gardening Projects Scotland

4 Drum Street,
Edinburgh, EH17 8QG
Tel: 0131-658-1096

Liz Ridder

Community Self Build (Scotland)

Queenslie Business Centre,
19 Blairtummock Road,
Glasgow, G33 4AN

Companies House

37 Castle Terrace,
Edinburgh, EH1 2EB
Tel: 0131-535-5800   Fax: 0131-535-5820

Mr. J. Henderson, *Registrar*

*The main functions are the incorporation and
striking off companies and registration of
documents and also the provision of company
information to the public for which purpose
compliance is enforced.**

Companions of Britain's Rheumatic and Arthritic Sufferers (COBRA)

59 Hyndland Street,
Glasgow, G11 5PS
Tel: 0141-357-1163

Company of Scottish Cheesemakers

Station House,
St Enoch Square,
Glasgow, G1 4DL
Tel: 0141-221-4838   Fax: 0141-221-4647

John Russell, *Manager*

Comunn Na Clarsach

22 Durham Road South,
Edinburgh, EH15 3PD
Tel: 0131-664-5584   Fax: 0131-468-1223

Mr. Alistair R. Cockburn, *Administrator*

Comunn Na Gàidhlig

5 Mitchell's Lane,
Inverness, IV2 3HQ
Tel: 01463-234138   Fax: 01463-237470

Mr. Allan Campbell

*This is Scotland's Gaelic Language Develop-
ment Agency established in 1984 to co-
ordinate the revival of Gaelic at all levels and
sectors in Scotland.* *

Concern Worldwide

Level 2,
80 Buchanan Street,
Glasgow, G1 3HA
Tel: 0141-221-3610   Fax: 0141-221-3708

Mr. David Welch

*Concern Worldwide is a non-denominational
voluntary organisation devoted to the relief,
assistance and advancement of peoples in
need in less developed countries of the world.* *

Confederation of British Industry Scotland

Beresford House,
5 Claremont Terrace,
Glasgow, G3 7XT
Tel: 0141-332-8661

Confederation of Passenger Transport UK

41 Laigh Road,
Newton Mearns,
Glasgow, G77 5EX
Tel: 0141-639-4984   Fax: 0141-616-0866

P. Thompson, *Scottish Regional Secretary*

*The Confederation of Passenger Transport UK
(CPT) is the national trade association
representing bus, coach and fixed track
operators.* *

Confederation of Scottish Counselling Agencies: COSCA

64 Murray Place,
Stirling, FK8 2BX
Tel: 01786-475140   Fax: 01786-446207

Conference of Religious Congregations in Scotland

15D Hill Street,
Glasgow, G3 6RN
Tel: 0141-332-3094   Fax: 0141-332-3094

Sister Winifred Connolly, *FMM General
Secretary*

*The Conference is a church organisation
representing men and women of Roman
Catholic religious congregations in Scotland.* *

Connections

26 Ashburton Road,
Glasgow, G12 0LZ
Tel: 0141-334-5846   Fax: 0141-621-1220

Mr. Ian Holland

Scotland's alternative health magazine. Also run the Scottish Alternative Health exhibitions in Glasgow and Edinburgh every year. *

Contact the Elderly in Scotland

361 Albert Drive,
Glasgow, G41 5PH
Tel: 0141-427-0827   Fax: 0141-427-0827

Ms. Elspeth Horsman

Small groups of volunteers with cars take frail and lonely older members to tea in volunteer hosts' homes one Sunday afternoon a month. *

Contemporary Music Making for Amateurs

Flat 7,
85 Polwarth Terrace,
Edinburgh, EH11 1NN
Tel: 0131-455-4631   Fax: 0131-455-4232

Colin Johnson, *Scottish Co-ordinator*

Coping with Hysterectomy and Menopausal Problems (CHAMP)

10 Howard Crescent,
Dunfermline, KY11 4QQ
Tel: 01383-729377

Ms. Una Ross, *Chairwoman*

Voluntary self-help group giving information and support to women before and after hysterectomy and those with menopausal problems. Monthly meetings in Dunfermline with speakers including doctors, psychologists, dieticians, etc. *

Cosgrove Care

Cosgrove House,
6 St. John's Road,
Glasgow, G41 5EG
Tel: 0141-429-2327   Fax: 0141-429-6532

Ms. Linda Goldberg, *Chief Executive*

Cosgrove Care supports and cares for people with learning disabilities within the Jewish community in Scotland. Services are for both children and adults. *

Costume Society of Scotland

8 Lynedoch Place,
Edinburgh, EH3 7PX
Tel: 0131-226-5583

Kirstie P. Colam, *Honorary Secretary*

Monthly meetings in Edinburgh October to May; occasional visits to costume collections and places of costume interest. Funded by members' subscriptions. Annual magazine. *

Council for Hospitality Management Education

Dept. of Hospitality, Tourism & Leisure
  Management,
Glasgow Caledonian University,
Park Drive,
Glasgow, G3 6LP
Tel: 0141-337-4313   Fax: 0141-337-4500

Prof. D.A. Mogendorff, *Secretary*

Council for Music in Hospitals

10 Forth Street,
Edinburgh, EH1 3LD
Tel: 0131-556-5848   Fax: 0131-556-0225

Ms. Alison Frazer, *Director*

Council for Scottish Archaeology

c/o National Museums of Scotland,
Chambers Street,
Edinburgh, EH1 1JF
Tel: 0131-225-7534   Fax: 0131-558-8834

Dr. Shannon Fraser, *Director*

*The Council for Scottish Archaeology is an
independent voluntary organisation which
promotes informed opinion concerning the
study and conservation of Scotland's archaeological heritage and has a membership of
individuals, societies and organisations in
order to do this.* *

Countryside in and Around Towns Network

Scottish Natural Heritage,
Caspian House,
Clydebank Business Park,
Clydebank, G81 2NR
Tel: 0141-951-4488   Fax: 0141-951-4510

Ms. Helen Robertson, *Network Officer*

Court of Session

Parliament House,
Parliament Square,
Edinburgh, EH1 1RQ
Tel: 0131-225-2595   Fax: 0131-225-8213

Mrs. G. McKeand, *Deputy Principal Clerk of
Session*

Court of the Lord Lyon King of Arms

H.M. New Register House,
Edinburgh, EH1 3YT
Tel: 0131-556-7255   Fax: 0131-557-2148

Mrs. C.G.W. Roads, *Lyon Clerk*

Cricket Society of Scotland

5 Riverside Road,
Eaglesham,
Glasgow, G76 0DQ

A.J. Robertson

*The Society aims to promote interest in cricket,
primarily by holding meetings addressed by
cricketers past and present, or by others
involved in the game.* *

Crime Concern Scotland

Messrs. Harper,
The Ca'd'oro,
45 Gordon Street,
Glasgow, G1 3PE
Tel: 0141-226-5661   Fax: 0141-226-5662

Criminal Injuries Compensation Authority

Tay House,
300 Bath Street,
Glasgow, G2 4JR
Tel: 0141-331-2726   Fax: 0141-331-2287

Mr. R. Armour

The Authority is responsible for operating the Government's Criminal Injuries Compensation Scheme which provides lump sum compensation to innocent victims of crimes of violence in Great Britain. *

Crofters Commission

4–6 Castle Wynd,
Inverness, IV2 3EQ
Tel: 01463-663450   Fax: 01463-711820

Mr. B. MacDonald, *Information Officer*

Our prime objective is to promote a thriving crofting community by regulating and developing crofting. We also advise the Secretary of State on crofting matters. *

Crossroads (Scotland) Care Attendant Schemes

4th floor,
24 George Square,
Glasgow, G2 1EG
Tel: 0141-226-3793   Fax: 0141-221-7130

Mr. Jack Ryan, *Chief Executive*

The leading voluntary sector provider of domiciliary care for carers in Scotland. Care is provided locally by 53 local schemes and managed by volunteers. *

Crown Estate Commissioners – Scottish Office

10 Charlotte Square,
Edinburgh, EH2 4DR
Tel: 0131-226-7241   Fax: 0131-220-1366

Mr. M.J. Gravestock, *Crown Estate Receiver, Scotland*

The Crown Estate manages a variety of interests including agricultural, forestry, foreshore and seabed. Crown Estate consent is required for any activities involving its resources. *

Crown Office

25 Chambers Street,
Edinburgh, EH1 1LA
Tel: 0131-226-2626   Fax: 0131-226-6910

Rt. Hon. the Lord Rodger of Earlsferry

Crusaid Scotland

25 Queensferry Street,
Edinburgh, EH2 4QS
Tel: 0131-225-8918   Fax: 0131-220-4033

Mr. David McNally, *Director*

*Crusaid Scotland raises and distributes funds
for prevention, education and care in the
fields of HIV infection and AIDS.* *

Cyclists' Touring Club Scotland

24 New Bridge Street,
Ayr, KA7 1JX

Mr. Drew Moyes, *Secretary*

Cystic Fibrosis Trust

Princes House,
5 Shandwick Place,
Edinburgh, EH2 4RG
Tel: 0131-221-1110

Ms. Helen Macfarlane

*Cystic Fibrosis Trust funds research, clinical
and community support through the Trust's
Family and Adult Support Service (FASS).
FASS offers emotional, practical and
financial support, advice and advocacy to
cystic fibrosis families and information to
professionals and the general public.* *

D

Dalmatian Club of Scotland

Mansefield,
Glebe Road,
Kilbirnie,
Ayrshire, KA25 6HX
Tel: 01505-683402

Mrs. C. Whyte

Dance School of Scotland

Knightswood Secondary School,
60 Knightswood Road,
Glasgow, G13 2XD
Tel: 0141-954-9124

Head of Dance

David Hume Institute

21 George Square,
Edinburgh, EH8 9LD
Tel: 0131-650-4633

Dr. Hector L. MacQueen, *Exec. Director &
Secretary*

Deaf Women's Health Project

55 Shieldhill Gardens,
Altens Cove,
Aberdeen, AB12 3JY
Tel: 01224-891425

Ms. Kathleen Cameron

DeafBlind UK

21 Alexandra Avenue,
Lenzie,
Glasgow, G66 5BG
Tel: 0141-777-6111   Fax: 0141-775-3311

Mrs. Drena O'Malley, *Development Manager, Scotland*

DeafBlind UK's objective is to help deafblind adults to live as useful members of any community in which they may find themselves. For 70 years DeafBlind UK has been bringing deafblind people together in clubs, holidays, outings and in any way possible to reduce their isolation. There is a 24-hour free helpline: 0800-132320 and our website is http://www.deafblindscotland.org.uk. *

Deer Commission for Scotland

Knowsley,
82 Fairfield Road,
Inverness, IV3 5LH
Tel: 01463-231751   Fax: 01463-712931

Mr. Andy Rinning, *Director*

The Government's adviser and lead agency on all deer matters in Scotland. *

Dementia Services Development Centre

University of Stirling,
Stirling, FK9 4LA
Tel: 01786-467740   Fax: 01786-466846

Mrs. Averil Harrison, *Information Officer*

The Centre exists to extend and improve services for people with dementia and their carers. Provides information development assistance, conferences and seminars, publications and training to any manager, planner or provider of services in the statutory, voluntary or private sector. *

Democracy for Scotland

Regent Road,
Edinburgh, EH7 5BL
Tel: 0131-558-3088

Department for Education and Employment, Redundancy Payments Service

Grayfield House,
5 Bankhead Avenue,
Sighthill,
Edinburgh, EH11 4AF
Tel: 0131-458-3322

Department for Education and Employment, Employment Service

Argyle House,
3 Lady Lawson Street,
Edinburgh,
EH3 9SD
Tel: 0131-229-9191

Department of Environment, Transport and Regions – Scottish Traffic Area

J Floor,
Argyle House,
3 Lady Lawson Street,
Edinburgh, EH3 9SE
Tel: 0131-529-8500   Fax: 0131-529-8501

J.R. Bannister, *Administrative Director*

Scottish Traffic Area issues operator licences to operators of lorries, buses and coaches, registers local bus services and enforces compliance with rules and regulations pertaining to these functions. *

Department of Transport – Vehicle Registration Office

Saughton House,
Spur E,
Broomhouse Drive,
Edinburgh, EH11 3XE
Tel: 0131-443-5833

M. McIver, *Area Manager*

Depression Alliance Scotland

3 Grosvenor Gardens,
Edinburgh, EH12 5JU
Tel: 0131-467-3050   Fax: 0131-467-7701

Ms. Rona Harkin, *Administrator for Scotland*

To provide support, understanding and information for those suffering from depression and for their carers, co-operate with caring professions, and raise public awareness about the illness. *

Design Business Association, Scotland

5 Gayfield Square,
Edinburgh, EH1 3NW
Tel: 0131-556-9115   Fax: 0131-556-9116

Mr. Andrew Hunter, *Chairman*

To promote, support and represent the business of design to industry and commerce worldwide. Be the influential voice of design consultancies synonymous with an assurance of design professionalism. *

Dietitians Scotland

Queen Margaret College,
Clerwood Terrace,
Edinburgh, EH12 8TS
Tel: 0131-317-3523   Fax: 0131-317-3528

Dr. Fred Pender, *Chairperson*

Dietitians Scotland is a focus for collective views of State Registered Dietitians in Scotland. The group facilitates development of dietetic practice through collaboration across Scotland. *

Direct Marketing Association (UK) Limited

41 Comely Bank,
Edinburgh, EH4 1AF
Tel: 0131-315-4422   Fax: 0131-315-4433

Jo Scobie, *Manager, Scottish Office*

The DMA is the main trade association in direct marketing. It represents the best interests of the direct marketing industry and gives the consumer trust and confidence in it. *

Disability Information Scotland (Disablement Information Advice Line)

Braid House,
Labrador Avenue,
Howden East,
Livingston,
West Lothian, EH54 6BU
Tel: 01506-433468   Fax: 01506-431201

Mrs. M. McDonald, *Scottish Officer*

Disability Information Scotland is a free service informing and advising on all aspects of disability. We enable all people with disabilities to gain full independence and access to all services in order to promote full participation in all walks of life. *

Disability Scotland

Princes House,
5 Shandwick Place,
Edinburgh, EH2 4RG
Tel: 0131-229-8632   Fax: 0131-229-5168

Ms. Kirsten Anne Ferguson

*Disability Scotland aims to be the national
representative voice of the disability equality
movement in Scotland. Services include an
enquiry service, information directories, DS
Data on CD-ROM and an accessible internet
site.* *

Disabled Drivers Association (Scottish Area)

51 Margaretvale Drive,
Larkhall,
Lanarkshire, ML9 1QH
Tel: 01698-881201   Fax: 01698-881201

Mr. James Ritchie, *Scottish Area Secretary*

*Free information on all aspects of mobility for
disabled drivers and passengers. Membership
£10 annually and discounts on all major
ferries.*

Disablement Income Group – Scotland (DIG)

5 Quayside Street,
Edinburgh, EH6 6EJ
Tel: 0131-558-2811

Mr. Jack F. McGregor

*A national charity providing free welfare
benefits, advisory and advocacy service to
disabled people in Scotland. Membership is
optional – fee £5 per annum.* *

Disfigurement Guidance Centre/Laserfair

P.O. Box 7,
Cupar,
Fife, KY15 4PF
Tel: 01337-870281   Fax: 01337-870310

Mr. Peter or Mrs. D. Trust, MBE

*Information for patients with birthmarks or
other forms of disfigurement.* *

Dog Aid Society of Scotland

60 Blackford Avenue,
Edinburgh, EH9 3ER
Tel: 0131-668-3633

Ms. Margaret Anderson, *Secretary*

*We rehome dogs and give general advice on
training, feeding, choosing a dog and
bereavement counselling. Help is given with
veterinary treatment, spaying and neutering.* *

Domestic Heating Council

2 Walker Street,
Edinburgh, EH7 3LB
Tel: 0131-225-2255   Fax: 0131-226-7638

Down's Syndrome Association Scotland

see Scottish Down's Syndrome Association

Driving Standards Agency, Scottish Region

P.O. Box 288,
Newcastle-upon-Tyne, NE99 1WD
Tel: 0131-529-8580   Fax: 0131-529-8589

Mr. A. Wilkinson, *Scottish Manager**

Duke of Edinburgh's Award Scheme

69 Dublin Street,
Edinburgh, EH3 6NS
Tel: 0131-556-9097   Fax: 0131-557-8044

Miss Janet Shepherd, *Secretary for Scotland*

*A challenging leisure time programme for
14–25 year olds consisting of three levels,
bronze, silver and gold, with four sections,
Service in the Community, Skills, Physical
Recreation and Expeditions. (There is a fifth
section at gold level - Residential).**

Dyslexia Institute (Scotland)

74 Victoria Crescent Road,
Dowanhill,
Glasgow, G12 9JN
Tel: 0141-334 4549   Fax: 0141-339-8879

Mrs. E. MacKenzie

ENABLE

6th Floor,
7 Buchanan Street,
Glasgow, G1 3HL
Tel: 0141-226-4541   Fax: 0141-204-4398

Mr. Norman Dunning, *Director*

*A voluntary organisation concerned with the
rights and needs of people with learning
disabilities and their families. Local branches
throughout Scotland.* *

Earl Haig Fund Scotland

New Haig House,
Logie Green Road,
Edinburgh, EH7 4HR
Tel: 0131-557-2782   Fax: 0131-557-5819

Cameron Whyte

*The Earl Haig Fund Scotland provides
financial and other assistance to ex-Armed
Service veterans and their dependants in need
in Scotland.* *

Early Music Forum of Scotland

Glen Cottage,
63 Holburn Street,
Aberdeen, AB10 6BR
Tel: 01224-580024

Dr. Charles Foster, *Chairman*

*The Early Music Forum of Scotland provides its
members with regular newsletters, detailing
Early Music concerts and courses held
throughout Scotland.* *

Ecclesiastical History Society

Department of History (Medieval),
University of Glasgow,
Glasgow, G12 8QQ
Tel: 0141-330-4087   Fax: 0141-330-5056

Mr. M.J. Kennedy, *Honorary Secretary*

*International society which promotes the study
of ecclesiastical history by holding two
conferences yearly and by publishing annually
Studies in Church History.* *

Edictal Citations & Office

2 Parliament Square,
Edinburgh, EH1 1RQ
Tel: 0131-225-2595

Mrs. E.E. Dickson, *Keeper*

Educational Institute of Scotland

see The Educational Institute of Scotland.

Electoral Reform Society in Scotland

17/10 Gillsland Road,
Edinburgh, EH10 5DA
A. Burns/J. Gilmour/J. McGowan-Smith,

E

Electrical & Plumbing Industries Union

c/o TGWU,
290 Bath Street,
Glasgow, G2 4LD
Tel: 0141-332-7321

Electrical Power Engineers Association

30 New Street,
Musselburgh,
Edinburgh, EH21 6JP
Tel: 0131-665 4487

Elkhound Association of Scotland

10 Barnton Place,
Glenrothes,
Fife, KY6 2PS
Tel: 01592-755365

Miss A. Charleston

Employee Ownership Scotland

Building 1, Unit D8,
Templeton Business Centre,
Templeton Street,
Glasgow, G40 1DA
Tel: 0141-554-3797   Fax: 0141-554-5163

Mr. Hugh Donnelly, *Executive Director*

*We assist the start up of employee-owned businesses; rescues from factory closure or receiverships; employee buyouts of family businesses; business plan production; legal and financial structuring. ***

Employers in Voluntary Housing

Suite 109,
Baltic Chambers,
50 Wellington Street,
Glasgow, G2 6NF
Tel: 0141-248-8254

Employers' Association for Scottish Further Education Colleges

c/o Falkirk College of Technology,
Grangemouth Road,
Falkirk, FK2 9AD

John W. Sellars, *Chief Executive*

Employment Medical Advisory Service

Belford House,
59 Belford Road,
Edinburgh, EH4 3UE
Tel: 0131-247-2000   Fax: 0131-247-2121

L. Williams, *Regional Director*

Employment Service

Office for Scotland,
Argyle House,
3 Lady Lawson Street,
Edinburgh, EH3 9SD
Tel: 0131-221-4000   Fax: 0131-221-4004

A.R. Brown, *Director*

Energy Action Scotland

Suite 4A,
Ingram House,
227 Ingram Street,
Glasgow, G1 1DA
Tel: 0141-226-3064   Fax: 0141-221-2788

Ms. Ann Loughrey, *Director*

Energy Action Scotland is the national charitable organisation promoting energy efficiency solutions, and affordable warmth in the domestic sector. *

Energy Design Advice Scheme

15 Rutland Square,
Edinburgh, EH1 2BE
Tel: 0131-228-4414   Fax: 0131-228-2188

Mrs. J. Chalmers, *Administrative Director*

Provide advice on energy and environmental design to building design terms. This is a government-financed initiative, and much of the advice is free. *

Engender

c/o One Parent Families Scotland,
13 Gayfield Square,
Edinburgh, EH1 3NX
Tel: 0131-558-9596   Fax: 0131-557-9650

Camilla Kidner

Engender is an information, research and networking organisation for women in Scotland. We publish an annual statistical audit of women's positions and a newsletter for members. *

Engineering Council

105 West George Street,
Glasgow, G2 1PB
Tel: 0141-248-3030

Engineering Education Association

Science Designs Limited,
Unit 27, Kirkhill Place,
Kirkhill Industrial Estate,
Dyce,
Aberdeen, AB1 0GU
Tel: 01224-773320   Fax: 01224-773320

Mrs. Gillian Lomas

EEA directs and manages education/industry schemes to attract young people into engineering. Membership of EEA is free and open to organisations and individuals as participants, supporters or sponsors. *

Engineers' & Managers' Association

30 New Street,
Musselburgh,
East Lothian, EH21 6JP
Tel: 0131-665-4487   Fax: 0131-665-7513

Ms. A. Douglas, *National Officer*

A trade union – professional services for professional people. *

English Setter Society of Scotland

54 James Street,
Alva,
Clackmannanshire, FK12 5AJ
Tel: 01685-722279

Mrs. C. Normansell

English Speaking Union – Scotland (ESU)

23 Atholl Crescent,
Edinburgh, EH3 8HQ
Tel: 0131-229-1528   Fax: 0131-229-1533

Mr. Richard Wickins, *Administrator*

The ESU is an educational charity, it administers several scholarships and takes an interest in schools' debating. For further information contact the Administrator. *

English Springer Spaniel Club of Scotland

Hillswick,
Abercromby Road,
Castle Douglas,
Kirkcudbrightshire, DG7 1BA
Tel: 01556-502430

Mr. G. Ford

Enterprise Music Scotland

Westburn House,
Westburn Place,
Aberdeen, AB2 5DF
Tel: 01224-620025   Fax: 01224-620027

Ronnie Rae, *Executive Director*

Epilepsy Association of Scotland

48 Govan Road,
Glasgow, G51 1JL
Tel: 0141-427-4911   Fax: 0141-419-1709

Mrs. Judy Cochrane

Our helpline no. is 0141-427-5225. *

Equal Opportunities Commission (Scottish Office)

Stock Exchange House,
7 Nelson Mandela Place,
Glasgow, G1 2RN
Tel: 0141-248-5833   Fax: 0141-248-5834

Mrs. Morag Alexander, *Director*

e-mail: moraga@eoc.org.uk. *

Erskine Hospital

Bishopton,
Renfewshire, PA7 5PU
Tel: 0141-812-1100   Fax: 0141-812-3733

Col. Martin Gibson, O.B.E.

Caring for ex-Service men and women throughout Scotland. This 80 year old charity provides care to over 400 residents per year. Facilities include: veterans' cottages; holiday home in Dunoon; physiotherapy and occupational and speech therapy. *

Estuarine & Coastal Sciences Association

Department of Biological Science,
University of Stirling,
Stirling, FK9 4LA
Tel: 01786-467755 Fax: 01786-464994

Dr. D.S. McLusky, *Honorary Secretary*

*The principal European organisation for the
study of the science of estuaries and coasts.
Organises meetings and publications on
estuaries, as well as workshops for training.* *

European Association of Professional Secretaries (EAPS)

Scottish Committee,
Bank of Scotland,
The Mound,
Edinburgh
Tel: 0131-243-5846

Karen Burnside

European Desalination Society

c/o Department of Mechanical Engineer-
ing,
University of Glasgow,
Glasgow, G12 8QQ
Tel: 0141-776-5221 Fax: 0141-776-1772

Dr. W.T. Hanbury

European Flexible Intermediate Bulk Container Association

140 Camphill Road,
Broughty Ferry,
Dundee, DD5 2NF
Tel: 01382-480049 Fax: 01382-480130

H.M. Speirs

*An international association of manufacturers,
distributors and suppliers of flexible interme-
diate bulk containers formed to promote
trade, to protect and encourage the interests of
members.* *

European Movement (Scottish Council)

see The European Movement (Scottish Council)

Ex-Services Mental Welfare Society

Hollybush House,
Hollybush,
by Ayr, KA6 7EA
Tel: 01292-560214 Fax: 01292-560871

Wing Commander D. Devine

*Hollybush House provides remedial treatment,
convalescence and respite care for ex-Service
men and women who suffer from some form
of psychiatric illness or stress disorder.
Clients normally stay for periods of one to
three weeks.* *

Eye to Eye

Lochty Farm,
Arncroach,
Anstruther,
Fife, KY10 2SA
Tel: 01333-720227

Mrs. Valerie Nicol

Eye to Eye is a support group for people who are about to go through the traumatic experience of having an eye removed. It gives patients the opportunity of speaking to, or meeting with, someone who has already been through this. *

Faculty of Actuaries in Scotland

23 St. Andrew Square,
Edinburgh, EH2 1AQ
Tel: 0131-557-1575

W. Wallace Mair, *Secretary*

Faculty of Advocates

Advocates Library,
Parliament House,
Edinburgh, EH1 1RF
Tel: 0131-226-5071   Fax: 0131-225-3642

Mr. Iain G. Armstrong, *Clerk of the Faculty*

The professional body regulating the practice of law at the Scottish Bar and part of the College of Justice in Scotland. *

Faculty of Homoeopathy: Scotland

Glasgow Homoeopathic Hospital,
1000 Great Western Road,
Glasgow, G12 0NR
Tel: 0141-337-1824

Fair Play for Children in Scotland

Unit 29,
6 Harmony Row,
Govan,
Glasgow, G51 3BA
Tel: 0141-425-1140   Fax: 0141-425-1140

Mr. Ross Dunn

Fairbridge in Scotland

Norton Park,
57 Albion Road,
Edinburgh, EH7 5QY
Tel: 0131-475-2303

Ms. Elizabeth Roy

Fairbridge offers long-term personal development programmes, enabling young people from inner cities to equip themselves with the skills needed to meet the opportunities and responsibilities of society. *

Families of Murdered Children

Basement,
40 Carlton Place,
Glasgow, G5 9TW
Tel: 0141-420-3883

Mrs. J. Barclay

Where to find help and speak to people who understand the trauma being experienced. Please feel free to call us at any time; home visits can also be arranged. *

Family Care

21 Castle Street,
Edinburgh, EH2 3DN
Tel: 0131-225-6441   Fax: 0131-225-6441

Ms. Linda Paterson, *Director of National Services*

Family Care is a charity and voluntary social work agency which provides national and local services for children and families, and people whose lives are affected by adoption. *

Family Law Association

17 Grampian Court,
Beveridge Square,
Livingston,
West Lothian, EH54 6QF
Tel: 01506-417737   Fax: 01506-460613

Sheriff A.G. Johnston, *Hon. President*/L. Di
   Biasio, *Secretary**

Family Mediation Scotland (FMS)

127 Rose Street South Lane,
Edinburgh, EH2 4BB
Tel: 0131-220-1610   Fax: 0131-220-6895

Ms. Elizabeth Foster, *Director*

*Family Mediation is a voluntary process which
   encourages a focus on children's needs after
   separation and divorce and provides parents
   and professionals with essential support.* *

Family Planning Association Scotland

Unit 10, Firhill Business Centre,
76 Firhill Road,
Glasgow, G20 7BA
Tel: 0141-576-5088

Anne Marie McKay, *Director*

*Advancing the sexual health and reproductive
   rights and choices of all through advocacy,
   lobbying, education and information.
   Telephone helpline 0141-576-5088.* *

Farming and Wildlife Advisory Group (FWAG) Scotland

Rural Centre,
Westmains of Ingliston,
Newbridge,
Midlothian, EH28 8NZ
Tel: 0131-472-4080   Fax: 0131-472-4083

Hilary Barker, *Scottish Operations Manager*

*The FWAG advises farmers, crofters and land
   managers on wildlife/habitat conservation,
   environmentally sensitive farming methods
   and availability of grants. We are of charitable status and have 25 professional advisory
   staff.* *

Fast Forward Positive Lifestyles

4 Bernard Street,
Edinburgh, EH6 6PP
Tel: 0131-554-4300   Fax: 0131-554-4330

Mr. Simon Jaquet

*Fast Forward is a national voluntary organisa-
   tion promoting health by, with and for young
   people, focusing on the prevention of drug,
   alcohol and tobacco misuse.* *

Federation of Children's Book Groups

6 Bryce Place,
Currie,
Midlothian, EH14 5LR
Tel: 0131-449-2713

Alison Dick

Federation of Civil Engineering Contractors

Empire House,
131 West Nile Street,
Glasgow, G1 2RX
Tel: 0141-332 5586

Federation of Independent Advice Centres (Scottish Region)

c/o Rights Office Fife,
4 Abbey Park Place,
Dunfermline,
Fife, KY12 7PD
Tel: 01383-739256   Fax: 01383-051709

Mr. Dave Milliken

Federation of Master Builders (Scottish Office)

540 Gorgie Road,
Edinburgh, EH11 3AL
Tel: 0131-455-7997

Federation of Recorded Music Societies, Scottish Group

11 Regent Place,
Balfour,
Kirkcaldy,
Fife, KY2 5HE
Tel: 01592-262727

Miss I.F. Page, *Secretary*

There are ten affiliated Societies. Two annual conferences are run under the auspices of the group. All affiliates welcome new members and visitors. For further details, please contact the above. *

Federation of Scottish Schools Sports Associations

Westwood House,
Gorgie Road,
Edinburgh

Charles R. Raeburn, *Chair*

Federation of Scottish Skateboarders

16 Northwood Park,
Livingstone, EH54 8BD
Tel: 01506-415308

Kenneth Omond, *Secretary*

F

Federation of Scottish Theatre Limited

2 Ferguson Green,
Musselburgh, EH21 6XB
Tel: 0131-665-1761   Fax: 0131-665-1761

Mr. Hamish Glen, *Chairman/*Heather
Baird, *Administrator*

The Federation of Scottish Theatre exists to advance the interests of professional Scottish theatre at home and abroad. Lobbying, PR campaigns, membership services and support are all within its remit. *

Federation of Small Businesses

Union Chambers,
114 Union Street,
Glasgow, G1 3QQ
Tel: 0141-221-0775   Fax: 0141-221-5954

Mr. John Downie

The Federation of Small Businesses is a campaigning pressure group which exists to promote and protect the interests of all who are either self-employed or run their own business. *

Federation of Student Nationalists

6 North Charlotte Street,
Edinburgh, EH2 4JH
Tel: 0131-226-3661

Feed the Minds

41 George IV Bridge,
Edinburgh, EH1 1EL
Tel: 0131-226-5254   Fax: 0131-225 8861

Scottish Secretary

Feed the Minds is an agency of the British churches supporting literacy and communication programmes of churches in the developing world and in Eastern Europe. *

Fèisean nan Gàidheal

Nicolson House,
Somerled Square,
Portree,
Isle of Skye, IV51 9EJ
Tel: 01478-613355   Fax: 01478-613399

Arthur Cormack, *Development Officer*

Fèisean nan Gàidheal is an umbrella body for the 27 community festivals, known as feisan, which take place throughout Scotland. *

Fibromyalgia Association of Scotland

13 Pitkerro Drive,
Dundee, DD4 8AF
Tel: 01382-50067   Fax: 01382-864183

Mr. Andy Dawson

Fire Brigades Union

4th Floor,
52 St. Enoch Square,
Glasgow, G1 4AA
Tel: 0141-221-2309   Fax: 0141-204-4575

Mr. T. Tierney, *Regional Secretary*

First Bite

St. George's West Church,
8 Shandwick Place,
Edinburgh, EH2 4RT
Tel: 0131-225-7993   Fax: 0131-225-7993

Ms. Rebecca Kilbey

*First Bite, formed in 1988, presents live,
movement-based theatre with a strong visual
element to young people throughout central
Scotland and north-west England. All
programmes concern the personal and social
development of young people.* *

Fish Conservation Centre

Easter Cringate,
Stirling, FK7 9QX
Tel: 01896-451312

Dr. Peter S. Maitland, *Consultant*

Fishmongers' Company

Fala Acre,
Fala Village,
Pathhead,
Midlothian, EH37 5SY
Tel: 01875-833246   Fax: 01875-833246

W.F. Beattie, MBE, *Inspector for Scotland*

*Charged with the protection of wild salmon
throughout Scotland and warranted by the
Secretary of State for Scotland.* *

Fitness Scotland

Caledonia House,
South Gyle,
Edinburgh, EH12 9DQ
Tel: 0131-317-7243

Ms. Irene M. Thom

Flatcoated Retriever Club of Scotland

29 Fairmile Avenue,
Edinburgh, EH10 6RL
Tel: 0131-445-2052

Ms. K. Munro, *Secretary*

*The FCRC, founded in 1985, aims to encour-
age the wellbeing of the breed, responsible
ownership and the working, training and
showing of the breed. Training, shows and
events are held each year.* *

Flax and Linen Association (GB)

Robertson-Coupar and Co.,
1 Bank Street,
Dundee, DD1 1RN
Tel: 01382-25691

Flexible Intermediate Bulk Container Association

140 Camphill Road,
Broughty Ferry,
Dundee, DD5 2NF
Tel: 01382-480049   Fax: 01382-480130

Hendry M. Speirs

*To promote the trade and to protect and
advance the interests of the Association and
its members.* *

Foresight: Association for the Promotion of Preconceptual Care

Camerons,
Midton Road,
Howwood,
near Glasgow, PA9 1AG
Tel: 01505-704567

Margaret Cameron*

Forest Authority (Scotland)

Portcullis House,
21 India Street,
Glasgow, G2 4PL
Tel: 0141-248-3931   Fax: 0141-226-5007

Dr. A.J. Low, *Chief Conservator*

Forestry Commission

231 Corstorphine Road,
Edinburgh, EH12 7AT
Tel: 0131-334-0303   Fax: 0131-334-3047

Information Division

Forthtell

8 Baileyfield Road,
Portobello,
Edinburgh, EH15 1DL
Tel: 0131-669-5275

Mr. Iain McGregor, *Secretary*

Promotes awareness of Hebrew origins of Scottish people and traditions through Bible exposition in media and public meetings. Upholds monarchy and Declaration of Arbroath, 1320. *

Forum of Private Business (Scotland)

27 Campbell Street,
Helensburgh, G84 8YG
Tel: 01436-671990

Forward Scotland

c/o Scottish Power,
St. Vincent Crescent,
Glasgow, G3 8LT
Tel: 0141-567-4334   Fax: 0141-567-4339

Mr. George Chalmers

Forward Scotland is an organisation committed to furthering sustainable development in Scotland. It works in partnership with a wide variety of communities and organisations. *

Foundation for Skin Research

The Lauriston Building,
The Royal Infirmary,
Edinburgh, EH3 9YW
Tel: 0131-536-2042   Fax: 0131-229-8769

Ms. Moira Gray

The Foundation for Skin Research is a national charity supporting clinical and laboratory research into the cause, treatment and prevention of skin disease. The aim is to attract funds to field a committed team of scientists and clinicians to tackle the many problems posed by skin diseases. *

Fox Terrier Club of Scotland

32 Castle Wynd,
Quarter,
Hamilton, ML3 7XD
Tel: 01698-458736

Mr. J. McGhie

Fraser of Allander Institute for Research on the Scottish Economy

University of Strathclyde,
204 George Street,
Glasgow, G1 1XW
Tel: 0141-552 4400

Free Church of Scotland

The Mound,
Edinburgh,
EH1 2LS
Tel: 0131-226-4978

The Principal Clerk

Free Presbyterian Church of Scotland

16 Matheson Road,
Stornoway,
Isle of Lewis, HS1 2LA
Tel: 01851-702755   Fax: 01851-702755

Rev. J. MacLeod, *Clerk of Synod**

Freight Transport Association - Scottish Office

Hermes House,
Melville Terrace,
Stirling, FK8 2ND
Tel: 01786-471910   Fax: 01786-450412

Friends of Historic Scotland

Lonmore House,
Salisbury Place,
Edinburgh, EH9 1SH
Tel: 0131-668-8635   Fax: 0131-668-8888

Membership section of Historic Scotland. Friends join on an annual or life basis and receive a range of membership benefits. *

Friends of the Earth Scotland (FOE Scotland)

72 Newhaven Road,
Edinburgh, EH6 5QG
Tel: 0131-554-9977   Fax: 0131-554-8656

Mr. Lang Banks, *Information Officer*

Friends of the Earth Scotland is committed to the conservation, restoration and sustainable use of the environment for the benefit of the community. *

Frontier Youth Trust Scotland

11 Queens Crescent,
Glasgow, G4 9AS
Tel: 0141-332-7208

Mrs. Margaret Hunter

GMB

Fountain House,
1/3 Woodside Crescent,
Glasgow, G3 7UJ
Tel: 0141-332-8641   Fax: 0141-332-4491

Mr. R. Parker, *Regional Secretary*

The GMB's purpose is to improve the quality of life for all our members and their families, widening horizons and bringing new opportunities into reach. *

GSD Club of Scotland

Glenview,
Tarholm,
Auchinchruive,
by Ayr, KA6 5HY
Tel: 01292-521129

Mrs. E. Young

Gaelic Books Council

see The Gaelic Books Council

Galloway Cattle Society of Great Britain and Ireland

15 New Market Street,
Castle Douglas,
Kirkcudbrightshire, DG7 1HY
Tel: 01556-502753   Fax: 01556-502753

A.J. McDonald, *Chief Executive* *

Gamblers Anonymous

c/o Pearce Institute,
Pearce Street,
Glasgow, G51 3UU
Tel: 0141-630-1033

Game Conservancy Scottish Research Trust

15 Atholl Crescent,
Edinburgh, EH3 8HA
Tel: 0131-228-3777   Fax: 0131-228-3878

Mr. Ian Hogg, *Manager*

Game Conservancy Trust

see The Game Conservancy Trust

Garden History Society – Scottish Group

Washington House,
Main Street,
Ardler,
Blairgowrie,
Perthshire, PH12 8SR
Tel: 0131-337-1747   Fax: 0131-337-8174

Christopher Dingwall, *Conservation Officer*

Gardeners' Royal Benevolent Society

Rosemount,
38 Ecclesmachan Road,
Uphall,
West Lothian, EH52 6JR
Tel: 01506-853758

Miss M. Wardlaw, *Development Officer, Scotland**

Gas Association of Scotland

British Gas Transco,
13 Kingsfield,
Linlithgow, EH49 7SJ
Tel: 01506-847778

Mr. Mike Scales, *President*

Gender Dysphoria Scotland

48 Gordon Avenue,
Poltonhall,
Bonnyrigg,
Midlothian, EH19 2PQ
Tel: 0131-654-1460

Ms. Janice Pevoy

General Assembly of the Church of Scotland

see The General Assembly of the Church of Scotland

General Dental Practitioners' Association

1 Bellevue Place,
Edinburgh, EH7 4BS

General Register Office for Scotland

New Register House,
Edinburgh, EH1 3YT
Tel: 0131-334-0380   Fax: 0131-314-4400

Mr. J. Meldrum, *Registrar General*

Government department with responsibility for the registration of births, deaths and marriages; production of population and vital statistics; and the taking of censuses of population.*

General Teaching Council for Scotland

Clerwood House,
96 Clermiston Road,
Edinburgh, EH12 6UT
Tel: 0131-314-6000   Fax: 0131-314-6001

Ian Clark*

Gestalt Trust

22 Woodend Drive,
Glasgow, G13 1QS
Tel: 0141-959 3100

Mr. Richard Cotter

Gingerbread Scotland

Community Central Halls,
304 Maryhill Road,
Glasgow, G20 7YE
Tel: 0141-353-0953   Fax: 0141-332-7198

Mr. Ritchie Smith

Girls' Brigade in Scotland

see The Girls' Brigade in Scotland

Goethe-Institut, German Cultural Institute

3 Park Circus,
Glasgow, G3 0AX
Tel: 0141-332-2655   Fax: 0141-333-1630

Susanne Abegg, *Director*

The services provided include language tuition, teacher training, liaison work with schools, a cultural programme (films, exhibitions, concerts etc.) and a lending library open to the public. There is a home page available on: http://www.goethe.de/gr/gla. *

Golden Retriever Club of Scotland

Woodlands,
Balmaha,
Loch Lomond, G63 0JQ
Tel: 01360-870435   Fax: 01360-870436

Mrs. M. Murray *

Goldenhar Syndrome Support Group Hemifacial Microsomia

54 Neil Street,
Greenock,
Renfrewshire, PA16 9HZ
Tel: 01475-650526

Mrs. Aileen Wilson, *Coordinator*

The group offers information and support to affected members. Newsletters and family weekends are available. *

Gordon Setter Club of Scotland

2 Eden Valley Row,
Freuchie,
Fife, KY7 7EU
Tel: 01337-585120

Mrs. G. Vick

Grand Lodge of Ancient Free & Accepted Masons of Scotland

(The Grand Lodge of Scotland),
96 George Street,
Edinburgh, EH2 3DH
Tel: 0131-225-5304   Fax: 0131-225-3953

Mr. C. Martin McGibbon, *Grand Secretary*

Governing body of masonic lodges in Scotland. Formed in 1736. A musem and library facility is open to the public Monday to Friday (excluding public holidays). *

Grapevine Audio Magazine & Newspaper for the Blind

5 Dunvegan Avenue,
Castlepark Estate,
Larbert, FK5 4TF
Tel: 01324-556064   Fax: 01324-556064

Yvonne M. Taylor, *Chairman*

Free C90 cassette irrespective of geographical location featuring a vast selection – world news, braille books, arts/crafts, police and benefit agency advice, gardening, travel, adventure, stories, etc. Registered charity no. SCO 07849. *

Graphical, Paper & Media Union

Graphical House,
222 Clyde Street,
Glasgow, G1 4JT
Tel: 0141-221-7730   Fax: 0141-248-7085

Mr. D. Munro, *Branch Secretary*

Griffon Bruxellois Club

14 Forres Avenue,
Dundee, DD3 0EJ
Tel: 01382-814987

Mrs. C. Marshall

Guide Association Scotland

16 Coates Crescent,
Edinburgh, EH3 7AH
Tel: 0131-226-4511   Fax: 0131-220-4828

Miss Sally Pitches, *Executive Director*

Part of a worldwide organisation dedicated to enabling girls to achieve their full potential through a stimulating, enjoyable programme of activities, delivered by trained volunteers. *

Guide Dogs for the Blind Association (GDBA)

Princess Alexandra House
Dundee Road,
Forfar, DD8 1JA
Tel: 01307-463531   Fax: 01307-465233

Mr. J. Duncan, *Controller–Scotland and N. Ireland*

To provide greater independence and mobility to visually impaired people through the provision of a guide dog and other rehabilitation services. *

Guild of Taxidermists

c/o Glasgow Museum & Art Gallery,
Kelvingrove,
Glasgow, G3 8AG
Tel: 0141-287-2671   Fax: 0141-287-2690

Duncan Ferguson

*The Guild's aims and objectives are to raise
and maintain the professional status and
standards of taxidermy.* *

H.M. Chief Inspector of Prisons for Scotland

Saughton House,
Edinburgh, EH11 3XA
Tel: 0131-244-8481

C.B. Fairweather, *H.M. Chief Inspector*

H.M. Customs & Excise

Scotland Collection
44 York Place,
Edinburgh,
EH1 3JW
Tel: 0131-469-2000

Campbell Arnott, *Collector*

H.M. Inspectorate of Constabulary

2 Greenside Lane,
Edinburgh, EH1 3AH
Tel: 0131-244-5614   Fax: 0131-244-5616

Sir William Sutherland, *Chief Inspector*

H.M. Inspectorate of Fire Services

Saughton House,
Edinburgh, EH11 3XD
Tel: 0131-244-2342   Fax: 0131-244-2564

A.N. Morrison, *H.M. Chief Inspector*

The Fire Service Inspectorate advises the Secretary of State for Scotland, the Scottish Office Home Department and local authorities on fire brigade and fire-related matters. *

H.M. Inspectorate of Mines (Scotland and East England District)

Silver House,
Silver Street,
Doncaster, DN1 9HR
Tel: 01302-368165   Fax: 01302-326521

R. Stevenson, *Principal District Inspector*

HM Inspectorate of Mines is an operating division of the Health and Safety Executive which has responsibilities for inspection and enforcement of Statute within the deep mining industry. *

HELP (Scotland)

60 The Pleasance,
Edinburgh, EH8 9TG
Tel: 0131-556-9497

Habitat Scotland

Hazelmount,
Heron Place,
Portree,
Isle of Skye, IV51 9EU
Tel: 01478-612898   Fax: 01478-613254

Mr. J. Graeme Robertson, *Director*

The independent research charity established in 1977 to promote the conservation, restoration and sustainable use of the environment for the benefit of all. *

Haemochromatosis Society

4 Mincher Crescent,
Motherwell, ML1 2RZ
Tel: 01698-269381

Mrs. Mary Burns, *Scottish Representative*

Our aim is to raise the awareness of genetic haemochromatosis (iron overload) and to counsel others with this disorder. *

Haggis Hurling Association

5 Castle Terrace,
Edinburgh, EH1 2DP
Tel: 0131-228-6262

Robin Dunseath, *Haggis Master*

Halliwick Association of Swimming Therapy

26 Carfrae Gardens,
Edinburgh, EH4 3SS
Tel: 0131-336-2357

Mrs. J. Ness, *Regional Secretary*

Aims to teach people with disabilities to swim for either leisure or recreation purposes. National organisation also provides education and training. *

Handbell Ringers of Great Britain

Scottish Regional Association,
Claganach,
1a Stirling Road,
Dunblane,
Perthshire, FK15 9EP
Tel: 01786-825387   Fax: 01786-825387

Mr. Malcolm C. Wilson, *Chairman*

Serving the needs of ringers of handbells, belleplates and handchimes throughout Scotland through workshops, ringer rallies, publications and newsletters. Over 50 groups throughout Scotland. *

Harris Tweed Authority

6 Garden Road,
Stornoway,
Isle of Lewis, HS1 2QJ
Tel: 01851-702269   Fax: 01851-702600

Ian A. Mackenzie, *Chief Executive & Secretary*

Administer the certification trademark and promote and protect the interests of the industry. Supply information packs to students. *

Hayfield Rehabilitation Unit for the Deaf

260 Moffat Street,
Glasgow, G5 0ND
Tel: 0141-429-0335   Fax: 0141-420-1990

Mr. R. Reid

Head Injuries Trust for Scotland

Unit 14,
39 Durham Street,
Glasgow, G41 1BS
Tel: 0141-427-7055   Fax: 0141-427-7454

Meta Evans, *Information & Training Officer*

HITS provides community-based rehabilitation, support, advice and information to people with a head injury, families and carers from three service areas throughout Scotland. *

Headteachers' Association of Scotland

Faculty of Education,
University of Strathclyde,
Southbrae Drive,
Glasgow, G13 1PP
Tel: 0141-950-3298   Fax: 0141-950-3434

Mr. James B.O. McNair, *General Secretary*

The professional association for headship teams in Scottish secondary schools. *

Health Service Commissioner for Scotland and Parliamentary Commissioner for Administration

28 Thistle Street,
Edinburgh, EH2 1EN
Tel: 0131-225-7465   Fax: 0131-226-4447

Mr Michael Buckley, *Commissioner*

Health and Safety Executive

Lord Cullen House,
Fraser Place,
Aberdeen, AB25 3UB
Tel: 01224-252500   Fax: 01224-252525

Hearing Dogs for Deaf People

29 Craighiehall Crescent,
West Freelands,
Erskine,
Renfrewshire, PA8 7DD
Tel: 0141-812-6542

Mrs. M. Arthur

To train dogs to alert deaf people to everyday sounds, while also giving them companionship and independence. *

Heating and Ventilating Contractors' Association (Scottish Region)

Bush House,
Bush Estate,
Penicuik,
Midlothian, EH26 0SB
Tel: 0131-445-5580

H

Help the Aged

Heriot House,
Heriothill Terrace,
Edinburgh, EH7 4DY
Tel: 0131-556-4666   Fax: 0131-557-5115

Ms. Elizabeth Duncan

*Charity offering grant aid and fundraising
management to voluntary and charitable
groups working with vulnerable older people.
SeniorLine on 0800-65 00 65 offers advice
and information on resources.* *

Hepatitis C Support and Information Group

P.O. Box 14466,
Glenrothes,
Fife, KY7 6WA
Tel: 01573-470359   Fax: 01573-470359

Ms. Feyona McFarlane

*This group can offer confidential support,
information, advocacy and counselling.* *

Her Majesty's Industrial Pollution Inspectorate (Scotland)

27 Perth Street,
Edinburgh, EH3 5RB
Tel: 0131-244-3062   Fax: 0131-244-2903

R. Thom

Heraldry Society of Scotland

25 Craigentinny Crescent,
Edinburgh, EH7 6QA

S. Emerson, *Treasurer*

*To encourage the study and practice in Scotland
of heraldry and allied subjects, both indig-
enous and international by arranging
lectures, discussions, visits, publications and
exhibitions.* *

Herring Buyers' Association Limited

46 Moray Place,
Edinburgh, EH3 6BQ
Tel: 0131-225-4548

E. Leedham, *Manager*

High Blood Pressure Foundation

Department of Medicine,
Western General Hospital,
Edinburgh, EH4 2XU
Tel: 0131-332-9211   Fax: 0131-537-1012

Ms. Rosalind Newton, *Director*

*Improving basic understanding, assessment,
treatment and public awareness of high blood
pressure and, in so doing, help promote the
welfare of people with high blood pressure.* *

High Court of Justiciary

Lawnmarket,
The Royal Mile,
Edinburgh, EH1 1RQ
Tel: 0131-225-2595   Fax: 0131-240-6915

T. Fyffe, *Deputy Principal Clerk of Justiciary*

*Supreme Criminal Court in Scotland. The
High Court site at the above address and at
various other Court Houses throughout
Scotland.* *

Highland Cattle Society

59 Drumlanrig Street,
Thornhill,
Dumfries, DG3 5LY
Tel: 01848-330438   Fax: 01848-331183

A.H.G. Wilson, *Secretary* *

Highlands and Islands Tape Service

38 Ardconnel Street,
Inverness, IV3 6EX
Tel: 01463-242600

*Recording and distributing tapes of local and
national newspapers.* *

Historic Scotland

Longmore House,
Salisbury Place,
Edinburgh, EH9 1SH
Tel: 0131-668-8600

Mrs. Marion Fry, *Education Officer*

Historical Houses Association for Scotland

c/o Blairquhan Estate Office,
Maybole,
Fife, KA19 7LZ
Tel: 01655-770239   Fax: 01655-770278

Ms. Kate Anderson

Home Education Advisory Service

10 Chalton Road,
Bridge of Allan,
Stirling, FK9 4DX
Tel: 01786-832042   Fax: 01786-831066

Mrs. Brenda Holliday

*HEAS is a national home education charity
dedicated to giving advice and practical
support for families who wish to educate
their children at home.* *

Home-Start UK

84 Drymen Road,
Bearsden,
Glasgow, G61 2RH
Tel: 0141-942-3450   Fax: 0141-942-3479

Ms. Martha Simpson, *Assistant Director
(Scotland)*

Hospital Christian Fellowship of Scotland

49 Priestfield Crescent,
Edinburgh, EH16 5JH
Tel: 0131-667-4494

Hospitality Industry Trust Scotland (HIT Scotland)

Scottish Office,
P.O. Box 7,
Penicuik, EH26 9NN
Tel: 01968-660727   Fax: 01968-660727

The Scottish Organiser

Hospitality Training Foundation

Capital House,
9 Logie Mill,
Edinburgh, EH7 4HG
Tel: 0131-558 9909   Fax: 0131-557-8846

Ms. Anneliese Archibald, *Head of HTF Scotland*

HTF is the national training organisation representing the hospitality industry. *

Hotel & Catering International Management Association

85 Argyle Way,
Dunblane,
Perthshire, FK15 9DY
Tel: 01786-822697

Housing Association Ombudsman for Scotland

2 Belford Road,
Edinburgh, EH4 3BL
Tel: 0131-220-0599   Fax: 0131-220-0577

Mr. John Richards, *Ombudsman*

Examines complaints of maladministration from tenants, sharing owners and customers of housing associations and co-operatives registered with Scottish Homes, and certain other landlords. *

Howard League for Penal Reform

c/o Faculty of Advocates,
Parliament Square,
Edinburgh, EH1 1RP
Tel: 0131-226 4381   Fax: 0131-226-4381

Ms. Laura Irvine

Humanist Society of Scotland

17 Howburn Place,
Aberdeen, AB11 6XT
Tel: 01224-573034

Mr. George D. Rodger, *Honorary Secretary*

The HSS seeks to represent the interests of the approximately one million people in Scotland who live moral lives without religious belief. Scottish charity no. SCO 26570. *

Huntington's Chorea Association

22 Craigs Crescent,
Edinburgh, EH12 8HT
Tel: 0131-339-7970

Ms. Jessie W. Forbes

ICFM Scotland (Institute of Charity Fundraising Managers)

Events and Fundraising Management
  Scotland,
Events House,
9 Fairley Street,
Glasgow, G51 2SN

Mr. Trevor Jones

ISIS (Scotland)

Scottish Council of Independent Schools,
21 Melville Street,
Edinburgh, EH3 7PE
Tel: 0131-220-2106

Ms. Judith Sischy, *Director*

Illustrators in Scotland

26 Nethergate South,
Crail,
Fife, KY10 3TY
Tel: 01333-450316   Fax: 01333-450513

Mr. David Sim

Immigration Advisory Service

115 Bath Street,
Glasgow, G2 2SZ
Tel: 0141-248-2956   Fax: 0141-221-5388

Mrs. Rheba Glazier

*IAS is a national charity providing free advice
  and representation in immigration and
  asylum matters and appeals.* *

Immigration Appellate Authority – Scotland

5th floor,
Portcullis House,
21 India Street,
Glasgow, G2 4PZ
Tel: 0141-221-3489   Fax: 0141-221-3532

Pamela McMullen, *Office Manager*

*The IAA is an independent tribunal which
  considers appeals against decisions made by
  the Home Secretary or an Entry Clearance
  Officer.* *

Imperial Cancer Research Fund

Scottish Appeals Centre,
Wallace House,
Maxwell Place,
Stirling, FK8 1JU
Tel: 01786-446689   Fax: 01786-446691

Mr. Laurence Brady

*The largest independent cancer research
  organisation in Europe, dedicated to finding
  a cure for most cancers, and saving lives.
  Almost totally dependent on voluntary
  contributions.* *

Implanted Defibrillator of Scotland (IDAS)

6 Argyll Street,
Brechin,
Angus, DD9 6JL
Tel: 01356-622554

Mr. Peter Slater, *Secretary*

Independent Federation of Nursing in Scotland

18 Overton Park,
Strathaven, ML10 6UW
Tel: 01357-523001   Fax: 01357-522546

Irenee F. O'Neill, *General Secretary*

IFONS is the only trade union/professional organisation born in Scotland, run by Scottish nurses and providing the full range of services to all grades of nursing/midwifery staff working in Scotland. *

Independent Schools Information Service

21 Melville Street,
Edinburgh, EH3 7PE
Tel: 0131-220-2106   Fax: 0131-225-8594

Independent Television Commission

Scottish Office,
123 Blythswood Street,
Glasgow, G2 2AN
Tel: 0141-226-4436   Fax: 0141-226-4682

Brian Marjoribanks, *Officer for Scotland*

The regulatory body of independent television, satellite and cable. *

Independent Tribunal Service

Wellington House,
134–136 Wellington Street,
Glasgow, G2 2XL
Tel: 0141-353-1441   Fax: 0141-353-2440

The Independent Tribunal Service is a Government body whose task is to arrange social security, medical, disability, vaccine damage and child support appeal tribunals. *

Industrial Society

4 West Regent Street,
Glasgow, G2 1RW
Tel: 0141-332-2827   Fax: 0141-332-9096

Industrial Tribunals for Scotland

The Eagle Building,
215 Bothwell Street,
Glasgow, G2 7TS
Tel: 0141-204-0730   Fax: 0141-204-0732

Inland Revenue

FICO (Scotland),
Trinity Park House,
South Trinity Road,
Edinburgh, EH5 3SD
Tel: 0131-551-8127   Fax: 0131-552-0746

Ms. Louise Clayton, *Assistant Director, FICO*

FICO (Scotland), a division of Inland Revenue Financial Intermediaries and Claims Office, deals with Scottish charities, Scottish Trusts and larger estates of UK deceased persons. *

Institut Français D'Écosse

13 Randolph Crescent,
Edinburgh, EH3 7TT
Tel: 0131-225-5366   Fax: 0131-220-0648

*Language courses and cultural events. ***

Institute for Environmental History

St. Andrews University,
St. John's House,
St. Andrews, KY16 9QW
Tel: 01334-463300   Fax: 01333-311193

T.C. Smout

*The Institute exists to encourage the study of people's interaction with the environment during the past 10,000 years by publication, conferences and postgraduate study. ***

Institute of Auctioneers & Appraisers in Scotland

P.O. Box 13811,
Penicuik, EH26 0YB
Tel: 01968-677227

Miss Muriel J. Gordon, *Secretary**

Institute of Bankers in Scotland

20 Rutland Square,
Edinburgh, EH1 2DE
Tel: 0131-229-9869

Institute of Biology, Scottish Branch

c/o Quintiles Scotland,
Heriot Watt University,
Research Park,
Riccarton,
Edinburgh, EH14 4AP
Tel: 0131-451-5511

Ms. Ruth Clague, *Scottish Branch Secretary*

Institute of Chartered Foresters

7a St. Colme Street,
Edinburgh, EH3 6AA
Tel: 0131-225-2705   Fax: 0131-220-6128

Mrs. M.W. Dick, *Executive Director*

*The Institute of Chartered Foresters is the representative professional body for the forestry profession in the UK and EU. ***

Institute of Energy – Scottish Branch

c/o NIFES Consulting Group,
8 Woodside Terrace,
Glasgow, G3 7UY
Tel: 0141-332-2453

A. L. Hannah, *Branch Chairman*

Institute of Food Science and Technology (Scottish Branch)

Glasgow Scientific Services,
64 Everard Drive,
Glasgow, G21 1XG
Tel: 0141-562-2203   Fax: 0141-563-5129

Dr. Charles McDonald

To serve the public interest by furthering food science and technology to all relevant aspects of the supply of safe, wholesome food nationally and internationally. *

Institute of Hydrology

Unit 2,
Alpha Centre,
Stirling Innovation Park,
Stirling
Tel: 01786-447612

Institute of Information Scientists (Scottish Branch)

Building Design Partnership,
5 Blythswood Square,
Glasgow, G2 4AD
Tel: 0141-226-5291   Fax: 0141-221-0720

Mr. Don Kelman

Institute of Licensed Trade Stocktakers

16 Comely Bank Place,
Edinburgh, EH4 1DU
Tel: 0131-315-2600   Fax: 0131-315 4346

Mr. Bruce Thompson, *Secretary*

The Institute is the only national body representing stocktakers in the UK. With over 400 members it is represented nationwide, also in Ireland and Europe. *

Institute of Local Television

13 Bellevue Place,
Edinburgh, EH7 4BS
Tel: 0131-557-8610   Fax: 0131-557-8608

Lyndsey Bowditch, *Secretary*

Institute of Management

21 Deanston Gardens,
Doune, FK16 6AZ
Tel: 01786-841133

Institute of Occupational Medicine

8 Roxburgh Place,
Edinburgh, EH8 9SU
Tel: 0131-667-5131   Fax: 0131-667-0136

Ms. A. Boyle, *Information Officer*

Research, consultancy and training in: health, hygiene and safety at work; occupational and environmental health, hygiene and epidemiology; hearing loss; ergonomics; respiratory diseases; asbestos; asbestosis; silica; pneumoconiosis; personal protective equipment; stress at work. *

Institute of Piping

16–24 Otago Street,
Glasgow, G12 8JH
Tel: 0141-334-3587   Fax: 0141-337-3014 *

Institute of Plumbing (Scotland)

Bellfield Mill Cottage,
Kinross,
Tayside, KY13 7NL
Tel: 01577-862910

Mr A.G. Brunton, IEng, MIPE, MIP, RP,
Scottish Chairman

*The Institute of Plumbing is a professional body
pursuing its major object of raising the science
and practice of plumbing in the public
interest.* *

Institute of Practitioners in Advertising, Scottish Branch

Covey Advertising,
1 Fountainhall Road,
Edinburgh, EH9 2NL
Tel: 0131-667-7770

Victor Covey, *Chairman*

Institute of Public Relations (Scottish Branch)

Catchline PR,
40 High Street,
Kirkcaldy, KY1 1LU
Tel: 01592-643200

David Wallace, *Chairman*

Institute of Quarrying (Scotland)

45 Stamperland Avenue,
Clarkston,
Glasgow, G76 8EX

W.F. Crooks, *Secretary*

Institution of Engineers & Shipbuilders in Scotland

1 Atlantic Quay,
Broomielaw,
Glasgow, G2 8JE
Tel: 0141-248-3721

Mr. I. Ramsay

Institution of Professionals, Managers & Specialists

18 Melville Terrace,
Stirling, FK8 2NQ
Tel: 01786-465999   Fax: 01786-466516

Mr. A. Denney, *Regional Secretary*

Institution of Structural Engineers (Scottish Branch)

4 Dixon Road,
Helensburgh, G84 9DW
Tel: 01436-675100

Mr. D.J. Nicoll, *Honorary Secretary*

*A chartered professional society devoted to the
promotion and advancement of structural
engineering.* *

Institution of Water Officers, Scottish Branch

Water Services Department,
Bullion House,
Invergowrie,
Dundee, DD2 5BB

L. Scobie

International Council of Hides & Skins Traders Associations

Dalriach House,
Tummel Bridge, PH16 5NZ
Tel: 01882-634241   Fax: 01882-634321

A.D. Cox

International Hospital Christian Fellowship in Ireland and Scotland

55 Chattan Avenue,
Causewayhead,
Stirling, FK9 5RF
Tel: 01786-62809

International League for the Protection of Horses (Scottish Branch)

Belwade Farm,
Aboyne,
Aberdeenshire, AB34 5DJ
Tel: 01339-887186   Fax: 01339-887051

Ms. Eileen Gillen

*A rehabilitation centre for all Scotland's
   unwanted or uncared-for horses.* *

International Otter Survival Fund

Broadford,
Isle of Skye, IV49 9AQ
Tel: 01471-822487

Mr. Paul Yoxon, *Head of Operations*

*IOST is concerned with preserving the world's
   13 species of otter. In Scotland it runs an
   ongoing research programme and a rehabilitation centre for orphaned and injured otters.
   e-mail: iost@aol.com.* *

International PEN Scottish Centre

see PEN, Scottish Centre

International Stress Management Association (UK Branch)

55 Beechwood Drive,
Glasgow, G11 7EU
Tel: 0141-339-5624   Fax: 0141-950-3539

Mr. Andrew T. Gordon

International Voluntary Service (IVS)

7 Upper Bow,
Edinburgh, EH1 2JN
Tel: 0131-226-6722   Fax: 0131-226-6723

Mr. Neil Harrower

*Aims to promote peace, justice and understand-
   ing, mainly by offering volunteering opportunities on international workcamps. Volunteers do socially useful work to help those in
   need.* *

Interserve (Scotland)

12 Elm Avenue,
Lenzie,
Glasgow, G66 4HJ
Tel: 0141-776-2943   Fax: 0141-777-8146

Mrs. Ellen Cooke, *Administrative Secretary*

Intervention Board Executive Agency

Saughton House,
Broomhouse Drive,
Edinburgh, EH11 3XA
Tel: 0131-244-8382   Fax: 0131-244-8117

P.R. Drummond, *Regional Verification Manager*

The Scottish region verification office. *

Irish Red & White Setter Club of Scotland

Rodoghvit New School House,
Culsalmond,
Insch,
Aberdeenshire, AB52 6UH
Tel: 01464-841317

Mrs. P. Ralston

Irish Setter Club of Scotland

Harcombes,
Macbie Hill,
by West Linton,
Peeblesshire, EH46 7AZ
Tel: 01968-660526   Fax: 01968-660526

Mr. B.M. Marshall

To promote and encourage the improvement and wellbeing of Irish Setters and responsible ownership thereof; to hold shows under Kennel Club regulations. *

Irish Terrier Club of Scotland

Foxhead Farmhouse,
Hillhead, by Cowie,
Stirlingshire, FK7 7DJ
Tel: 01786-813308

Mrs. C. Lamb

Iron & Steel Trades Confederation

20 Quarry Street,
Hamilton,
Lanarkshire, ML3 7AR
Tel: 01698-422924   Fax: 01698-286332

Mr. J. Brandon, *Scottish Officer*

Islamic Council of Scotland

30 Clyde Place,
Glasgow, G5 8AA

Mr Bashir Man

Israel Information Office in Scotland

222 Fenwick Road,
Glasgow, G46 6UE
Tel: 0141-620-0940   Fax: 0141-620-0940

Dr. Ezra Golombok

News, information and speakers on Israeli politics, history, tourism, etc. Internet website updated daily: http://www.isrinfo.demon.co.uk. *

Issue Scotland (The National Fertility Association)

21 Castle Street,
Edinburgh, EH2 3DN
Tel: 0131-225-2464

JIT Club Scotland

14 & 20 Hardengreen Business Centre,
Dalkeith,
Edinburgh, EH22 3NU
Tel: 0131-654 2992

Japan Society of Scotland

48 The Ness,
Dollar,
Clackmannanshire, FK14 7EB
Tel: 01259-742978   Fax: 01259-742978

Mrs. Marion Moir, *Secretary*

Japanese Akita Club of Scotland

92 Mungalhead Road,
Bainsford,
Falkirk, FK2 7JG
Tel: 01324-631084

Mr. G. Gemmell

Jewish Blind Society (Scotland)

May Terrace,
Giffnock,
Glasgow, G46 6LD
Tel: 0141-638-0066

Mrs. C. Blake

We make sure our clients receive the standard of care they deserve from qualified professionals. *

Jewish Care Scotland

May Terrace,
Giffnock,
Glasgow, G46 6LD
Tel: 0141-620-1800   Fax: 0141-620-1088

Mrs. Ethne Woldman

To provide social work services to vulnerable individuals and families within the Jewish community. *

John Muir Trust

12 Wellington Place,
Leith, EH6 7EQ
Tel: 0131-554-0114   Fax: 0131-555-2112

Joint Negotiating Committee for Chief Officials of Local Authorities (Scotland) Employers' Side

Helenic House,
87/97 Bath Street,
Glasgow, G2 2ER
Tel: 0141-332-0006

Junior Chamber (of Commerce) Scotland

Central Scottish Chamber of Commerce,
Haypark Business Centre,
Marchmont Avenue,
Polmont,
Falkirk, FK2 0NZ
Tel: 01324-718000   Fax: 01324-713027

Ms. Lynne Mallice

Justice and Peace Scotland

65 Bath Street,
Glasgow, G2 2BX
Tel: 0141-333-0238   Fax: 0141-333-0238

Ms. Maryanne Ure

Justice and Peace Scotland advises the Scottish bishops on matters of social justice, human rights, peace, disarmament and development, and promotes action through local groups. *

Jute Importers' Association Limited

c/o Sidlaw Textiles Limited,
Manhattan Works,
Dundonald Street,
Dundee, DD3 7PY
Tel: 01382-450645   Fax: 01382-462903

A.G. Scott, *Chairman*

KEEP WELL Services

28 Forth Street,
Edinburgh, EH1 3LH
Tel: 0131-556 3190   Fax: 0131-557-1620

Ms. Dorothy Walster

Keepwell Services are targeted at those over 50. They include EXTEND basic exercise training, the Pet Fostering Service Scotland, staff in-service training and counselling. *

Keep Scotland Beautiful

7 Melville Terrace,
Stirling, FK8 2ND
Tel: 01786-471333   Fax: 01786-464611

J. Robert Dickson, *Director*

Key Housing Association

Savoy Tower,
77 Renfrew Street,
Glasgow, G2 3BZ
Tel: 0141-332-7472   Fax: 0141-332-7498

Mr. Jim Kearns

In small scale, integrated housing developments throughout Scotland, we provide support to meet the individual needs of people with learning difficulties. *

Kids in Need and Distress KIND (Scotland)

Balbeg House,
Balbeg Estate,
Straiton,
Maybole,
Ayrshire, KA19 7NN
Tel: 01655-770644

Mr. Steven Yip, *Secretary*

KIND provides week long social educational breaks for disadvantaged children giving them a chance to experience another side of life and to show them that they and life do have more to offer. *

King George's Fund for Sailors

HMS Caledonia,
Rosyth,
Dunfermline, KY11 2XH
Tel: 01383-419969   Fax: 01383-419969

The Area Organiser

KGFS raises funds for the nautical charities that support the Royal Navy, the Merchant Navy and the fishing fleets. *

Kirk Care Housing Association

3 Forres Street,
Edinburgh, EH3 6BJ
Tel: 0131-225-7246   Fax: 0131-226-4551

Mrs. Mary Docherty, *Housing Assistant*

LEAD Scotland (Linking Education and Disability)

Queen Margaret College,
Clerwood Terrace,
Edinburgh, EH12 8TS
Tel: 0131-317-3439   Fax: 0131-339-7198

Ms. Rona Connolly, *Director*

LEAD Scotland exists to empower and enable physically disabled and/or sensorily-impaired adults in Scotland to access education, training and lifelong learning opportunities. *

LEPRA (British Leprosy Relief Association)

The Beehive,
Dolphinton,
near West Linton,
Edinburgh, EH46 7HH
Tel: 01968-682369   Fax: 01968-682356

Mrs. Rosalind Kerry, *Regional Manager*

LETS Link Scotland

38 Queen Street,
Tayport,
Fife, DD6 9LQ
Tel: 01382-553109   Fax: 01382-553109

Mr. Mark Johnston

LINKS – Scottish Episcopal Church Mission Association

21 Grosvenor Crescent,
Edinburgh, EH12 5EE
Tel: 0131-225-6357   Fax: 0131-341-7247

Mrs. Margaret A. Deas, *Provincial Secretary*

A voluntary organisation aiming to stimulate awareness of the worldwide partnership of Christians, and to support overseas mission by prayer and donations. *

Labrador Club of Scotland

46 Orchard Street,
Galston,
Ayrshire, KA4 8EL
Tel: 01563-820270

Mrs. A.M. Pollock

There are various Club events – the championship show, open shows and field trials which include a two-day open stake and two novice stakes. *

Ladies' Golf Union

The Scores,
St. Andrews,
Fife, KY16 9AT
Tel: 01334-475811   Fax: 01334-472818

Mrs. J. Hall, *Administrator*

The governing body of amateur golf in Great Britain and Ireland. *

Land Reform Scotland

The Chalmer,
Mill of Towie,
Cullen,
Buckie,
Banffshire, AB56 4TA
Tel: 01542-841842   Fax: 01542-841842

Mr. Peter Gibb, *Coordinator*

Campaigning for fundamental social justice through radical land and tax reform. *

Lands Tribunal for Scotland

1 Grosvenor Crescent,
Edinburgh, EH12 5ER
Tel: 0131-225-7996   Fax: 0131-226-4812

Mr. Neil Tainsh, *Clerk*

A judicial body determining a range of questions relating to land valuation; discharge of land obligations; council house purchase disputes; disputed compensation following compulsory purchase, etc. *

Landscape Institute Scotland

5 Coates Crescent,
Edinburgh, EH3 7AL
Tel: 0131-226-3939

Sue Gray, *Secretary*

Law Society of Scotland

26 Drumsheugh Gardens,
Edinburgh, EH3 7YR
Tel: 0131-226-7411   Fax: 0131-225-2934

Ms. Gillian Meighan, *Media Relations Officer*

The Law Society of Scotland is the governing body of the Scottish legal profession. It promotes the interests of both practising solicitors and the public. Website is http://www.lawscot.org.uk. *

Lawyers Christian Fellowship

see The Lawyers Christian Fellowship

Legal Defence Union Limited

17 Ainslie Place,
Edinburgh, EH3 6AU
Tel: 0131-220-0116

Legal Services Agency (LSA)

3rd floor,
Fleming House,
134 Renfrew Street,
Glasgow, G3 6ST
Tel: 0141-353-3354   Fax: 0141-353-0354

Mr. Paul Brown, *Principal Solicitor*

Legal Services Agency Limited is a charitable community-based law centre. It aims to tackle unmet legal needs through training, research, publications and casework by means of seminars, publishing and distributing leaflets and raising actions in courts and tribunals throughout Scotland. *

Leonard Cheshire in Scotland

20/21 Woodside Place,
Glasgow, G3 7QF

Ms. Dot Pringle

Leprosy Mission (Scotland)

89 Barnton Street,
Stirling, FK8 1HJ
Tel: 01786-449266   Fax: 01786-449266

Leukaemia & Cancer Children's Fund

14 Featherhall Place,
Edinburgh, EH12 7TN
Tel: 0131-316-4149   Fax: 0131-316-4060

Ms. Shannon Douglas

Leukemia Research Fund in Scotland

43 Westbourne Gardens,
Glasgow, G12 9XQ
Tel: 0141-339-0690   Fax: 0141-339-0690

Mrs. Mulholland, *Secretary*

The Leukaemia Research Fund works to prevent, improve diagnosis and cure all forms of leukaemia and related cancers of the blood in children and adults. *

Lhasa Apso Club of Scotland

Brook Bank Cottage,
by Craigie,
Kilmarnock,
Ayrshire, KA1 5LX
Tel: 01563-860207

Mr. J.B. Watson, *Honorary Secretary*

The main objectives of the Club are to promote and encourage the general welfare of the Lhasa Apso and responsible ownership of the breed. *

Linguistics Association of Great Britain

Programme in Literary Linguistics,
University of Strathclyde,
Glasgow, G1 1XH
Tel: 0141-552-4400   Fax: 0141-552-3493

Dr. Nigel Fabb, *Honorary Secretary*

Link Overseas Exchange

Ogstoun House,
Gordonstoun,
Elgin,
Moray, IV30 2RF
Tel: 01343-835910   Fax: 01343-835966

Mrs. V. Greaves

Link is a Scottish charity that gives young people the opportunity to live and work overseas for a period of six months. By living in the local community, volunteers have a chance to increase their knowledge and understanding of different cultures. e-mail: link@gordonstoun.org.uk. *

L

Lip Reading Teachers

Adult Basic Education Unit,
South Bridge Resource Centre,
Infirmary Street,
Edinburgh, EH1 1LT
Tel: 0131-558-3545

Ms. Sarah Kilbey

Live Music Now! (Scotland)

14 Lennox Street,
Edinburgh, EH14 1QA
Tel: 0131-332-6356   Fax: 0131-332-6356

Ms. Carol Main

*Live Music Now! was founded in 1977 by Lord
Menuhin with the two-fold aim of giving
young musicians experience in performing,
while simultaneously bringing live music of
an extremely high standard to disadvantaged
and deprived people throughout our communities.* *

Lloyds TSB Foundation for Scotland

Henry Duncan House,
120 George Street,
Edinburgh, EH2 4LH
Tel: 0131-225-4555

Andrew Muirhead/Connie Williamson

*The Foundation awards grants to registered
charities that operate in the fields of training
and education, social and community needs
and scientific and medical research.* *

Local Authority (Scotland) Accounts Advisory Committee

8 North West Circus Place,
Edinburgh, EH3 6ST
Tel: 0131-220-4316   Fax: 0131-220-4305

Mr. Ian P. Doig, *Secretary*

Local Government Boundary Commission for Scotland

3 Drumsheugh Gardens,
Edinburgh, EH3 7QJ
Tel: 0131-538-7510

Mr. R. Smith, *Secretary*

Local Government Ombudsman for Scotland

23 Walker Street,
Edinburgh, EH3 7HX
Tel: 0131-225-5300   Fax: 0131-225-9495

Mr. Frederick C. Marks, *Ombudsman*

Local Government Property Commission (Scotland)

3 Drumsheugh Gardens,
Edinburgh, EH3 7QJ
Tel: 0131-538-7410   Fax: 0131-538-7240

Professor Gordon S. Milne, *Chairman*

Locate in Scotland

120 Bothwell Street,
Glasgow, G2 7JP
Tel: 0141-248-2700   Fax: 0141-221-5129

Kevin Clark, *Interim Director*

*Joint venture organisation of Scottish Enterprise
and The Scottish Office for the attraction of
inward investment to Scotland.**

London Stock Exchange –
Scotland

Stock Exchange House,
P.O. Box 141,
Glasgow, G2 1BU
Tel: 0141-221-7060   Fax: 0141-221-3184

Mr. Stephen Robertson, *Senior Manager,
Scotland**

Look Scotland

10 Magdala Crescent,
Edinburgh, EH12 5BE
Tel: 0131-313-5711   Fax: 0131-313-1875

Ms. Carolyn Finlayson, *Development Officer*

Lord's Day Observance
Society

9 Kingsburgh Road,
Edinburgh, EH12 6DZ
Tel: 0131-337-6007

Lord's Taverners Scottish
Region

34 Queen's Crescent,
Edinburgh, EH9 2BA
Tel: 0131-667-0111

Loyal Orange Institution of
Scotland

108a Beith Street,
Glasgow, G11 6AR
Tel: 0141-400-1690   Fax: 0141-400-1690

Mr. Jack Ramsay, *Grand Secretary*

*Fraternal organisation whose objects are to
promote the reformed faith and uphold the
constitutional monarchy and the union of
Great Britain-Northern Ireland.**

Lubavitch Foundation of
Scotland

8 Orchard Drive,
Giffnock,
Glasgow, G46 7NR
Tel: 0141-638-6116   Fax: 0141-628-6478

Rabbi and Mrs. Chaim Jacobs

M.E. Association – Scotland (GB)

52 St. Enoch Square,
Glasgow, G1 4AA
Tel: 0141-204-3822   Fax: 0141-204-1673

Miss C. Reynolds, *Office Administrator*

M.E. Foundation (Scotland)

8 Inverleith Gardens,
Edinburgh, EH5 3PU
Tel: 0131-478-7879

Ms. Lynn McCormack, *President, Help Group*

METCOM Training (National Foundry & Engineering Training Association)

Savoy Tower,
77 Renfrew Street,
Glasgow, G2 3BZ
Tel: 0141-332-0826   Fax: 0141-332-5788

A.Y. Simpson, *Secretary*

METCOM Training is a national membership-based training organisation with a background in mechanical and foundry engineering and engineering construction. *

MISSION (Scotland)

9 Upper Gray Street,
Edinburgh, EH9 1SN
Tel: 0131-667-1605

Rev. Daniel Foley

MacMillan Cancer Relief

9 Castle Terrace,
Edinburgh, EH1 2DP
Tel: 0131-229-3276   Fax: 0131-228-6710

Mr. Ian Gibson, *Regional Director*

MacMillan works with the NHS and others to provide expert nursing and medical care for people who have cancer and their families. *

Macaulay Land Use Research Institute

Craigiebuckler,
Aberdeen, AB15 8QH
Tel: 01224-318611   Fax: 01224-311556

Dr. Sue Bird, *External Affairs Officer*

Government-funded research institute (Scottish Office). A premier centre in Europe for research on land use and environmental science. Its aim is to develop sustainable systems of land use. *

Malt Distillers Association of Scotland

see The Malt Distillers Association of Scotland

Maltese Club of Scotland

18 Robinson Drive,
Worksop,
Nottinghamshire, S80 1AT
Tel: 01909-475578

Mr. P. Moorby

Manic Depression Fellowship Scotland

7 Woodside Crescent,
Glasgow, G3 7UL
Tel: 0141-331-0440   Fax: 0141-331-0366

Ms. Kathleen Flanigan*

Manufacturing, Science & Finance

1 Woodlands Terrace,
Glasgow, G3 6DD
Tel: 0141-331-1216   Fax: 0141-331-1835

Mr. I. Fulton, *Designated Officer*

Marfan Association UK

Scottish Support Group,
1 Borden Road,
Jordanhill,
Glasgow, G13 1RB
Tel: 0141-954-8068

Mrs. Christine Mitchell

Supports sufferers and their families, provides information to medical and other caring professionals and fosters research. *

Marie Curie Cancer Care Scotland

21 Rutland Street,
Edinburgh, EH1 2AH
Tel: 0131-229-8332   Fax: 0131-229-9887

Mr. Peter Laidlaw, *Secretary*

Market Research Society in Scotland

T.L. Dempster,
Hermyon House,
Bothwell Road,
Uddington,
Glasgow, G71 7HA
Tel: 01698-811444

Alistair McCrae, *Secretary*

Marriage Counselling Scotland

105 Hanover Street,
Edinburgh, EH2 1DJ
Tel: 0131-225-5006   Fax: 0131-220-0639

Mrs. Frances Love, *Director* *

Meat and Livestock Commission (Scottish HQ)

3 Atholl Place,
Perth, PH1 5ND
Tel: 01738-627401   Fax: 01738-621367

Alistair Donaldson, *General Secretary*

Medau Society of Great Britain & Northern Ireland

Shieling of Blebo,
Pitscottie,
Fife, KY15 5TX
Tel: 01334-828623

Ms. Rosalind Garton, *Scottish Representative*

The governing body promoting the Medau method of movement to music for women, which exercises without strain and develops confidence and grace in movement. *

Medical Action for Global Security

51 Marchmont Road,
Edinburgh, EH9 1HT
Tel: 0131-229-3511

Dr. C.M. Bronte-Stewart

Medical and Dental Defence Union of Scotland (MDDUS)

120 Blythswood Street,
Glasgow, G2 4EH
Tel: 0141-221-5858   Fax: 0141-228-1208

Dr. Ian G. Simpson, *Chief Executive* *

Meningitis Association Scotland

9 Edwin Street,
Glasgow, G51 1ND
Tel: 0141-427-6698   Fax: 0141-427-6698

Mrs. E.E. McKiernan, *Chairperson*

Promotion of awareness of meningitis and provision of services such as specialist equipment for victims, research funding, support group for bereaved families, provision of literature. There is a network throughout Scotland and a 24-hour helpline. *

Meningitis Research Foundation (MRF)

133 Gilmore Place,
Edinburgh, EH3 9PP
Tel: 0131-228-3322   Fax: 0131-221-0300

The Meningitis Research Foundation works actively with families affected by meningitis and septicaemia to fight the disease by promoting public awareness and by funding scientific research. *

Mental Health Foundation Scotland

24 George Square,
Glasgow, G2 1EG
Tel: 0141-572-0125   Fax: 0141-572-0246

Ms. Lynda M. Somerville, *Director*

MHF Scotland works with, and on behalf of, people with mental health problems or learning disabilities, their carers and professionals in the field. *

Mental Welfare Commission for Scotland

K Floor,
Argyle House,
3 Lady Lawson Street,
Edinburgh, EH3 9SH
Tel: 0131-222-6111   Fax: 0131-222-6112

Mr. D. Hogg, *Secretary*

*Exercises protective functions in respect of
people with a mental disorder.* *

Meteorological Office

Scottish Climate Office,
220 St. Vincent Street,
Glasgow, G2 5QD
Tel: 0141-303-0110   Fax: 0141-303-0101

*Past weather enquiries, from actual data to
analyses which provide design information or
enable specific events to be placed into
perspective.* *

Methodist Church in Scotland

20 Inglewood Crescent,
East Kilbride, G75 8QD
Tel: 01355-237411   Fax: 01355-237411

Rev. T. Alan Anderson, *Chairman*

Micro Anophthalmic Children's Society (MACS)

10 Mugdrum Place,
Newburgh,
Cupar,
Fife, KY14 6DD
Tel: 01337-840754   Fax: 01337-840754

Mr. Peter Attenborough

*MACS is a support group for families of
children born with anophthalmia (absence of
eyes), microphthalmia (small eyes) and
coloboma (a structural defect of the eyes).* *

Millennium Forest for Scotland Trust

91 Mitchell Street,
Glasgow, G1 3LN
Tel: 0141-204-2001   Fax: 0141-204-2222

Mrs. Penny Cousins, *Director*

*MFST is a charitable trust whose aim is to
promote the restoration and regeneration of
Scotland's native woods as an important part
of our natural heritage, and to bring them
back into management for the widest possible
public benefit.* *

Mime Forum (Scotland)

112 West Bow,
Grassmarket,
Edinburgh, EH1 2HH
Tel: 0131-225-2237

Minerals Engineering Society

Scottish Section,
8 Langton Gardens,
East Calder,
West Lothian, EH53 0DZ

E.R. Sim, *Secretary*

Mining Institute of Scotland (formerly Institute of Mining & Metallurgy)

26 Durness Avenue,
Bearsden,
Glasgow, G61 2AL
Tel: 0141-942-7348

Dr. D.O. Davies

Miscarriage Association

23 Castle Street,
Edinburgh, EH2 3DN
Tel: 0131-220-3841   Fax: 0131-220-3841

Ms. Morag Kinghorn, *Scottish Coordinator*

Miscarriage Association Support Group

15 Clerwood Bank,
Edinburgh, EH12 8PZ
Tel: 0131-334-8883   Fax: 0131-539-1135

Ms. Morag Kinghorn, *Scottish Coordinator*

Mission Aviation Fellowship

Challenge House,
29 Canal Street,
Glasgow, G4 0AD
Tel: 0141-332-5222   Fax: 0141-332-5222

Mr. Matthew McKinnon

The work of MAF is to speed the spread of the good news of Jesus Christ in word and deed, which meets deepest human need. *

Mission Scotland

9 Canal Street,
Glasgow, G4 0AB
Tel: 0141-333-1282   Fax: 0141-333-1282

Mrs. Myra Cathcart

Missions to Seamen, Scotland

Containerbase,
Gartsherrie Road,
Coatbridge,
Lanarkshire, ML5 2DS
Tel: 01236-440132

Mrs. L.C. Boyd, *Administration Manager*

Caring for seafarers regardless of race, rank or creed. *

Modern Studies Association

1F3, 12 Broughton Road,
Edinburgh, EH7 4EB
Tel: 0131-556-2580

Mr. Gavin Black, *Secretary*

*A professional association of modern studies
teachers established in 1972, which aims to
promote and enhance the teaching of modern
studies in schools in Scotland.* *

Money Advice Scotland

Suite 306,
Pentagon Centre,
36 Washington Street,
Glasgow, G3 8AZ
Tel: 0141-572-0237   Fax: 0141-572-0237

Mrs. Yvonne Gallacher

*Money Advice Scotland, the national organisa-
tion was set up in 1989 and exists to
represent the views of all those involved in
money advice, encourage development of free,
independent, impartial money advice services
and provide a forum for discussions between
voluntary, statutory, independent and finance
industry organisations.* *

Morris Minor Owners' Club (Scotland)

Laundry Cottage,
Darleith,
Cardross,
Dumbarton, G82 5PG
Tel: 01389-841572

Ms. Flora Leckie, *Secretary*

Mountain Bothies Association

26 Rycroft Avenue,
Deeping St. James,
Peterborough, PE6 8NT
Tel: 01778-345062

Mr. Ted Butcher, *Information Secretary*

*To maintain simple unlocked shelters in remote
country for the use and benefit of all those
who love wild and lonely places.* *

Mountain Rescue Committee of Scotland

12 Hazel Avenue,
Dundee, DD2 1QD
Tel: 01382-68193

Mr. A.C. Ingram, *Secretary*

Mountaineering Council of Scotland

4a St. Catherine's Road,
Perth, PH1 5SE
Tel: 01738-638227   Fax: 01738-442095

Mr. Kevin Howett, *National Officer*

*The national governing body for the sport of
hillwalking and mountaineering in Scotland.
As a representative body for our members, we
aim to promote and protect their interests.* *

Multiple Sclerosis Centre

Unit 16,
Chapel Street Industrial Estate,
Glasgow, G20 9BD
Tel: 0141-945-3344

Mrs. Margaret Neill, *Financial Administrator*

The provision in a relaxed atmosphere of daily
support and therapies including counselling,
physiotherapy, aromatherapy, reflexology for
those affected by multiple sclerosis and their
carers. *

Multiple Sclerosis Society in Scotland

2A North Charlotte Street,
Edinburgh, EH2 4HR
Tel: 0131-225-3600   Fax: 0131-220-5188

Mr. T.J. Hope Thomson

Its aims are to provide for and promote the
welfare of people with multiple sclerosis and
their families, to provide advice and informa-
tion and to fund medical research in Scot-
land. The Society has 45 local branches and
maintains two holiday homes. *

Muscular Dystrophy Group

Room 262,
11 Bothwell Street,
Glasgow, G2 6NL
Tel: 0141-221-4411

Muscular Dystrophy Group Scottish Council

3rd floor,
Princes House,
5 Shandwick Place,
Edinburgh, EH2 4RG
Tel: 0131-221-0066   Fax: 0131-221-0066

Mr. Ken Brown, *Director*

Research, counselling and care for families and
individuals affected by neuromuscular
conditions. *

Music in Scotland Trust Limited

11 Sandyford Place,
Sauchiehall Street,
Glasgow, G3 7NB
Tel: 0141-204-3520

Musicians' Union

11 Sandyford Place,
Sauchiehall Street,
Glasgow, G3 7NB
Tel: 0141-248-3723   Fax: 0141-204-3510

Mr. I. Smith, *Scottish Organiser*

Europe's largest representative organisation for
musicians. Offering a wide range of services,
including legal, accountancy, tax advice as
well as free contract vetting, public liability
insurance and much more. *

NASPCS, the Charity for Incontinent & Stoma Children

51 Anderson Drive,
Valley View Park,
Darvel,
Ayrshire, KA17 0DE
Tel: 01560-322024

Mr. John Malcolm, *National Organiser*

To provide a contact and information service for
parents on all aspects of coping with a child
with either a colostomy, ileostomy or
urostomy. We also try to give advice on the
incontinence often encountered with bowel
and bladder problems and enable families to
contact others in a similar situation for
mutual support and advice. *

NCH Action for Children, Scotland

17 Newton Place,
Glasgow, G3 7PY
Tel: 0141-332-4041   Fax: 0141-332-7002

The Director

NHBC – Scotland (National House-Building Council)

42 Colinton Place,
Edinburgh, EH10 5BT
Tel: 0131-313-1001

Helen McCallum

National Association for Colitis & Crohn's Disease (NACC)

2 Wester Coates Gardens,
Edinburgh, EH12 5LT
Tel: 0131-346-1747   Fax: 0131-346-1747

Mrs. Gillian Hamer-Hodges

We offer support, in a one-to-one setting,
medical and general lectures and local and
national newsletters. Information booklets
are sent to all members. *

National Association for Gifted Children in Scotland (NAGCS)

8 Drymen Place,
Lenzie,
Glasgow, G66 5HL
Tel: 0141-776-1798

Ms. Alison Hore, *Secretary*

NAGCS brings together and supports teachers,
parents and others interested in educational
provision for gifted children as well as their
social and emotional development. *

National Association for Patient Participation

51 Crollshillock Place,
Newtonhill,
Stonehaven, AB39 3RF
Tel: 01569-731020

Mrs. Angela Broad

National Association of Accordion & Fiddle Clubs

63 Station Road,
Thankerton,
Biggar, ML12 6NZ
Tel: 01899-308327

Charles Todd, *Secretary*

71 member clubs, mostly in Scotland and the north of England, promote and encourage all types of accordion and fiddle music, with the emphasis on traditional Scottish and Irish music. *

National Association of Cigarette Machine Operators

Scottish Section,
Taylor Vending & Wholesale,
60 Ferry Street,
Montrose, DD10 8BY
Tel: 01674-76446

David Taylor

National Association of Colliery Overmen, Deputies and Shotfirers (Scottish Area)

19 Cadzow Street,
Hamilton,
Midlothian, ML3 6EE
Tel: 01698-284981

Mr. R. Letham

National Association of Educational Guidance for Adults

1a Hilton Road,
Milngavie,
Glasgow, G62 7DN
Tel: 0141-956-5950   Fax: 0141-956-6020

Anne Docherty, *General Secretary*

National Association of Hospital Play Staff Scotland (NAHPSS)

The Croft,
Rait,
Perthshire, PH2 7RT
Tel: 01821-670261

Ms. Jane Greig, *Chairperson*

National Association of Roofing Contractors

see Scottish Decorators' Federation

National Association of Scaffolding Contractors, Scottish Section

see Scottish Decorators' Federation

National Association of Schoolmasters/Union of Women Teachers

5th floor,
Stock Exchange House,
7 Nelson Mandela Place,
Glasgow, G2 1QY
Tel: 0141-229-5790   Fax: 0141-229-5799

Ms. C. Fox

The only UK teachers' trade union providing advice, support and representation to teachers in nursery, primary and secondary education. Membership benefits include legal support and financial assistance in times of hardship. *

National Association of Specialist Contractors

see Scottish Decorators' Federation

National Association of Toy and Leisure Libraries/Play Matters

10 Suffolk Road,
Edinburgh, EH16 5NR
Tel: 0131-662-4454

Ms. Joy Blakeney

National Association of Youth Orchestras

Ainslie House,
11 St. Colme Street,
Edinburgh, EH3 6AG
Tel: 0131-539-1087   Fax: 0131-539-1069

Miss Carol Main, *Director*

Formed in 1961 to represent youth orchestras throughout the UK and to foster their development. Organises Annual Festival of British Youth Orchestras in Edinburgh and Glasgow. *

National Asthma Campaign Scotland

21 Coates Crescent,
Edinburgh, EH3 7AF
Tel: 0131-226-2544   Fax: 0131-226-2401

Ms. Marjory O'Donnell, *Head of Development*

The National Asthma Campaign is the independent UK charity working to conquer asthma, in partnership with people with asthma and all who share their concern, through a combination of research, education and support. *

National Autistic Society

111 Union Street,
Glasgow, G1 3TA
Tel: 0141-221-8090

Mr. Mike Collins

National Baton Twirling Association of Scotland

19 Pollock Walk,
Dunfermline, KY12 9DA

Bill Clarke, *Secretary*

National Bible Society of Scotland

7 Hampton Terrace,
Edinburgh, EH12 5XY
Tel: 0131-337-9701   Fax: 0131-337-0641

Mrs. Pauline Hurst, *Assistant General Secretary*

The Bible Society's aim is to make the Bible available to people worldwide in a language they can understand and at a price they can afford to pay. *

National Board for Nursing, Midwifery and Health Visiting for Scotland

22 Queen Street,
Edinburgh, EH2 1NT
Tel: 0131-226-7371   Fax: 0131-225-9970

Mr. D.C. Benton, *Chief Executive*

The National Board is a statutory body responsible for maintaining and developing standards of professional educational provision for nurses, midwives and health visitors in Scotland. *

National Canine Defence League

Rescue Centre,
Dovecotwell, by Glencaple,
Dumfries, DG1 4RH
Tel: 01387-770346   Fax: 01387-770242

Mrs. Jean Coupland

The NCDL exists to protect and defend all dogs from abuse and cruelty, abandonment and any form of mistreatment, both in the UK and abroad. The charity seeks to achieve this through its nationwide rescue centres, education and advocacy work and welfare campaigns. *

National Centre for Play

Moray House Institute,
Cramond Campus,
Edinburgh, EH4 6JD
Tel: 0131-312-8088   Fax: 0131-312-6335

The Secretary *

National Childbirth Trust

Stockbridge Health Centre,
1 India Place,
Edinburgh, EH3 6EH
Tel: 0131-225-9191

Ms. Kathy McGlew

Concerned with pregnancy and childbirth, we offer antenatal classes, breastfeeding counselling, parent and baby groups for postnatal support. A fee is charged for classes but all other services are free and there is an information pack available. *

National Commission for Social Care (Catholic Church)

1/2, 15c Hill Street,
Glasgow, G3 6RE
Tel: 0141-572-0115   Fax: 0141-572-0115

Mr. David McCann*

National Convention of Mental Health Charities in Scotland

Suite 48,
Fountain Business Centre,
Ellis Street,
Coatbridge, ML5 3AA
Tel: 01698-351615

Mr. Richard Anderson

National Cooperage Federation

Dundashill Cooperage,
1 Dundashill,
Glasgow, G4 9UE
Tel: 0141-353-0732   Fax: 0141-353-1627

Charles H. Alcorn, *Secretary & Treasurer*

National Council of Women – Scottish Standing Committee

49 Keir Street,
Bridge of Allan, FK9 4QJ
Tel: 01786-832064

National Deaf Children's Society (NDCS)

100 Norfolk Street,
Glasgow, G5 9EJ
Tel: 0141-420-3555   Fax: 0141-420-3442

Mrs. Veronica Rattray, *Scottish Development Officer*

NDCS provides information and advice on all aspects of childhood deafness, providing practical support through our network of regional staff and trained local representatives. Our telephone number is voice/text. *

National Eczema Society (Scotland)

P.O. Box 2,
Arbroath, DD1 4YG
Tel: 01241-853407   Fax: 01241-853407

Ms. S. Manknell

Information and support to those affected by eczema and relevant professionals. Holidays for youngsters, run jointly with National Asthma Campaign. Research support. Limited welfare fund. *

National Farmers' Union of Scotland

The Rural Centre,
West Mains,
Ingliston,
Newbridge,
Midlothian, EH28 8LT
Tel: 0131-472-4000   Fax: 0131-472-4010

Professional agricultural organisation which monitors, protects and promotes the interests of members – Scottish farmers, growers and crofters. Powerful lobbying role. *

National Federation of Demolition Contractors

13 Woodside Crescent,
Glasgow, G3 7UP
Tel: 0141-353-2637   Fax: 0141-331-1684

J.A. Williams, *Scottish Secretary*

National Federation of Music Societies (Scotland)

9 Beamsburn,
Kilmarnock, KA3 1RN
Tel: 01563-520538

Miss Isobel Crawford

National Federation of Retail Newsagents

6a Weir Street,
Falkirk, FK1 1RB
Tel: 01324-625293

National Federation of Roofing Contractors (Scottish Office)

13 Woodside Crescent,
Glasgow, G3 7UP
Tel: 0141-332-7144   Fax: 0141-331-1684

National Federation of Spiritual Healers

Herdsmans Hill,
off Knockbuckle Road,
Kilmacolm,
Renfrewshire, PA13 4JS
Tel: 01505-873144

Mrs. Liz Carnie, *Secretary*

Contact or distant healing. There are healer development groups, courses, classes and/or general information. *

National Foster Care Association (NFCA)

1 Melrose Street,
off Queen's Crescent,
Glasgow, G4 9BJ
Tel: 0141-332-6655   Fax: 0141-353-1135

Ms. Margaret Reid, *Administrator*

National Foster Care Association exists to improve the standard of foster care services to children and young people who cannot live with their own families. *

National Gaelic Arts Agency/Proiseact nan Ealan

10 Shell Street,
Stornoway,
Isle of Lewis, HS1 2BS
Tel: 01851-704493/703440   Fax: 01851-704734

Mr. Malcolm MacLean, *Director*

The National Gaelic Arts Agency/Proiseact nan Ealan designs, develops and delivers strategic projects and fulfils an advocacy and networking role across the arts and Gaelic world. *

National Galleries of Scotland

13 Heriot Row,
Edinburgh, EH3 6HP
Tel: 0131-556-8921   Fax: 0131-556-9972

Mr. T.P.P. Clifford, *Director*

National Joint Council for Local Authorities' Administrative, Professional, Technical and Clerical Services – Employers' Side

Rosebery House,
9 Haymarket Terrace,
Edinburgh, EH12 5XZ
Tel: 0131-474-9200   Fax: 0131-474-9292

Mr. Dan Brown

*The employers' side of the National Joint
Council is drawn from elected members of
local authorities in Scotland and represents
all 32 councils in Scotland in national pay
bargaining.* *

National Joint Council for Local Authorities' Administrative, Professional, Technical and Clerical Services – Employees' Side

Helenic House,
87/97 Bath Street,
Glasgow, G2 2ER
Tel: 0141-332-0006

National League of the Blind and Disabled

15 Lilybank Avenue,
Halfway,
Cambuslang,
Glasgow, G72 8QP
Tel: 0141-641-2017

Mr. W. Walker, *Secretary*

National Library of Scotland

George IV Bridge,
Edinburgh, EH1 1EW
Tel: 0131-226-4531   Fax: 0131-220-6662

Mr. I.D. McGowan, *Librarian*

National Lottery Charities Board

Norloch House,
36 King's Stables Road,
Edinburgh, EH1 2EJ
Tel: 0131-221-7100   Fax: 0131-221-7120

Mr. John Rafferty, *Director for Scotland*

*The Board distributes a proportion of lottery
money to charities, voluntary and community
groups throughout Scotland. Organisations
can apply for a grant to a number of different
programmes, depending on the nature of their
projects.* *

National Metal Trades Federation

77 Renfrew Street,
Glasgow, G2 3BZ
Tel: 0141-332-0826   Fax: 0141-332-5788

Mr. A. Shaw, *Secretary**

National Monuments Record of Scotland

John Sinclair House,
16 Bernard Terrace,
Edinburgh, EH8 9NX
Tel: 0131-662-1446   Fax: 0131-662-1477

Mr. R.J. Mercer, *Secretary and Curator*

National Museum of Antiquities

1 Queen Street,
Edinburgh, EH2 1JD
Tel: 0131-225-7534

National Museums of Scotland

The Royal Museum of Scotland,
Chambers Street,
Edinburgh, EH1 1JF
Tel: 0131-225-7534   Fax: 0131-220-1870

Ms. Mary Bryden, *Head of Public Affairs*

National Network of Community Businesses

Society Place,
West Calder,
West Lothian, EH55 8BA
Tel: 01506-871370   Fax: 01506-873079

Ms. Kay Caldwell

*Information and networking service for those
involved in community business and community economic development.**

National Playbus Association

John Cotton Business Centre,
172 Easter Road,
Edinburgh, EH7 5QE
Tel: 0131-661-7559   Fax: 0131-661-7559

Mr. Hugo Whitaker, *Development Officer
(Scotland)*

*Promotes, supports and facilitates the develop-
ment of mobile community resources throughout Scotland.**

National Playing Fields Association (Scotland)

20 Queen Street,
Edinburgh, EH2 1JX
Tel: 0131-225-4307   Fax: 0131-225-5763

Mr. Stephen Barr, *Secretary/Treasurer*

*We are a charity tasked by Royal Charter with
the protection and preservation of playing
fields and recreational space.**

National Prayer Breakfast for Scotland

c/o National Bible Society for Scotland,
7 Hampton Terrace,
Edinburgh, EH12 5JD
Tel: 0131-337-3331

Mrs. Molly McArther, *Administrator*

National Rett Syndrome Association

15 Tanzieknowe Drive,
West Greenlees,
Cambuslang,
Glasgow, G72 8RG
Tel: 0141-641-7662

Ms. Isobel Allan, *President*

National Schizophrenia Fellowship (Scotland)

40 Shandwick Place,
Edinburgh, EH2 4RT
Tel: 0131-226-2025   Fax: 0131-225-7552

Mr. Ian Harper, *Information Officer*

*NSF (Scotland) is a national charity providing advice, information and support to people affected by mental illness, including drop-in centres and employment support.**

National Seminary in Scotland

Scotus College,
2 Chester Road,
Bearsden,
Glasgow, G61 4AG
Tel: 0141-942-8384   Fax: 0141-943-1767

National Society for Clean Air and Environmental Protection

c/o City of Glasgow Council,
Environmental Services Department,
20 India Street,
Glasgow, G2 4PF
Tel: 0141-287-6530

Ms. Clare Carruthers, *Administration Officer*

National Theatre for Scotland Campaign

Netherbow Theatre,
43–5 High Street,
Edinburgh, EH1 1SR
Tel: 0131-556-2647

*A loose federation of organisations including the Saltire Society, Arts and Democracy Forum, Equity, Scottish Society of Playwrights, etc., committed to the creation of a National Theatre Company for Scotland.**

National Trust for Scotland

5 Charlotte Square,
Edinburgh, EH2 4DU
Tel: 0131-226-5922   Fax: 0131-243-9501

Mr. Trevor A. Croft, *Director*

*The National Trust for Scotland is a conservation charity responsible for preserving and presenting to the public over 100 examples of Scotland's magnificent heritage of architecture, scenic beauty and historic sites.**

National Union of Civil & Public Servants

6 Hillside Crescent,
Edinburgh, EH7 5DY
Tel: 0131-556-0407

National Union of Journalists

114 Union Street,
Glasgow, G1 3QQ
Tel: 0141-248-6648   **Fax:** 0141-248-2473

Mr. P. Holleran, *Scottish Organiser* *

National Union of Knitwear, Footwear & Apparel Trades

5 St. Marnock Street,
Kilmarnock, KA1 1DZ
Tel: 01563-527476   **Fax:** 01563-537851

Mr. J. Steele, *District Secretary*

National Union of Mineworkers: Scotland Area

Unit 9,
The Enterprise Centre,
Dryden Road,
Loanhead, EH20 9LZ
Tel: 0131-440-1844   **Fax:** 0131-440-0844

Mr. S. Dickson

National Union of Rail, Maritime & Transport Workers

180 Hope Street,
Glasgow, G2 2UE
Tel: 0141-332-1117   **Fax:** 0141-333-9583

Mr. P. McGarry

We are the Scottish section of the RMT, representing members in the offshore and gas industry, shipping ferry operators, private engineering companies of the former B.R.B. railways, road haulage, transport, catering, etc. *

National Union of Students Scotland (NUS)

11 Broughton Market,
Edinburgh, EH3 6NU
Tel: 0131-556-6598   **Fax:** 0131-557-5679

Ms. Carole Ewart

National Youth Orchestra of Scotland

see The National Youth Orchestra of Scotland

National Youth Theatre of Scotland

13 Somerset Place,
Glasgow, G3 7JT

The Administrator

Neil Gunn Society

25 Newton Avenue,
Wick,
Caithness, KW1 5LJ
Tel: 01955-602607

Mrs. Jess M. Campbell, *Secretary*

Network Scotland

The Mews,
57 Ruthven Lane,
Glasgow, G12 9JG
Tel: 0141-357-1774   Fax: 0141-334-0299

Mr. David Dougan

*Telephone helplines, database management,
   counselling, fulfilment and despatch.* *

Network of Individuals and Campaigns for Humane Education

Department of Psychology,
University of Stirling,
Stirling, FK9 4LA
Tel: 01786-467677

Network of Voluntary Organisations in Aids/HIV

P.O. Box 5000,
Glasgow, G12 9BL

Mary Mantell, *Chairman*

Neurofibromatosis Association

31 Doune Crescent,
Larbert, FK5 4TR
Tel: 01324-554788

Miss Aileen Barrowman

*We now have a Family Support Worker at
   Duncan Guthrie Unit, Yorkhill Hospital,
   Glasgow. Telephone 0141-201-0504.* *

No Frontiers – Scottish Humanitarian Relief Aid

2 Gairnieston Cottages,
Gairnieston,
Turriff,
Aberdeenshire, AB53 7RP
Tel: 01888-551303   Fax: 01888-551303

Mr. Robert Milne

*A non-denominational voluntary organisation
   committed to assistance of all vulnerable
   groups in/from zones of conflict. Long-
   lasting, sustainable aid and refugee advice.* *

Nordoff Robins Music Therapy in Scotland

35 Moray Place,
Edinburgh, EH3 6BX

The Chairperson

OFFER Scotland (Office of Electricity Regulation)

48 St Vincent Street,
Glasgow, G2 5TS
Tel: 0141-248-5917

OYC Scotland (Ocean Youth Club Scotland)

Kip Marina,
Inverkip, PA16 0AS
Tel: 01475-521294   **Fax:** 01475-521294

Mrs. Bet Phillips, *Area Manager*

Office of the Social Security and Child Support Commissioners

23 Melville Street,
Edinburgh, EH3 7PW
Tel: 0131-225-2201   **Fax:** 0131-220-6782

E. Barschtschyk, *Secretary*

Applications for leave to appeal and appeals on questions of law from social security appeal tribunals, disability appeal tribunals and medical appeal tribunals in social security cases and from child support appeal tribunals in child support cases. *

Officers' Association Scotland

Haig House,
1 Fitzroy Place,
Glasgow, G3 7RG
Tel: 0141-221-8141   **Fax:** 0141-204-0939

Lt Col JSD Robertson DL, *Secretary*

The Association aims to relieve distress among all those who have held a commission in the naval, military or air forces, their widows and dependants and corresponding women's and nursing services. It also offers advice on re-employment to ex-officers. *

Offshore Contractors' Association

12 Queens Road,
Aberdeen, AB15 4ZT
Tel: 01224-645450   **Fax:** 01224-645452

I.M. Bell, *Chief Executive*

The Offshore Contractors' Association is the head representative body for the UK's oil and gas contracting and supply industry. *

Offshore Manufacturers' & Constructors' Association

1 Melville Crescent,
Edinburgh, EH3 7HW
Tel: 0131-226-2470   **Fax:** 0131-226-2471

William E. Allison, *Chief Executive*

Old English Sheepdog Club of Scotland

Laigh Armsheugh Cottage,
Doura,
Irvine, KA11 2AU
Tel: 01294-850364   Fax: 01294-850364

Mrs. J. Burns

The object of the Club is to further the interests of the breed in Scotland and support shows for the purpose of stimulating public interest. *

One Parent Families Scotland (OPFS)

13 Gayfield Square,
Edinburgh, EH1 3NX
Tel: 0131-556-3899   Fax: 0131-557-9650

Ms. Sue Robertson, *Director*

*National charity representing the interests of Scotland's 170,000 one parent families. There are publications, training, advice and library available.
Website on http://www.gn.ape.org/opfs.* *

One Parent Family Holidays

Kildonan Courtyard,
Barrhill,
Girvan, KA26 0PS
Tel: 01465-821288   Fax: 01776-889500

Mr. Colin Chatfield

As a member of the Group Travel Organisers Association, we have been organising holidays for families since 1976. A practical range of holidays are offered where families travel as part of a small group. *

Ordnance Survey

Grayfield House,
5 Bankhead Avenue,
Edinburgh, EH11 4AE
Tel: 0131-442-3985   Fax: 0131-442-4780

Mr. G.E. Little, *Account Manager*

Ordnance Survey is Britain's national mapping agency and is responsible for the production and maintenance of a wide range of maps in both conventional and digital form. *

Organisation of Chartered Physiotherapists in Private Practice

Aberdeen Physiotherapy,
99 Westburn Road,
Aberdeen, AB25 6SG
Tel: 01224-626266   Fax: 01224-641137

Ms. Linda Duncan/Rosemary Clark

Special interest group of the Chartered Society of Physiotherapy. *

Outright Scotland – Advocating Gay Equality

58a Broughton Street,
Edinburgh, EH1 3SA
Tel: 01592-655392 or 0131-558-1683

Mr. Ian Dunn, *Convenor*

National Gay Rights campaign, advocating LGB equality. Main work is 'EQUALITY 2000' and working with the Scottish Parliament. Active member of the International Lesbian and Gay Association (ILGA). *

Outward Bound Scotland

Loch Eil Centre,
Achdalieu,
Corpach,
Fort William, PH33 7NN
Tel: 01397-772866   **Fax:** 01397-773905

Mr. Geoff Hewitt

*The Scottish centre for the Outward Bound
Trust. Development and adventure courses
for 11–60+. Mountain-based and sea-based
skills courses. SQA, RYA, SMLTB accredited. AALA licence.* *

Over-Count Drugs Information and Advice Agency

20 Brewery Street,
Dumfries, DG1 2RP
Tel: 01387-770404   **Fax:** 01387-770404

Mr. David Grieve, *Project Director*

*Information, advice and support for misusers of
non-prescription, over-the-counter drugs and
medicines. Professional product misuse
database, treatment programmes, lecture
services and publications available.* *

Oxfam in Scotland

Floor 5,
Fleming House,
134 Renfrew Street,
Glasgow, G3 6ST
Tel: 0141-331-2724   **Fax:** 0141-331-2264

Mr. Ian Gray, *Acting Head of Campaigns*

PATH (Scotland)

c/o Skillnet, Unit 4,
Abbeymount Techbase,
2 Easter Road,
Edinburgh, EH7 5AN

PBC (Primary Biliary Cirrhosis) Foundation

The Dean,
Longniddry,
East Lothian, EH32 0PN
Tel: 01875-853552   Fax: 01875-852155

Mrs. Collette Thain, *Chairman**

PEN, Scottish Centre

15a Lynedoch Street,
Glasgow, G3 6EF
Tel: 0141-564-1958   Fax: 0141-564-1958

Mr. Simon Berry, *Acting Secretary*

Part of a writers' association with 130 centres world-wide, open to those professionally engaged in writing. Recognised by UNESCO as the voice of the international community of writers.*

PHAB Scotland

5a Warriston Road,
Edinburgh, EH3 5LQ
Tel: 0131-558-9912   Fax: 0131-558-9913

Ms. Maggie Hunter or *Chief Executive*

The main aim of PHAB Scotland is the empowerment of people with a physical disability, to encourage their inclusion in social, leisure, educational and vocational activities.*

Pain Association Scotland

Cramond House,
Cramond Glebe Road,
Edinburgh, EH4 6NS
Tel: 0131-312-7955

Mr. David Falconer, *National Organiser*

The Association provides through a network of local groups community-based pain management strategies for all sufferers of chronic pain.*

Pain Concern UK (Scottish Contact)

P.O. Box 13256,
Haddington,
East Lothian, EH41 4YD
Tel: 01620-822572

Ms. Heather Wallace

Information and support for chronic pain sufferers. Publications include newsletter, factsheet and leaflets on chronic pain.*

Paintings in Hospitals (Scotland)

Princess Margaret Rose Hospital,
Frogston Road West,
Edinburgh, EH10 7ED
Tel: 0131-536-4836   Fax: 0131-536-4836

Ms. Sarah Hall

Paintings in Hospitals Scotland, a registered charity, purchases paintings and original works of art to place in hospitals, homes and other healthcare organisations.*

P

Papillon Club of Scotland

117 Cheviot Road,
Kirkcaldy, KY2 6BE
Tel: 01592-260872

Mr. E. Whitehill

Parent Network Scotland

15 Saxe Coburg Place,
Edinburgh, EH3 5BR
Tel: 0131-332-0893

Josephine Macleod

Parents Forever Scotland

P.O. Box 23,
Kirkcaldy, KY1 1SS
Tel: 01333-352034

Mr. John Bernard

Parkinson's Disease Society of the United Kingdom, Scottish Resource

10 Claremont Terrace,
Glasgow, G3 7XR
Tel: 0141-332-3343   Fax: 0141-332-3343

Mrs. Sheila Scott

The Society's mission is the conquest of Parkinson's disease and the alleviation of the suffering and distress it causes, through effective research, education, welfare and communication. *

Parole Board for Scotland

Calton House,
5 Redheugh's Rigg,
Edinburgh, EH12 9HW
Tel: 0131-244-8755

Ian McNee, *Chairman*

Passport Office for Scotland

3 Northgate,
96 Milton Street,
Cowcaddens
Glasgow, G4 0BB
Tel: 0141-332-0271

Pensions Appeal Tribunals for Scotland

20 Walker Street,
Edinburgh, EH3 7HS
Tel: 0131-220-1404   Fax: 0131-225-2596

Mrs. L.E. Young, *Secretary*

The Tribunals hear and decide appeals against the rejection and assessment, by the Department of Social Security, of war pension claims. *

Penumbra

Gogar Park,
167 Glasgow Road,
Edinburgh, EH12 9BG
Tel: 0131-317-1337   Fax: 0131-317-1410

Mr. Peter Kampman

People First (Scotland)

45 York Place,
Edinburgh, EH1 3HP
Tel: 0131-558-9855   Fax: 0131-558-9866

Ms. Andrea Ridley, *Support Coordinator/ Administrator*

People First (Scotland) is the independent national self-advocacy organisation for people with learning difficulties in Scotland. It is linked to the international People First Movement. *

People's Dispensary for Sick Animals (PDSA)

Unit A16, Clyde Workshops,
Fullarton Road,
Glasgow, G32 7TX
Tel: 0141-641-5511

Ms. Lynn Crawford

To provide free veterinary treatment to sick and injured animals whose owners cannot afford private veterinary fees. *

Performing Rights Society

3 Rothesay Place,
Edinburgh, EH3 7SL
Tel: 0131-226-5320   Fax: 0131-220-4541

Jim McNeilage

Personal Investment Authority

108 Dundas Street,
Edinburgh, EH3 6RQ
Tel: 0131-557-6760

Perthes Association Scotland

29 Leander Crescent,
Deanpark Estate,
Renfrew, PA4 0XB
Tel: 0141-885-0001   Fax: 0141-561-0001

Ms. Muriel Buchanan

Pet Fostering Service Scotland

P.O. Box 6,
Callander, FK17 8ZU
Tel: 01877-331496   Fax: 01877-330996

Ms. Anne Docherty, *Treasurer*

PFSS has volunteers throughout Scotland who look after pets of elderly people unable to care for their pets temporarily because of an emergency such as illness/hospitalization. *

Phoenix (Scotland) Trust

278 High Street,
Glasgow, G4 0QT
Tel: 0141-553-2353

Ms. Anne Shearer

Phoenix Cancer Foundation

c/o Glasgow Council for Voluntary
    Services,
11 Queen's Crescent,
Glasgow, G4 9BW
Tel: 0141-332-2444   Fax: 0141-332-0175

Phoenix House

586 Keppochhill Road,
Glasgow, G22 5HS
Tel: 0141-332-0121   Fax: 0141-332-0117

Mr. Phil Hogben/Mr. John Perry

*This residential project is open to male and
females aged 18+ who are experiencing
problems with drugs and/or alcohol. A
detoxification service is also available.* *

Piobaireachd Society

16–24 Otago Street,
Glasgow, G12 8JH
Tel: 0141-334-3587   Fax: 0141-334-358

Dugald MacNeill, *Honorary Secretary* *

Planning Aid for Scotland (PAS)

Bonnington Mill,
72 Newhaven Road,
Edinburgh, EH6 5QG
Tel: 0131-555-1565   Fax: 0131-467-7830

Ms. Hilda Hand, *Project Manager*

*PAS is a voluntary charitable company giving
free advice on town and country planning to
community councils and community groups or
individuals unable to pay for private
consultations. e-mail: pas@sol.co.uk.* *

Play in Scottish Hospitals

15 Smith's Place,
Edinburgh, EH6 8NT
Tel: 0131-553-2189

Jennifer Gibb, *Executive Secretary*

Playback Recording Service for the Blind

Centre for Sensory Impaired,
17 Gullane Street,
Glasgow, G11 6AH
Tel: 0141-334-2983   Fax: 0141-334-2983

Mr. Peter Fraser, *Coordinator*

*Playback is a comprehensive recording service
providing newspapers, magazine, reading
service and tape library. Over 40,000 tapes
are sent out each month with 20 regular
publications such as* Playback Magazine.
The Sunday Mail *and* Daily Record
newspapers are sent out weekly. *

Poetry Association of Scotland

The Orchard,
Muirton,
Auchterarder,
Perthshire, PH3 1ND
Tel: 01764-662211

Mr. Robin Bell, *General Secretary*

*A registered charity founded in 1924 to promote
public readings of the best poery from all over
the world. Events are mainly at The
Netherbow Centre, High Street, Edinburgh.* *

Pointer Club of Scotland

Beechwood,
Balloch Road,
Alexandria,
Dunbartonshire, G83 8JZ
Tel: 01389-59666

Mrs. P. Tibbs

Poodle Club of Scotland

6 Avon Grove,
Cramond,
Edinburgh, EH4 6RF
Tel: 0131-312-8622

Mrs. K.B. Douglas

Positive Action in Housing Limited

6th Floor,
98 West George Street,
Glasgow, G2 1PJ
Tel: 0141-353-2220   Fax: 0141-353 3882

Ms. Anee la Mirza

*We are working with communities and housing
providers in Scotland to enable everyone to
have an equal chance to live in good quality,
affordable and safe housing, free from
discrimination and the fear of racial harass-
ment and violence.**

Positive Housing

c/o GCVS,
11 Queen's Crescent,
Glasgow, G4 9AS
Tel: 0141-332-2444   Fax: 0141-332-0175

Poverty Alliance

see The Poverty Alliance

Premenstrual Syndrome Support Group

Family Planning Services,
Dean Terrace,
Edinburgh, EH4 1NL
Tel: 0131-332-7941   Fax: 0131-332-2931

Sister Lora Green, *Senior Nurse*

Press Association

4th floor,
96 Warroch Street,
Glasgow, G3 8BL
Tel: 0141-221-8521

Press Standards Board of Finance

30 George Square,
Glasgow, G2 1EG
Tel: 0141-222-3957   Fax: 0141-248-2362

A. Graham Thomson, *Secretary & Treasurer*

Pride Scotland

58a Broughton Street,
Edinburgh, EH1 3SA
Tel: 0131-556-8822   Fax: 0131-556-8822

Ms. Laura Norris, *Human Resources Director*

P

Prince's Scottish Youth Business Trust

6th floor, Mercantile Chambers,
53 Bothwell Street,
Glasgow, G2 6TS
Tel: 0141-248-4999   Fax: 0141-248-4836

Mr. David Cooper

*PSYBT is a charity with an enterprise flavour
providing seedcorn finance and support to
young Scots aged 18–25 to set up and
continue their own businesses.* *

Prince's Trust – Action in Scotland

see The Prince's Trust – Action in Scotland

Prince's Trust Volunteers

see The Prince's Trust Volunteers

Princess Royal Trust for Carers

see The Princess Royal Trust for Carers

Prison Fellowship Scotland

P.O. Box 366,
101 Ellesmere Street,
Hamiltonhill,
Glasgow, G22 5QS
Tel: 0141-332-8870   Fax: 0141-332-8870

Mr. Allan Grant, *Director*

*Supporting the work of the Church and
chaplains in serving the needs of prisoners,
ex-prisoners and their families.* *

Private Legislation Procedure for Scotland

50 Frederick Street,
Edinburgh, EH2 1EX
Tel: 0131-226-6499

Nigel M.P. Morrison, *Counsel*

Procurator Fiscals' Society

Stuart House,
181–201 High Street,
Linlithgow, EH49 7EW
Tel: 01506-844556   Fax: 01506-670102

David Green, *Secretary*

Producers Alliance for Cinema and Television [PACT] Scotland

Dowanhill,
74 Victoria Crescent Road,
Glasgow, G12 9JN
Tel: 0141-339-5660   Fax: 0141-339-5799

Margaret Scott, *Manager*/Emma Valentine,
Asst. Manager

*PACT is a trade alliance for independent film
and television production companies. e-mail:
pact@cqm.co.uk.* *

Professional Association of Teachers

4/6 Oak Lane,
Edinburgh, EH12 6XH
Tel: 0131-317-8282   Fax: 0131-317-8111

R.J.S. Christie, *Secretary for Scotland*

Professional Golfers' Association

Glenbervie Golf Club,
Stirling Road,
Larbert,
Falkirk, FK5 4SJ

Mr. Peter Lloyd, *Scottish Region Secretary*

Professional Sales Association Scotland

Independent Finance Centre,
67 Causeyside Street,
Paisley, PA1 1YT
Tel: 0141-848-5454   Fax: 0141-848-7999

Mr. Brian Evans

Property Managers Association Scotland Ltd

2 Blythswood Square,
Glasgow, G2 4AD
Tel: 0141-248-4672   Fax: 0141-221-9270

Mr. James Millar

The trade association of property managers which represents their interests in legislative matters, provides educational opportunities and sets standards for the profession. *

Public Services Tax and Commerce Union

Edinburgh Centre,
6 Hillside Crescent,
Edinburgh, EH7 5DY
Tel: 0131-556-0407   Fax: 0131-557 5613

Mr. P. Kelly

A trade union representing 18,000 members in Scotland, the majority working in the civil service, including the Inland Revenue. The Union is affiliated to the STUC. *

Pyrenean Mountain Dog Club of Scotland

1 Pitcorthie Mains,
Colinsburgh,
Leven,
Fife, KY9 1JX
Tel: 01333-340672

Mrs. J. Henderson

The Pyrenean Mountain Dog Club of Scotland exists to promote the breed in Scotland through shows and activities and to help and advise newcomers to the breed. *

Quality Scotland Foundation

13 Abercromby Place,
Edinburgh, EH3 6LB
Tel: 0131-556-2333

Quarriers

Homelea,
Bridge of Weir,
Renfrewshire, PA11 3SX
Tel: 01505-612224   Fax: 01505-613906

Mr. Gerald E. Lee

Queen's Nursing Institute, Scotland

31 Castle Terrace,
Edinburgh, EH1 2EL
Tel: 0131-229-2333   Fax: 0131-229-0443

Mr. G.D.C. Preston, *Director* *

RAFT – Relatives and Friends Talking

Drug Project,
Southern General Hospital,
1345 Govan Road,
Glasgow, G51 4TF
Tel: 0141-201-1956   Fax: 0141-201-1969

Mr. Bobby Ross/Ms. Liz Webber *

REMAP (Scotland)

Maulside Lodge,
Beith,
Ayrshire, KA15 1JJ
Tel: 01294-832566   Fax: 01294-832374

Mr. John Golder, *National Organiser*

REMAP (Scotland), charity no. SCO 09141, has 17 panels who produce aids for disabled people when no suitable appliance is commercially available. Their services are free. *

RNIB Scotland (Royal National Institute for the Blind)

10 Magdala Crescent,
Edinburgh, EH12 5BE
Tel: 0131-313-1498   Fax: 0131-313-1875

Ms. Elizabeth Kennedy, *Liaison Officer*

Rail Users' Consultative Committee for Scotland

249 West George Street,
Glasgow, G2 4QE
Tel: 0141-221-7760   Fax: 0141-221-3393

The Secretary

Railway Development Society (Scotland)

2 Clark Road,
Inverkeithing,
Fife, KY11 1AW
Tel: 01383-416319

Mr. David Hansen, *Honorary Secretary*

The Railway Development Society campaigns for improved and expanded rail services for passengers and freight. *

Railway Society of Scotland

7 Elm Grove,
Dunfermline, KY11 5AA
Tel: 01383-728132

Ian MacKenzie, *General Secretary*

Railway Staff Association for Scotland

Junction Road,
Kirkcaldy, KY1 2BH
Tel: 01592-652007

Ramblers' Association (Scotland)

Crusader House,
Haig Business Park,
Markinch,
Fife, KY7 6AQ
Tel: 01592-611177   Fax: 01592-611188

Ms. Linda Johnson, *Executive Officer*

Rathbone Community Industry Scotland

C.I. Building,
Scott Street,
Motherwell, ML1 1LP
Tel: 01698-252326   Fax: 01698-251400

Mr. Gerry Gallagher, *Director*

Reality at Work Scotland (RAW)

6 Rochdale Place,
Kirkintilloch,
Glasgow, G66 1HZ
Tel: 0141-777-7656   Fax: 0141-777-7656

Ms. Pam Thomson, *Adminstrator*

Christian organisation working alongside other agencies across Scotland to support disadvantaged young people aged 9–18. RAW provides residential activity holidays and area-based befriending. *

Recycling Advisory Group Scotland (RAGS)

Unit 1,
60 Newhaven Road,
Edinburgh, EH6 5QT
Tel: 0131-553-3303   Fax: 0131-553-7077

Ms. Gillian Smith, *Group Coordinator*

RAGS is a multi-sector organisation representing and promoting the development of recycling and waste minimisation in Scotland. *

Reforesting Scotland

P.O. Box 1707,
Edinburgh, EH1 1YB
Tel: 0131-557-6997   Fax: 0131-557-9222

Adminstrator

Reformed Presbyterian Church of Scotland

17 George IV Bridge,
Edinburgh, EH1 1EE
Tel: 0131-220-1450

Rev. A. Sinclair Horne, *Clerk of Synod*

Regional Studies Association (Scottish Branch)

School of Town and Regional Planning,
University of Dundee,
Dundee, DD1 4HT

Mr. John McCarthy

Register of Clinical Hypnotherapists in Scotland

The Harvest Clinic,
201 St. George's Road,
Glasgow, G3 6JE
Tel: 0141-333-0878   Fax: 0141-333-0878

Ms. Angela Trainer

Holds listing of members of the British Society of Clinical Hypnosis and offers advice and referrals on matters relating to hypnotherapy and psychotherapy. BUPA and NHS provider. *

Registers of Scotland Executive Agency

Meadowbank House,
153 London Road,
Edinburgh, EH8 7AU
Tel: 0131-659-6111   Fax: 0131-459-1221

A.W. Ramage, *Chief Executive*

The Agency is responsible for Scottish public registers including the Land Register and Register of Sasines which provide for the registration of interests in land. *

Registry of Friendly Societies

58 Frederick Street,
Edinburgh, EH2 1NB
Tel: 0131-226-3224

Mr. James L.J. Craig, *Assistant Registrar*

Rehab Scotland

Melrose House,
15–23 Cadogan Street,
Glasgow, G2 6QQ
Tel: 0141-204-5700   Fax: 0141-229-5701

Mr. Bertie Hunt, *General Manager*

Religious Society of Friends (Quakers)

Quaker Link Scotland,
7 Victoria Terrace,
Edinburgh, EH1 2JL
Tel: 0131-225-4825   Fax: 0131-226-4392

Part of a worldwide religious body, originating in seventeenth century Britain. Worship based on silence and commitments to equality, peace, simplicity and integrity. *

Rent Assessment Panel for Scotland

48 Manor Place,
Edinburgh, EH3 7EH
Tel: 0131-226-1123

Mr. G.F. Robertson, *President*

Rent Registration Service for Scotland

Corunna House,
29 Cadogan Street,
Glasgow, G2 7AB
Tel: 0141-204-5881

Mr. J. Todd, *Chief Rent Officer*

Representation in Scotland, European Commission

9 Alva Street,
Edinburgh, EH2 4PH
Tel: 0131-225-2058   Fax: 0131-226-4105

Kenneth A. Munro, *Head of Representation in Scotland* *

Research Centre in Scottish History

Room 459, McCance Building,
University of Strathclyde,
Richmond Street,
Glasgow, G1 1XQ
Tel: 0141-548-4531

Professor Tom Devine, *Director*

Resource Use Institute Limited

Leewood,
Leewood Road,
Dunblane,
Perthshire, FK15 0DR
Tel: 01786-822161   Fax: 01786-823733

Miss Isabel Soutar, *Secretary*

The Resource Use Institute, founded in 1969, is a multi-disciplinary college of independent consultants devoted to the sustainable management of physical resources. It lays great emphasis on holistic thinking, on integration between sectors of the economy including the recycling of wastes, and on the preservation of cultural heritage. *

Retired Greyhound Trust (Scottish Division)

95 North Gyle Loan,
Edinburgh, EH12 8LB
Tel: 0131-539-0672

Mr. Don Ferguson

Retired Police Officers' (Scotland) Association

5 Lee Crescent,
Portobello,
Edinburgh, EH15 1LW

James B. Anderson, *General Secretary*

Rhodesian Ridgeback Club of Scotland

Middle Third House,
Newton of Pitcairns,
Dunning,
Perth, PH2 0RE
Tel: 01764-684021

Mr. R. Mason

The Rhodesian Ridgeback dog has its origins in Southern Africa. The Club furthers the interests of the breed, runs dog shows, promotes seminars and social activities. *

Richmond Fellowship Scotland

9 Sandyford Place,
Glasgow, G3 7NB
Tel: 0141-248-4818   Fax: 0141-248-8485

Mr. Peter Millar, *Director*

Road Haulage Association – Scottish Office

Roadway House,
17 Royal Terrace,
Glasgow, G3 7NY
Tel: 0141-332-9201

Roman Catholic Church in Scotland

Bishops' Conference of Scotland,
General Secretariat,
64 Aitken Street,
Airdrie, ML6 6LT
Tel: 01236-764061   Fax: 01236-762489

Rt. Rev. Mgr. Henry Docherty, *General Secretary*

Royal & Ancient Golf Club of St. Andrews

The Links,
St. Andrews, KY16 9JD
Tel: 01334-472112   Fax: 01334-477580

M.F. Bonallack, *Secretary*

A private members' club. The world governing body for the rules of golf and amateur status (except USA). *

Royal Academy of Engineering

c/o Department of Civil Engineering,
University of Strathclyde,
Glasgow, G4 0NG
Tel: 0141-553-4169   Fax: 0141-552-0067

Professor George Fleming, *Scottish Convenor*

Scottish Fellows of the Royal Academy of Engineering comprise senior captains of industry, active and retired, and meet on average four times per year. *

Royal Air Force Benevolent Fund

20 Queen Street,
Edinburgh, EH2 1JX
Tel: 0131-225-6421   Fax: 0131-220-0643

Director/Assistant Director

Provides relief from financial distress to past and present members of the Royal Air Force and their dependent relatives. *

Royal Air Forces Association

20 Queen Street,
Edinburgh, EH2 1JX
Tel: 0131-225-5221   Fax: 0131-220-0643

Mr. G.M. Halloran, *Director, Scottish Area*

RAFA is a Service charity providing advice and assistance on all aspects of welfare – convalescence, pensions, nursing care, etc. – for all serving and former RAF personnel. There are 5000 members and 27 branches in Scotland. *

Royal Automobile Club

200 Finnieston Street,
Glasgow, G3 8NZ
Tel: 0141-248-4444

Royal Blind Asylum & School

Box No. 500,
Gillespie Crescent,
Edinburgh, EH10 4HZ
Tel: 0131-229-1456   Fax: 0131-229-4060

J.B.M. Munro

Education, employment and nursing care for the visually impaired. *

Royal British Legion Scotland

New Haig House,
Logie Green Road,
Edinburgh, EH7 4HR
Tel: 0131-557-2782   Fax: 0131-557-5819

Major General J.D. MacDonald

Royal British Legion Women's Section

55 Warout Road,
Glenrothes,
Fife, KY7 4EP
Tel: 01592-759200

Mrs. A. Robertson, *Secretary/Treasurer* *

Royal Caledonian Curling Club

2 Coates Crescent,
Edinburgh, EH3 7AN
Tel: 0131-225-7083   Fax: 0131-220-6191

A.C.B Guild

Royal Caledonian Horticultural Society

6 Kirkliston Road,
South Queensferry, EH30 9LT
Tel: 0131-331-1011

Mr. Tom Mabbott, *Secretary*

*Founded in 1809, incorporated by Royal Charter 1824, 'for the purpose of forming a society for the improvement of horticulture in all its branches'. **

Royal Celtic Society

23 Rutland Street,
Edinburgh, EH1 2RU
Tel: 0131-228-6449   Fax: 0131-228-6987

J. Gordon Cameron, *Secretary & Treasurer*

*Founded in 1820, the Society's primary aims are to maintain and promote interest in the history, traditions, language and arts of the Highlands and Western Isles of Scotland. **

Royal College of General Practitioners, Scottish Council

2 Hill Square,
Edinburgh, EH8 9DR
Tel: 0131-667-3115   Fax: 0131-667-1060

Dr. George S. Dyker, *Honorary Secretary and Treasurer*

*The Royal College of General Practitioners draws its membership largely from General Practitioners throughout the UK. As a College we are primarily interested in services to our members and quality of care through education and research. Scottish Council coordinates College activities throughout Scotland. **

Royal College of Nursing Scottish Board

42 South Oswald Road,
Edinburgh, EH9 2HH
Tel: 0131-662-1010

Royal College of Physicians and Surgeons

234 St Vincent Street,
Glasgow, G2 5RJ
Tel: 0141-221-6072   Fax: 0141-221-1804

Royal Commission on the Ancient and Historical Monuments of Scotland

John Sinclair House,
16 Bernard Terrace,
Edinburgh, EH8 9NX
Tel: 0131-662-1446   Fax: 0131-662-1477

Mr. R.J. Mercer, *Secretary*

The aims of the RCAHMS are to survey and record Scotland's man-made environment; to compile and maintain records in the National Monuments Record of Scotland and to promote understanding by all appropriate means. *

Royal Environmental Health Institute of Scotland

3 Manor Place,
Edinburgh, EH3 7DH
Tel: 0131-225-6999   Fax: 0131-225-3993

Mr. Dave Watson, *Director of Professional Development*

The Institute is a professional body whose aims are to promote environmental health throughout Scotland and secure the proper qualifications and training within the discipline. *

Royal Fine Art Commission for Scotland

Bakehouse Close,
146 Canongate,
Edinburgh, EH8 8DO
Tel: 0131-556-6699   Fax: 0131-556-6633

Mr. Charles Prosser, *Secretary*

Established in 1927 to advise Government on the visual impact and quality of design of construction projects. Although financed by the Government, opinions are given impartially. *

Royal Highland & Agricultural Society of Scotland

Royal Highland Centre,
Ingliston,
Edinburgh, EH28 8NF
Tel: 0131-333-2444   Fax: 0131-333-5236

Mr. Hywel Davies, *Chief Executive* *

Royal Incorporation of Architects in Scotland

15 Rutland Square,
Edinburgh, EH1 2BE
Tel: 0131-229-7545   Fax: 0131-228-2188

Mr. Sebastian Tombs, FRIAS, RIBA, ACIArb, *Secretary*

The RIAS is the professional institute for all chartered architects in Scotland. It offers a wide range of services to architects and all those with an interest in the built environment. *

Royal Institution of Chartered Surveyors in Scotland

see The Royal Institution of Chartered Surveyors in Scotland

Royal Life Saving Society (Scottish Region)

30 Seres Road,
Clarkston,
Glasgow, G76 7QF
Tel: 0141-638-8271

Miss Janet Castro, *Secretary*

Royal Medical Society

Student Centre,
5/5 Bristo Square,
Edinburgh, EH8 9AL
Tel: 0131-650-2762

Mrs. P. Strong, *Secretary*

Medical student society, founded in 1737, for Edinburgh Medical School students. *

Royal Museum of Scotland

Chambers Street,
Edinburgh, EH1 1JF
Tel: 0131-225-7534   Fax: 0131-220-4819

Royal National Institute for Deaf People (RNID)

9 Clairmont Gardens,
Glasgow, G3 7LW
Tel: 0141-332-0343   Fax: 0141-331-2640

Ms. Dorothy Davidson, *Information Officer*

A national, registered charity, catering for deaf, deafened and hard of hearing people and their families and carers/professionals working with them. The RNID offers support, information, advice, communication support, deaf awareness training and communication training courses. *

Royal National Lifeboat Institution (RNLI)

Belleview House,
Hopetoun Street,
Edinburgh, EH7 4ND
Tel: 0131-557-9171   Fax: 0131-557-6943

Mrs. Maren Fitzgerald, *Organising Secretary*

Royal National Mission to Deep Sea Fishermen

3 Queen Margaret Road,
Glasgow, G20 6DP
Tel: 0141-946-4263

Royal Naval and Royal Marine Association

Heriot Hill House,
1 Broughton Road,
Edinburgh, EH7 4EW
Tel: 0131-556-2973

Royal Pharmaceutical Society of Great Britain, Scottish Executive

36 York Place,
Edinburgh, EH1 3HU
Tel: 0131-556-9386

Dr. G. Jefferson, *Secretary*

Royal School of Church Music

Scottish Area Branch,
36 Garriochmill Road,
Glasgow, G20 6LT
Tel: 0141-357-1966

The RSCM is an ecumenical organisation dedicated to promoting excellence in music and liturgy in Christian worship. *

Royal Scottish Academy

The Mound,
Edinburgh, EH2 2EL
Tel: 0131-225-6671   Fax: 0131-225-2349

Mr. Bruce Laidlaw, *Administrative Secretary*

The Royal Scottish Academy (founded 1826) is in the forefront in promoting contemporary Scottish art through its annual exhibition (April-July) and its students' exhibition (March). *

Royal Scottish Agricultural Benevolent Institution (RSABI)

see The Royal Scottish Agricultural Benevolent Institution (RSABI)

Royal Scottish Automobile Club

11 Blythswood Square,
Glasgow, G2 4AG
Tel: 0141-221-3850   Fax: 0141-221-3805

Mr. J.C. Lord, *Secretary*

Founded in 1899, the Club provides clubhouse services to its members and guests. It is involved in public policy matters and offers motoring services. *

Royal Scottish Automobile Club (Motor Sport) Limited

see The Royal Scottish Automobile Club (Motor Sport) Limited

Royal Scottish Country Dance Society

12 Coates Crescent,
Edinburgh, EH3 7AF
Tel: 0131-225-3854   Fax: 0131-225-7783

Miss Gill Parker, *Secretary*

The main objectives of the Royal Scottish Country Dance Society are to promote Scottish country dancing and thereby preserve the traditions of Scottish dancing. The Society runs classes for all levels, publishes instruction books and has recordings available. *

R

Royal Scottish Forestry Society

The Stables,
Dalkeith Country Park,
Dalkeith,
Midlothian, EH22 2NA
Tel: 0131-660-9480   Fax: 0131-660-9490

Mr. Michael Osborne, *Director*

Its major aim is 'the advancement of forestry in all its numerous branches' by organising meetings and conferences throughout Scotland and arranging excursions abroad. Tree planting by all landowners is encouraged and the interests of those involved in forestry in Scotland. *

Royal Scottish Geographical Society

40 George Street,
Glasgow, G1 1QE
Tel: 0141-552-3330   Fax: 0141-552-3331

Dr. David M. Munro, *Director and Secretary*

An educational charity founded in 1884 'to enhance the science of geography' by stimulating research, education, travel, exploration and debate on key global issues. *

Royal Scottish National Orchestra

73 Claremont Street,
Glasgow, G3 7JB
Tel: 0141-226-3868   Fax: 0141-221-4317

Mr. Simon Crookall, *Chief Executive*

Scotland's major symphony orchestra, performing a series of winter season and summer proms concerts throughout the country, touring abroad, recording and promoting educational and outreach work. e-mail: rsno@glasgow.almac.co.uk. *

Royal Scottish Pipers' Society

127 Rose Street Lane South,
Edinburgh, EH2 4BB
Tel: 01620-842146

M.J.B. Lowe, *Secretary*

A society for the encouragement of bagpipe playing and the general advancement and study of the great Highland bagpipe and its music. *

Royal Scottish Society of Arts (Science & Technology)

National Museum of Scotland,
Dept. of Science, Tech. & Working Life,
Chambers Street,
Edinburgh, EH1 1JF
Tel: 0131-225-7534   Fax: 0131-226-5949

Dr. A.D.C. Simpson, *Honorary Archivist*

Royal Scottish Society of Painters in Water Colours

29 Waterloo Street,
Glasgow, G2 6BZ
Tel: 070-50217502   Fax: 013552-65166

Roger Frame

Its object shall be to encourage and develop the art of painting in water colours and the appreciation of this art, and to arrange exhibitions or lectures as shall be decided by the Council of the Society. *

Royal Society for the Prevention of Accidents (RoSPA)

Slateford House,
53 Lanark Road,
Edinburgh, EH14 1TL
Tel: 0131-455-7457   Fax: 0131-443-9442

Mr. Michael A. McDonnell, *Road Safety Manager*

RoSPA is a registered charity and one of the world's leading safety organisations, dealing with home, road, occupational, water and leisure safety issues. *

Royal Society for the Relief of Indigent Gentlewomen of Scotland

see The Royal Society for the Relief of Indigent Gentlewomen of Scotland

Royal Town Planning Institute in Scotland

57 Melville Street,
Edinburgh, EH3 7HL
Tel: 0131-226-1909   Fax: 0131-226-1909

Mr. Graham Uren, *Director*

The RTPI is the UK organisation representing professional town planners. The RTPI in Scotland represents its Scottish members, provides a point of contact for the public in Scotland and promotes policy on the Scottish planning system. *

Royal United Kingdom Beneficent Association

P.O. Box 16058,
Glasgow, G12 8PG
Tel: 0141-339-7469   Fax: 0141-339-7469

Mrs. Mirren Graham

The Association gives a regular small additional income to men and women aged 60+ who come from a professional or similar background and are in need. *

Royal Yachting Association, Scotland

Caledonia House,
South Gyle,
Edinburgh, EH12 9DQ
Tel: 0131-317-7388   Fax: 0131-317-8566

Honorary Secretary

The governing body for the sport of sailing in Scotland. *

Royal Zoological Society of Scotland

see The Royal Zoological Society of Scotland

Rural Education and Development Association

Scottish Agricultural College,
Cleeve Gardens,
Oakbank Road,
Perth, PH1 1HF
Tel: 01738-36611   Fax: 01738-27860

J.B. Dakers

Rural Forum

Highland House,
46 St. Catherine's Road,
Perth, PH1 5RY
Tel: 01738-634565   Fax: 01738-638699

Mr. Dermot Grimson

Rural Forum is a membership organisation that seeks to promote practical approaches to integrated rural development and community participation in local development. Website: www.ruralforum.org.uk. *

SAC (Scottish Agricultural College)

West Mains Road,
Edinburgh, EH9 3JG
Tel: 0131-535-4078

Mr. Barry Sheppard, *Marketing Department*

Throughout Scotland SAC offers research, education, training and consultancy in the fields of food, land and the environment. Contact SAC's website at: http://www.sac.ac.uk. *

SALVO – The Scottish Arts Network

c/o Royal Lyceum Theatre,
30b Grindlay Street,
Edinburgh, EH3 9AD
Tel: 0131-228-3885   Fax: 0131-228-3955

Ruth Holloway, *Administrator*

SALVO, The Scottish Arts Network, promotes the advocacy and advancement of all the arts in Scotland and provides an information and consultancy service to its membership. *

SAOS Limited

Rural Centre,
West Mains,
Ingliston, Newbridge,
Midlothian, EH28 8NZ
Tel: 0131-472-4100   Fax: 0131-472-4101

Mr. E. Rainy Brown, *Chief Executive*

SAOS is the Scottish farming industry's own development organisation, assisting business co-operation and partnership in the food, agriculture and rural sectors, and providing consultancy. *

SCRAN (Scottish Cultural Resources Access Network)

Abden House,
1 Marchhall Crescent,
Edinburgh, EH10 4BL
Tel: 0131-662-1211   Fax: 0131-662-1511

Professor Bruce Royan, *Chief Executive*

A Millennium project spending £15 million to build a networked multimedia resource base for the teaching and celebration of human history and material culture in Scotland. *

SELECT

Bush House,
Bush Estate,
Midlothian, EH26 0SB
Tel: 0131-445-5577   Fax: 0131-445-5548

M.D. Goodwin, *Managing Director*

Scottish electrical contractors' trade association. *

SHARE

5 Finnieston Quay,
Glasgow, G3 8NH
Tel: 0141-204-1446   Fax: 0141-204-2316

SHARE is a membership organisation which provides training for the staff and voluntary committee members of housing associations and co-operatives. *

SSC – A Club for the Youth of Scotland

The Boyd Centre,
Dykehead,
Port of Menteith,
Stirling, FK8 3JY
Tel: 01877-385611   Fax: 01877-385616

Lizzie Rose

Founded on Christian principles, the SSC runs camps, weekly meetings and residential activities for 11–18 year olds, often with a focus on sports or outdoor activities. *

SSC Library

11 Parliament Square,
Edinburgh, EH1 1RF
Tel: 0131-225-6268   Fax: 0131-225-2270

Christine Wilcox, *Keeper of the Library*

A legal library open to members only. It holds all Scottish legal materials and a good selection of English material. *

SSC Society

7 Albyn Place,
Edinburgh, EH2 4NN

Mrs. Kathrine E.C. Mackie, *President*

Sacro

31 Palmerston Place,
Edinburgh, EH12 5AP
Tel: 0131-226-4222   Fax: 0131-225-1024

Ms. Susan Matheson, *Chief Executive*

Sacro (Scottish Association for the Care and Resettlement of Offenders) promotes community safety through innovative services which reduce offending and conflict, and by influencing change in criminal justice policy. *

Sailors' Orphan Society of Scotland

Cumbrae House,
15 Carlton Court,
Glasgow, G5 9JP
Tel: 0141-429-2181   Fax: 0141-429-4348

Mr. Alistair Thomson, *Honorary Secretary*

Saint Andrew Society

P.O. Box 84,
Edinburgh, EH3 8LG

Mrs. Rina Moore, *Honorary Secretary* *

Salmon and Trout Association

see The Salmon and Trout Association

Saltire Society

9 Fountain Close,
22 High Street,
Edinburgh, EH1 1TF
Tel: 0131-556-1836   Fax: 0131-557-1675

Mrs. Kathleen Munro, *Administrator*

Founded in 1936 to increase public awareness of Scotland's natural and cultural heritage at home and abroad. Membership is open to all who share this aim. e-mail: saltire@saltire.org.uk. Website: http://www.saltire.org.uk. *

Salvation Army

30 Rutland Square,
Edinburgh, EH1 2BW
Tel: 0131-221-9699   Fax: 0131-221-1482

Lt. Col. Cedric Sharp, *Secretary*

Samaritans Scottish Correspondence Branch

P.O. Box 9,
Stirling, FK8 2SA

Sargent Cancer Care for Children (Scotland)

Malcolm Sargent House,
158 South Street,
St. Andrews, KY16 9EG
Tel: 01334-470044   Fax: 01334-470144

Dr. Chris Brittain

Sargent Cancer Care for Children supports all young people with cancer, leukaemia or Hodgkin's disease and their families with counselling, financial help and practical care. *

Save our Seals Fund

62 Old Dumbarton Road,
Glasgow, G3 8RE
Tel: 0141-334-6014   Fax: 0141-445-6470

Mr. John F. Robins, *Secretary*

Established in 1996, the Save Our Seals Fund promotes the conservation of seals and the marine environment. *

Save the Children Scotland

Haymarket House,
2nd floor,
8 Clifton Terrace,
Edinburgh, EH12 5DR
Tel: 0131-527-8200   Fax: 0131-527-8201

Ms. Helen Tyrrell, *Community Health Adviser*

Schizophrenia Association of Great Britain

59 Barrington Drive,
Glasgow, G4 9ES
Tel: 0141-339-3705

Mrs. Anne Good, *Scottish Director*

Schizophrenia Fellowship (Scotland) – National

40 Shandwick Place,
Edinburgh, EH2 4RT
Tel: 0131-226-2025

S

Scoliosis Association

16 Kinrossie Terrace,
Downfield,
Dundee, DD3 9RL
Tel: 01382-815411

Mrs. Linda Muir, *Regional Secretary*

Scotcare National Brain Injury Rehabilitation Unit

Murdostoun Castle,
Bonkle,
Newmains,
Wishaw,
Motherwell, ML2 9ZB
Tel: 01698-384055

Scotch Malt Whisky Society Limited

The Vaults,
87 Giles Street,
Edinburgh, EH6 6BZ
Tel: 0131-554-3451   Fax: 0131-553-1003

Mr. P. Hills Dana, *Chairman*

Scotch Quality Beef & Lamb Association

c/o Rural Centre,
West Mains,
Ingliston,
Edinburgh, EH28 8NZ
Tel: 0131-333-5335   Fax: 0131-333-2935

Scotch Whisky Association

20 Atholl Crescent,
Edinburgh, EH3 8HF
Tel: 0131-222-9200   Fax: 0131-222-9248

Hugh Morison, *Director General*

The Scotch Whisky Association is the trade association representing the interests of Scotch whisky producers in promoting and protecting Scotch whisky worldwide. *

Scotland Against Being Ruled by Europe (SABRE)

8 Baileyfield Road,
Portobello,
Edinburgh, EH15 1DL
Tel: 0131-669-5275

Iain McGregor, *Secretary*

Founded 25 years ago as the Scottish Anti-Common Market Council, it campaigns for exit from the European Union, in association with the Anti-Maastricht Alliance, UK. *

Scotland China Association

25a Raeburn Place,
Edinburgh, EH4 1HU
Tel: 0131-332-7822   Fax: 0131-332-6784

Mr. Peter Lindow, *Secretary**

Scotland Patients Association

Gartincaber,
West Plean,
Bannockburn,
Stirling, FK7 8BA
Tel: 01786-818008   Fax: 01786-816400

Ms. Margaret Davidson, *Chief Executive*

*To help patients in their dealings with care
under the umbrella of the NHS. To give
advice and assistance when required and to
respond to queries and problems highlighted
by patients.* *

Scotland Russia Trust

8 Belmont Crescent,
Glasgow, G12 8EU
Tel: 0141-339-9706

Scotland United

P.O. Box 7575,
Glasgow, G3 6HT
Tel: 0141-331-1707

Scotland and Newcastle Lymphoma Group

Department of Public Health Sciences,
University of Edinburgh,
Medical School (R666),
Teviot Place,
Edinburgh, EH8 9AG
Tel: 0131-650-4382   Fax: 0131-650-6812

Miss K.S. MacLaren, *Administrative Secretary*

Scotland for Bosnia

Box 102,
Edinburgh, EH2 2HQ

Scotland's Alternative Skiers

32 Broomhill Avenue,
Aberdeen, AB10 6JY
Tel: 01224-324521

Ms. Carol Nickerson, *Club Secretary/
Treasurer*

*The SAS Club was founded in 1989 to help
provide skiing facilities, equipment and
opportunities for disabled people of all ages in
Scotland.* *

Scotland's Churches Scheme

'Dunedin',
Holehouse Road,
Eaglesham,
Glasgow, G76 0JF
Tel: 01355-302416   Fax: 01355-303181

Dr. Brian M. Fraser, *Director*

*Scotland's Churches Scheme is an inter-
denominational organisation encouraging the
opening of churches to visitors, providing
historical, architectural and artistic information. An annual guidebook is published of
over 400 open churches across Scotland.* *

Scotland's Gardens Scheme

31 Castle Terrace,
Edinburgh, EH1 2EL
Tel: 0131-229-1870   Fax: 0131-229-0443

Mr. R.S. St. Clair-Ford

Scotland's Gardens Scheme opens over 350 gardens in Scotland as listed in Gardens of Scotland, *the annual handbook of the Scheme published each February.* *

Scotland's National Watersports Centre

Cumbrae,
Isle of Cumbrae,
Ayrshire, KA28 0HQ
Tel: 01475-530757   Fax: 01475-530013

Annie Dippie

The Centre trains instructors and the national squad but also offers a complete range of courses at all levels in sailing, kayaking and sub-aqua. *

Scots Language Resource Centre Association

A. K. Bell Library,
2–8 York Place,
Perth, PH2 8EP
Tel: 01738-440199   Fax: 01738-477010

Mr. Stuart McHardy, *Director*

The SLRC promotes and supports all activities relating to the Scots language, creates educational resources and acts as an information nexus for all relevant activities. e-mail: slrc@sol.co.uk. *

Scots Language Society

c/o Scots Language Resource Centre,
A.K. Bell Library,
York Place,
Perth, PH2 8EP
Tel: 01738-440199

Ms. Maggie Myles

Scots Tung

27 Stoneyhill Avenue,
Musselburgh,
Midlothian, EH21 6SB
Tel: 0131-665-5440

R. Fairnie, *Secretary*

Scots Tung is a curn o Scots language upsteerers that eydentlie ettle tae uphaud an forder the staunin o the Scots leid. *

Scots at War Trust

Institute for Advanced Studies in the
   Humanities,
University of Edinburgh,
Hope Park Square,
Edinburgh, EH8 9NW
Tel: 0131-650-4671   Fax: 0131-668-2252

Dr. Diana M. Henderson, *Research Director*

The aims of the Scots at War Trust are to advance research, collate information and to educate the public of all ages in the history of Scots at war. Website: http://www-saw.arts.ed.ac.uk. *

Scottish (Horse) Racing Club

22 Mertoun Place,
Edinburgh,
EH11 1JX

Mike Sangster

Scottish AIDS Monitor

26 Anderson Place,
Edinburgh, EH6 5NP
Tel: 0131-557-3885   Fax: 0131-555-4857

Scottish Abortion Campaign

41 Cumlodden Drive,
Glasgow, G20 0JT
Tel: 0141-945-3943

Ms. Liz Armstrong

SAC is an independent organisation campaigning for a woman's right to free, safe, legal abortion on the NHS. *

Scottish Academy of Falconry

The Wigg,
Bonchester Bridge,
near Hawick

Scottish Accident Prevention Council (SAPC)

Slateford House,
53 Lanark Road,
Edinburgh, EH14 1TL
Tel: 0131-455-7457   Fax: 0131-443-9442

Mr. Michael A. McDonnell, *Secretary*

The SAPC aims to co-ordinate and stimulate accident prevention work within Scotland. A registered charity, it is closely linked to RoSPA. *

Scottish Action Against Bloodsports

P.O. Box 002,
Glenrothes,
Fife, KY61 2EZ

Mr. David Pritchard, *Press Officer*

Scottish Activity Holiday Association

Craigower Lodge,
Newtonmore,
Inverness-shire, PH20 1AT
Tel: 01540-673319   Fax: 01540-673319

The Administrator

Residential outdoor centre, capacity 50, offering a wide range of activities for all ages, schools, families, youth groups, companies etc. Mountain and water sports, ski-ing etc. are available. *

Scottish Adoption Advice Service (SAAS)

16 Sandyford Place,
Glasgow, G3 7NB
Tel: 0141-339-0772   Fax: 0141-248-8032

Ms. Joan Atherton/Ros McMillan

An independent advice service offering support
and counselling to all parties involved in
adoption. *

Scottish Adoption Association

2 Commercial Street,
Leith,
Edinburgh, EH6 6JA
Tel: 0131-553-5060   Fax: 0131-553-6422

Ms. Ann Sutton, *Director*

Recruitment of adoptive and permanent foster
families for children aged up to eight years.
Counselling of adoptive families, adopted
people and birth families. *

Scottish Adult Education Voluntary Organisations' Forum

c/o WEA Scotland,
Riddle's Court,
322 Lawnmarket,
Edinburgh, EH1 2PG
Tel: 0131-226-3456

Ms. Joyce Connon

SAEVOF seeks to advance the education of
adults in Scotland by supporting the volun-
tary organisations engaged in adult educa-
tion. *

Scottish Advisory Committee on Telecommunications (SACOT)

2 Greenside Lane,
Edinburgh, EH1 3AH
Tel: 0131-244-5576   Fax: 0131-244-5696

The Secretary

SACOT is an advisory committee to OFTEL
(Office of Telecommunications) and was
established to promote the interests of
telecommunications users in Scotland. *

Scottish Aeromodellers Association

2 Forth Avenue,
Kirkcaldy, KY2 5PN
Tel: 01592-260512

Mr. A. Gibson, *Secretary*

Scottish Agricultural College

West Mains Road,
Edinburgh, EH9 3JG
Tel: 0131-535-4078

Mr. Barry W. Sheppard

Scottish Agricultural Museum

RHAS Showground,
Newbridge,
Midlothian, EH28 8LY
Tel: 0131-333-2674

Scottish Agricultural Research Institutes (SARIS)

Pentlansfield,
Roslin,
Midlothian, EH25 9RF
Tel: 0131-445-3401   Fax: 0131-445-4035

Scottish Agricultural Rural Development Centre Limited

Newbridge,
Ingliston,
Edinburgh, EH28 8LT
Tel: 0131-335-3999

Scottish Agricultural Science Agency

82 Craigs Road,
East Craigs,
Edinburgh, EH12 8NJ
Tel: 0131-244-8890   Fax: 0131-244-8940

Ms. Lynda Clark

The aim of SASA is to provide expert scientific and technical advice and information on agricultural crops, horticultural crops and aspects of the environment. *

Scottish Agricultural Wages Board

Pentland House,
47 Robb's Loan,
Edinburgh, EH14 1TY
Tel: 0131-244-6392

Scottish Aid for Nicaragua

25–27 Elmbank Street,
Glasgow, G2 4PB

Scottish Aids Research Foundation (SARF)

Blood Transfusion Service,
The Royal Infirmary,
Edinburgh, EH3 9HB
Tel: 0131-229-7387   Fax: 0131-536-5352

Mrs. I. McKechnie*

Scottish Air Rifle & Pistol Association (SARPA)

45 Glenartney Court,
Glenrothes,
Fife, KY7 6YF
Tel: 01592-743929

Mr. E.B. Wallace, *Secretary*

SARPA is the field target governing body for Scotland. Air rifles are used to engage metal targets at various ranges up to 50 metres. *

Scottish Amateur Boxing Association

96 High Street,
Lochee,
Dundee, DD2 3AY
Tel: 01382-508261   Fax: 01382-509425

Mr. F. Hendry, *President/Executive Director*

S

Scottish Amateur Brass Band Association

85 Robert Smillie Crescent,
Larkhall,
Lanarkshire, ML9 1LE
Tel: 01698-882085

H.P. Walker, *Secretary*

Scottish Amateur Dancesport Association

93 Hillfoot Drive,
Bearsden,
Glasgow, G61 3TQ
Tel: 0141-563-2001   Fax: 0141-563-2001

Mrs. M. Fraser, *General Secretary*

The governing body for amateur dancesport in
*   Scotland. Dancesport comprises ballroom,*
*   Latin, disco and freestyle dancing.* *

Scottish Amateur Football Association

6 Park Gardens,
Glasgow, G3 7YF
Tel: 0141-333-0839

Mr. H. Knapp, *Secretary*

The governing body of amateur football in
*   Scotland.* *

Scottish Amateur Music Association

18 Craigton Crescent,
Alva,
Clackmannanshire, FK12 5DS
Tel: 01259-760249

Margaret W. Simpson, *Honorary Secretary*

SAMA's aim is to promote and stimulate
*   amateur music making. Courses for string*
*   orchestra, wind and brass band, traditional*
*   Scots fiddle, chamber music and recorder*
*   ensemble are organised, as is a biennial Scots*
*   song recital competition.* *

Scottish Amateur Rowing Association

18 Daniel McLaughlin Place,
Kirkintilloch, G66 2LH
Tel: 0141-775-0522

Ms. Rachel Clarke, *Secretary*

The governing body of rowing in Scotland. *

Scottish Amateur Swimming Association

Holmhills Farm,
Greenlees Road,
Cambuslang, G72 8DT
Tel: 0141-641-8818   Fax: 0141-641 4443

Mrs. Elaine Mackenzie, *Administration*
*   Manager*

151

Scottish Amateur Weight Lifters' Association

Shore Chambers,
24a Bernard Street,
Leith, EH6 6PP

Mr. Charles Revolta

Scottish Amateur Wrestling Association

Kelvin Hall International Sports Arena,
Argyle Street,
Glasgow, G3 8AW
Tel: 0141-334-3843   Fax: 0141-334-3843

Ms. Rhona Polak, *Administrator*

The governing body for amateur wrestling in Scotland, providing information/practical assistance to new/existing wrestling clubs. Also runs wrestling courses in schools, leisure centres. Presence at Highland Games.*

Scottish Ambulance College

Barony Castle,
Eddleston,
near Peebles, EH45 8QW
Tel: 01721-726-200   Fax: 01721-730-606

Mr. Gerry Kelly

Scottish Ambulance College provides a centre of excellence for training and education. Additionally, the college is an ideal high quality venue for conferences and meetings.*

Scottish Ambulance Service NHS Trust

National Headquarters,
Tipperlinn Road,
Edinburgh, EH10 5UU
Tel: 0131-447-7711

Scottish Ancestry Research Society

296 Albany Street,
Edinburgh, EH1 3QN
Tel: 0131-556-4220   Fax: 0131-556-4220

Scottish Anglers National Association

Caledonia House,
South Gyle,
Edinburgh, EH12 9DQ
Tel: 0131-339-8808   Fax: 0131-317-7192

Mr. D. Wilkie, *Administrative Officer*

Recognised by the Scottish Sports Council as the governing body for the sport of game fishing (e.g. salmon, sea trout, brown trout, grayling) in Scotland.*

Scottish Animal Rights Network

121 West Regent Street,
Glasgow, G2 2SD
Tel: 0141-221-2300

Scottish Antibody Production Unit (SAPU)

Law Hospital,
Carluke,
Lanarkshire, ML8 5ES
Tel: 01698-351161   Fax: 01698-359376

Dr. A.C. Munro, *Director*

Part of the NHS in Scotland, SAPU produces diagnostic reagents for hospital and associated laboratories, where they are used to test blood and other patient specimens. *

Scottish Arboricultural Society

4 Knightsbridge Road,
Dechmont,
Broxburn,
West Lothian, EH52 6LT

Scottish Archery Association

30 Gardner Street,
Partick,
Glasgow, G11 5NY
Tel: 0141-339-9188

Mr. B. Simpson, *Secretary*

Scottish Architectural Education Trust

108 Arkleston Road,
Paisley, PA1 3TZ
Tel: 0141-848-1589   Fax: 0141-848-1589

Ms. Samantha MacGregor, *Administrator*

The Trust's aim is to raise awareness amongst young people of architecture and the built environment by bringing architects and architecture into schools throughout Scotland. *

Scottish Artists & Artist Craftsmen

11 Rosefield Avenue,
Portobello,
Edinburgh, EH15 1AT
Tel: 0131-669-2799   Fax: 0131-669-0454

Sally Schofield, *Secretary*

Scottish Artists' Benevolent Association

2nd floor,
5 Oswald Street,
Glasgow, G1 4QR
Tel: 0141-248-7411   Fax: 0141-221-0417

R.C. Liddle, CA, *Secretary*

Object: to afford relief to distressed deserving artists – whether subscribers to the funds of the Association or not – their widow, orphans or dependants. *

Scottish Arts Council

12 Manor Place,
Edinburgh, EH3 7DD
Tel: 0131-226-6051 Fax: 0131-225-9833

Ms. C. Galey, *Senior Info. & Marketing Officer*

The Scottish Arts Council is the principal funding body for the arts in Scotland, distributing funds from Government and the National Lottery. *

Scottish Asian Action Committee

39 Napiershall Street,
Glasgow, G20 6EZ
Tel: 0141-341-0025 Fax: 0141-341-0020

Ms. Kam Sambhi, *Development Officer*

SAAC is an umbrella organisation affiliated to Citizens Advice Scotland and provides advice and information to black and ethnic minority communities in Glasgow and throughout Scotland. *

Scottish Assessors' Association

see The Scottish Assessors' Association

Scottish Association for Blind Bowlers

8 Homelea Place,
Kilmarnock, KA1 1UU
Tel: 01563-532287 Fax: 01294-471283

Mr. James Bircham, *Hon. Secretary/Treasurer*

The Association has approximately 20 blind bowling clubs in Scotland. There are seven national championships and various international competitions. Scotland also participates in the world championships which will next be held in Scotland in 2001. *

Scottish Association for Building Education & Training

c/o Reid Kerr College,
Renfrew Road,
Paisley, PA3 4DR

Scottish Association for Church Music

1 Auld Gavel Place,
Strathaven,
Lanarkshire, ML10 6DE
Tel: 0141-810-6296 Fax: 0141-810-7413

Scottish Association for Educational Management & Administration

St. Andrews College,
Drymen Road,
Glasgow, G61 4QA
Tel: 0141-943-3505   Fax: 0141-943-0106

Mr. Douglas McCreath, *Chairman*

SAEMA offers a forum for managers, teachers and others to share ideas and evaluate educational policy and practice. Its thrice-annual conferences on matters of contemporary interest are open to non-members. *

Scottish Association for Gestalt Education (SAGE)

29 Lauriston Street,
Edinburgh, EH3 9DQ
Tel: 0131-228-1183

Scottish Association for Language Teaching

Beath High School,
Foulford Road,
Cowdenbeath,
Fife, KY4 9BH
Tel: 01383-313000   Fax: 01383-313061

Jane Renton, *Chair*

SALT aims to promote the teaching and learning of foreign languages in Scotland. It has approx 700 members in all sectors of education. Annual conference at Stirling University, first Saturday of November. *

Scottish Association for Marine Science

Dunstaffnage Marine Laboratory,
P.O. Box 3,
Oban,
Argyll, PA34 4AD
Tel: 01631-62244   Fax: 01631-65518

Prof. J.B.L. Matthews, *Director & Secretary*

Scottish Association for Mental Health (SAMH)

Cumbrae House,
15 Carlton Court,
Glasgow, G5 9JP
Tel: 0141-568-7000   Fax: 0141-568-7001

Ms. Gerrie Grant, *Information Officer*

SAMH is the largest voluntary sector provider working in Scotland to challenge false stereotypes and improve care services for people with mental health problems. *

Scottish Association for Metals

c/o Optimat Limited,
Scottish Enterprise Technology Park,
Birniehill,
East Kilbride, G75 0QD
Tel: 01355-272800   Fax: 01355-272556

Dr. J.R. Wilcox, *Secretary*

The Association seeks to promote the achievement of the science and technology of metals, alloys and allied materials through a programme of technical meetings. *

Scottish Association for Music Education

Auchterderran Centre,
Woodend Road,
Cardenden,
Fife, KY5 0NE
Tel: 01592-414600   Fax: 01592-414641

Mr. Graeme Wilson

The Association exists to promote music in education and membership is open to all who work in music education in Scotland. *

Scottish Association for Natural Family Planning

The Archdiocesan Offices,
196 Clyde Street,
Glasgow, G1 4JY
Tel: 0141-221-0858   Fax: 0141-221-0858

The Secretary

Scottish Association for Public Transport

5 St. Vincent Place,
Glasgow, G1 2DH
Tel: 0141-639-3697   Fax: 0141-639-3697

Mr. M.J. Foreman, *Secretary*

Scottish Association for the Deaf

Clerwood House,
96 Clermiston Road,
Edinburgh, EH12 6UT
Tel: 0131-314-6075   Fax: 0131-314-6077

Mrs. L. Sutherland, *Administrator* *

Scottish Association for the Study of Delinquency

9 Caddlehill Street,
Greenock,
Renfrewshire, PA16 8TU
Tel: 01475-725982

Alexandra Kirkpatrick, *Honorary Secretary* *

Scottish Association of Advisers in Physical Education

Newton Advisers Centre,
Green Street Lane,
Ayr, KA8 8BH
Tel: 01292-260325

Malcolm Renny

Scottish Association of Amenity Supervisory Staff

27 Allan Avenue,
Deanpark,
Renfrew, PA4 0YN
Tel: 0141-886-6039

The Secretary

S

Scottish Association of Care Home Owners

Ashlea House,
Bracklinn Road,
Callander,
Perthshire, FK17 8EH
Tel: 01877-330799   Fax: 01877-330931

Dr. Colin M. Barron, *Chairman*

Represents owners of private residential and nursing homes. *

Scottish Association of Change Ringers Bell Restoration Fund

30 Orchard Court,
Dundee, DD4 9DB
Tel: 01382-502296

Mr. S.A. Elwell-Sutton, *Treasurer*

Scottish Association of Citizens Advice Bureaux

4 Park Gardens Lane,
Glasgow, G3 7YL
Tel: 0141-332-8341

Scottish Association of Community Education Staff

Gowanhill Neighbourhood Centre,
6 Daisy Street,
Glasgow, G42 8JL
Tel: 0141-423-2330   Fax: 0141-423-3815

Mr. Ian Robertson, *Secretary*

SACES is a voluntarily run Association, established by community educators to act as a voice for the field, on relevant issues of concern that affect those working in Scotland. *

Scottish Association of Directors of Leisure Services

Arts & Recreation Department,
Aberdeen City Council,
St Nicholas House
Broad Street,
Aberdeen, AB10 1XJ
Tel: 01224-522472

Brian Woodcock, *Honorary Chairman*

Scottish Association of Educational Technology Advisers

Auchterderran Staff Development Centre,
Woodend Road,
Cardenden,
Fife, KY5 0NE

Scottish Association of Family Conciliation Services

127 Rose Street Lane South,
Edinburgh, EH2 5BB
Tel: 0131-220-1610   Fax: 0131-220-6895

Susan Mathieson, *Director*

Scottish Association of Family History Societies

27 Woodend Drive,
Aberdeen, AB2 6YJ

Miss S. M. Speirs

Scottish Association of Geography Teachers

Lenzie Academy,
Myrtle Avenue,
Lenzie,
Glasgow, G66 4HR
Tel: 0141-776-6118   Fax: 0141-777-8121

J. Bruce

SAGT's aim is to further the development and teaching of geography. Publications include an annual journal, quarterly newsletter and occasional papers. An annual conference, excursions and pupil quizzes are held. *

Scottish Association of Health Councils

18 Alva Street,
Edinburgh, EH2 4QG
Tel: 0131-220 4101   Fax: 0131-220-4108

Ms. Patricia Dawson, *Director*

The SAHC seeks to be the national voice of the public on health matters. *

Scottish Association of Laryngectomees and those with Related Cancers (SALARC)

2nd floor,
30 Bell Street,
Glasgow, G1 1LG
Tel: 0141-552-3366   Fax: 0141-553-2686

Miss Jean Trautman, *Information Officer*

We provide information, practical and emotional support to sufferers of cancers of the head and neck, and can access legal and welfare benefits advice. *

Scottish Association of Law Centres

c/o Govan Law Centre,
Unit 31,
6 Harmony Row,
Govan,
Glasgow, G51 3BA
Tel: 0141-445-6451

Scottish Association of Leagues of Hospital Friends

37 Merchant Street,
Peterhead,
Aberdeenshire, AB42 1DU
Tel: 01779-474424

Mrs. Rose Reid, *Regional Chairman*

Scottish Association of Local Government Educational Psychologists

13 Kelvinside Gardens East,
Glasgow, G20 6BE
Tel: 0141-946-1075

Scottish Association of Local Sports Councils

Caledonia House,
South Gyle,
Edinburgh, EH12 9DQ
Tel: 0131-317-7200 Fax: 0131-317-7202

Ivor G. Henrichsen, *Administrator*

Scottish Association of Master Bakers

Atholl House,
4 Torphichen Street,
Edinburgh, EH9 3HP
Tel: 0131-229-1401 Fax: 0131-229-8239

Ian Hay, *Chief Executive*

The trading arm of the Association is SAMB, which is a trade and employers' association for the craft bakery industry in Scotland. *

Scottish Association of Milk Product Manufacturers

Phoenix House,
South Avenue,
Clydebank,
Glasgow, G81 2LG
Tel: 0141-951-1170 Fax: 0141-951-1129

K.J. Hunter, *Secretary*

Scottish Association of Psychoanalytic Psychotherapists

56 Albany Street,
Edinburgh, EH1 3QR
Tel: 0131-556-0924 Fax: 0131-556-2612

Scottish Association of Publishers' Educational Representatives

62 Dunvegan Avenue,
Elderslie,
Renfrewshire, PA5 9NL
Tel: 01505-325438

Mr. Drew Stewart, *Secretary*

Scottish Association of Sign Language Interpreters (SASLI)

31 York Place,
Edinburgh, EH1 3HP
Tel: 0131-557-6370 Fax: 0131-557-4110

Mrs. Doreen Mair, *Director*

The Association maintains a register of interpreters, assists with the training of those wishing to develop interpreting skills and can provide interpreter services when required. *

Scottish Association of Smallscale Broadcasters

13 Comely Bank Row,
Edinburgh, EH4 1EA
Tel: 0131-332-8270

The Director

Scottish Association of Speech & Drama Adjudicators

33 Hammersmith Road,
Aberdeen, AB10 6NA
Tel: 01224-314471

Mr. Alan Nicol, MBE, *Administrator**

Scottish Association of Spiritual Healers (SASH)

36 Ambrose Rise,
Dedridge,
Livingston,
West Lothian, EH54 6JT
Tel: 01506-413746

Mrs. E. Philp

We offer spiritual healing to the general public and aim to have a Scottish register of healers.*

Scottish Association of Staff Development Officers

Glasgow College of Building & Printing,
60 North Hanover Street,
Glasgow, G1 2BP
Tel: 0141-332-9969

Mr. Brian Filling, *Staff Development Officer*

Scottish Association of Track Statisticians

21 Bogton Avenue,
Muirend,
Glasgow, G44 3JJ
Tel: 0141-571-9243   Fax: 0141-571-9243

Mr. Colin Shields

The Association collates Scottish athletics performance statistics for track and field, road and cross-country running and publishes an annual yearbook of ranking lists and national records.*

Scottish Association of Volunteers Managers

c/o Volunteer Development Scotland,
80 Murray Place,
Stirling, FK8 2BX
Tel: 01786-479593

Mr. Brian Magee, *Membership Secretary*

Scottish Association of Watchmakers & Jewellers

29 Gauze Street,
Paisley,
PA1 1ES
Jim Gillougley, *Secretary*

Scottish Association of Writers

221 East Clyde Street,
Helensburgh,
Dunbartonshire, G84 7AU
Tel: 0141-334-3164

Scottish Association of Young Farmers' Clubs

Young Farmers' Centre,
Ingliston,
Edinburgh, EH28 8NE
Tel: 0131-333-2445   Fax: 0131-222-2488

Miss Fiona Bain, *National Secretary*

Scottish Athletics Federation

Caledonia House,
South Gyle,
Edinburgh, EH12 9DQ
Tel: 0131-317-7320   Fax: 0131-317-7321

Mr. N. Park, *Administrator*

*The management, promotion and development
   of athletics in Scotland. e-mail:
   saf@dial.pipex.com.* *

Scottish Auto-Cycle Union Limited

Block 2, Unit 6,
Whiteside Industrial Estate,
Bathgate,
West Lothian, EH48 2RX
Tel: 01506-630262   Fax: 01506-634972

Adam M. Brownlie, *Secretary*

*This is the governing body for motorcycle sport
   in Scotland which exists to promote the sport
   in a safe and enjoyable fashion to all those
   who administer, observe and participate in
   motorcycling.* *

Scottish Avalanche Information Service

Glenmore Lodge,
Aviemore,
Inverness-shire, PH22 1BR

Scottish Bach Consort

66 Main Street,
Killearn,
Stirlingshire, G63 9ND
Tel: 01360-550824   Fax: 01360-550588

Iain D. Beattie, *Director*

*The SBC is a professional ensemble taking
   quality performances of music to rural areas
   of Scotland, inviting your musicians as
   soloists and training tomorrow's musicians
   today. A Scottish ccharity no. SCO 53223.* *

Scottish Badminton Union

Cockburn Centre,
40 Bogmoor Place,
Glasgow, G51 4TQ
Tel: 0141-445-1218   Fax: 0141-425-1218

Miss A. Smillie, *Chief Executive*

*The governing body for the sport and recreation
   of badminton in Scotland.* *

Scottish Ballet

261 West Princes Street,
Glasgow, G43 9EE
Tel: 0141-331-2931   Fax: 0141-331-2629

Scottish Band of Hope Union

11 Newton Place,
Glasgow, G3 7PR
Tel: 0141-772-6871

Mrs. McDonald, *Office Secretary*

Scottish Baptist College

12 Aytoun Road,
Glasgow, G41 5RN
Tel: 0141-424-0747

Rev. Kenneth B.E. Roxburgh, BA, MTh,
PhD, *Principal*

*The College trains students towards a BD
degree in Theology and Pastoral Studies
validated by Paisley University. An alternative shorter course is available leading to a
Diploma of Practical Theology.* *

Scottish Baptist Men's Movement

21 Edenside,
Westerwood,
Cumbernauld, G68 0ER
Tel: 01236-738444

Mr Kenneth Stewart, *Secretary*

Scottish Basketball Association

Caledonia House,
South Gyle,
Edinburgh, EH12 9DQ
Tel: 0131-317-7260   Fax: 0131-317-7489

Ms. Alexandra Harvey, *Administration
Manager*

*Development and promotion of basketball in
Scotland at all levels and to represent Scottish
basketball internationally.* *

Scottish Basketmakers' Circle

Wee Darnhunch,
Glenbuck,
Ayrshire
Tel: 01290-661082

Ms. Lise Bech

*We promote basketmaking in Scotland –
teaching, making, exhibiting, researching and
demonstrating. We are a busy, active group
and our work ranges from traditional to
contemporary.* *

Scottish Bass Trust

6 West Garleton,
Haddington,
Edinburgh, EH41 3SL
Tel: 01620-822532   Fax: 01620-822532

Jennifer Sharp

*The Scottish Bass Trust provides opportunities
for double bass players to develop their skills;
promotes public performances involving the
instrument and commissions new bass
works.* *

Scottish Beagle Club

5 Dee Path,
Holytown,
Motherwell, ML1 4SX
Tel: 01698-834387

Mrs. J. Penman

Scottish Beekeepers' Association (SBA)

44 Dalhousie Road,
Kilbarchan,
Renfrewshire, PA10 2AT
Tel: 01505-702680

David Blair, *Publicity Convener*

The Association seeks to promote beekeeping within and beyond Scotland. *

Scottish Befriending Development Forum

CSV Befriending Project,
Bedford House,
50 Richardland Road,
Kilmarnock, KA1 3JS
Tel: 01563-544937

Ms. Shirley Haggerty

Scottish Bicycle Polo Association

16 Edminston Drive,
Linwood,
Paisley, PA3 3TD
Tel: 01505-328105

Mr. A. McGee, *Secretary*

Scottish Billiards & Snooker Association

P.O. Box 147,
Kirkcaldy, KY1 2HS
Tel: 01383-625373   Fax: 01383-625373

Mr. A.T. Craig, *Secretary*

The national governing body for the game in Scotland, accredited by the Scottish Sports Council and member of the Scottish Sports Association. *

Scottish Biodiversity Group

RSPB Scottish Headquarters,
17 Regent Terrace,
Edinburgh, EH7 5BN

Ms. Margaret Duncan

Scottish Biomedical Association

Unit 6/01 Kelvin Campus,
West of Scotland Science Park,
Glasgow, G20 0SP
Tel: 0141-945-1934   Fax: 0141-945-1591

G.W. Robertson, *General Secretary*

Scottish Biomolecules Group

Biotechnology Group,
Scottish Enterprise,
120 Bath Street,
Glasgow, G2 2EN
Tel: 0141-248-2700

Linda Wilson

Scottish Blind Golf Association

1010 Aitkenhead Road,
Glasgow, G44 4SB
Tel: 0141-632-3659

Ken Freeman

Scottish Board Sailing Association

Beinn Bhan,
Kilmory Road,
Lochgilphead,
Argyll, PA31 8SZ

Forbes Johnston

Scottish Bobath Association

see Bobath Scotland

Scottish Book Marketing Group

Scottish Book Centre,
137 Dundee Street,
Edinburgh, EH11 1BG
Tel: 0131-228-6866   Fax: 0131-228-4293

Mr. Allan Shanks

*The SBMG is a venture unique to Scotland set
up by the Scottish Publishers Association and
the Booksellers Association (Scottish branch).
Its aims are to promote Scottish books
through Scottish bookshops, libraries and arts
organisations to create a wider public
awareness of their quality and range.*

Scottish Book Trust

Scottish Book Centre,
137 Dundee Street,
Edinburgh, EH11 1BG
Tel: 0131-229-3663   Fax: 0131-228-4293

Lindsey Fraser

*An independent charity promoting books,
reading and writers throughout Scotland.* *

Scottish Bookmakers Protection Association

19 Waterloo Street,
Glasgow, G2 6BZ
Tel: 0141-221-0822

Scottish Border Collie Club

Blackshaw Farm,
West Kilbride,
North Ayrshire, KA23 9PG
Tel: 01294-829640

Mrs. J. Hastie

Scottish Border Terrier Club

2 Midhalket Cottage,
Halket,
by Dunlop,
Ayrshire, KA3 4EW
Tel: 01505-850313

Mr. W.I.L. Shorthose

*Members' club to promote the Border Terrier
through organising shows and other events.* *

Scottish Bosnia Relief

117 Saltmarket,
Glasgow,
G1 5LF
Tel: 0141-552-7770

Scottish Bowlers' Fellowship

101 West Nile Street,
Glasgow, G1 2RA

Gavin Taylor

Scottish Bowling Association

50 Wellington Street,
Glasgow, G2 6EF
Tel: 0141-221-8999   Fax: 0141-221-8999

W.S. Forbes, *Secretary*

*The governing body of the sport of lawn bowls in Scotland. **

Scottish Bowls Coaching Committee

Argyle Villa,
45 Bridge Street,
Tranent,
East Lothian, EH33 1AH
Tel: 01875-615953   Fax: 01875-615953

Mr. Graham Robertson, *National Coach*

*Undertakes the task of training bowls coaches throughout Scotland for the four national governing bodies. Coaches are trained at club and advanced levels. **

Scottish Boxer Club

High Kirkland,
Leswalt,
near Stranraer, DG9 0RH
Tel: 01776-870211

Mr. W.G. Miller

*The club organises three shows per year. Once a month there is a social section meeting where dogs can be trained and owners educated in all aspects of dog care and management. **

Scottish Braille Press

Craigmillar Park,
Edinburgh, EH16 5NB
Tel: 0131-662-4445   Fax: 0131-662-1968

Mr. J.H. Adams

*The Scottish Braille Press publishes and produces items in Braille, large print and audio. Tactile diagrams and material on disk can also be supplied. **

Scottish Broadcast & Film Training Unit

74 Victoria Crescent Road,
Dowanhill,
Glasgow, G12 9JN
Tel: 0141-334-2826   Fax: 0141-334-8132

Scottish Building Apprenticeship and Training Council

Woodside Crescent,
Glasgow, G3 7UP
Tel: 0141-332-7144

Scottish Building Contract Committee

27 Melville Street,
Edinburgh, EH3 7JF
Tel: 0131-226-2552

Mr. J.M. Arnott, *Secretary*

Scottish Building Contractors Association

4 Woodside Place,
Glasgow, G3 7QF
Tel: 0141-353-5050   Fax: 0141-332-2928

N.J. Smith, *Secretary*

An Association of employers in the building and construction industries in Scotland.*

Scottish Building Employers' Federation

13 Woodside Crescent,
Glasgow, G3 7UP
Tel: 0141-332-7144   Fax: 0141-331-1684

R.W. Campbell, *Director*

Scottish Bull Terrier Club

21 Elliot Crescent,
Calderwood,
East Kilbride, G74 3ET

Miss L. Shearer

Scottish Business in the Community

30 Hanover Street,
Edinburgh, EH2 2DR
Tel: 0131-220-3001   Fax: 0131-220-3003

Ms. Jennifer McCulloch, *Secretary*

Scottish Business in the Community is a charity whose purpose is to promote, in Scotland, business involvement with the community.*

Scottish Campaign Against a Federal Europe

Faculty of Social Sciences,
University of Glasgow,
Glasgow, G12 8QQ

Mr. Charles Woolfson, *Secretary*

Scottish Campaign for Nuclear Disarmament (CND)

15 Barrland Street,
Glasgow, G41 1QH
Tel: 0141-423-1222   Fax: 0141-423-1231

Mr. John Ainslie, *Administrator*

CND campaigns for the elimination of nuclear weapons with particular emphasis on British nuclear weapons which are all based in Scotland.*

Scottish Campaign for Public Angling

18/5 Restalrig Drive,
Edinburgh, EH7 6JX

D. Keith, *Secretary*

Scottish Cancer Registry

Information & Statistics Division of the
  NHS in Scotland,
Trinity Park House,
South Trinity Road,
Edinburgh, EH5 3SQ
Tel: 0131-551-8903   Fax: 0131-551-1392

Dr. D.H. Brewster

The Scottish Cancer Registry collects informa-
  tion on new cases of cancer in Scotland,
  enabling trends in cancer incidence and
  survival to be monitored. *

Scottish Canine Consultative Council

The Community Dog Training Centre,
43-49 Alexander Street,
Alexandria,
West Dunbartonshire, G83 0PG
Tel: 01389-755133   Fax: 01389-755133

Mr. George P. Cochrane, *Chairman*

The SCCC seeks to achieve a balance on the
  subject of dogs in society in a national sense
  which will be acceptable to the general public,
  the dog world and the authorities alike. *

Scottish Canoe Association

Caledonia House,
South Gyle,
Edinburgh, EH12 9DQ
Tel: 0131-317-7314   Fax: 0131-317-7319

Executive Officer

Recognized as the governing body for all
  Scottish kayaking and canoeing, the SCA
  promotes canoeing as a healthy, sustainable
  activity and competititve sport. *

Scottish Carpet Workers' Union

1125 Argyle Street,
Glasgow, G3 8ND
Tel: 0141-204-1911

Mr. R. Smillie

Scottish Cashmere Producers Association

8 Polton Bank Terrace,
Lasswade,
Midlothian, EH18 1JL
Tel: 0131-654-1305

Alison McPake

Scottish Cat Club

c/o 49 Drummond Hill,
Calderwood,
East Kilbride, G74 3AA

Scottish Catholic Historical Association

John S. Burns & Sons,
25 Finlas Street,
Glasgow, G22 5DS
Tel: 0141-336-8678

Prof. T.M. Devine, *Chairman*

Scottish Catholic International Aid Fund (SCIAF)

5 Oswald Street,
Glasgow, G1 4QR
Tel: 0141-221-4447   Fax: 0141-221-2373

Mr. Paul Chitnis

Scottish Cavalier King Charles Spaniel Club

9 Elm Grove,
Larbert,
Stirlingshire, FK5 3LP
Tel: 01324-553331

Mrs. E. Smith

The aim of the Club shall be to unite lovers of the breed, promoting the general interests of the Cavalier King Charles Spaniel. *

Scottish Central Fire Brigades Advisory Council

c/o The Scottish Office Home Department,
F1 Spur,
Saughton House,
Broomhouse Road,
Edinburgh, EH11 3XD
Tel: 0131-244-2166   Fax: 0131-244-2819

R.L. Knowles, *Secretary*

Advises the Secretary of State for Scotland on Fire Service matters. *

Scottish Centre for Children with Motor Impairments

Craighalbert Centre,
1 Craighalbert Way,
Cumbernauld,
Glasgow, G68 0LS
Tel: 01236-456100   Fax: 01236-736889

Dr. Liuemor Jernqvist

The Craighalbert Centre helps children under the age of seven who have cerebral palsy. It combines Peto's principles of conductive education with the national advice available on the curriculum in Scotland, to teach children everyday activities. *

Scottish Centre for Infection and Environmental Health

Ruchill Hospital,
Bilsland Drive,
Glasgow, G20 9NB
Tel: 0141-946-7120

Professor D. Reid, *Director*

Scottish Centre for Information on Language Teaching and Research

Pathfoot Building,
University of Stirling,
Stirling, FK9 4LA
Tel: 01786-467631   Fax: 01786-467632

Mrs Lottie Gregory, *Liaison Officer*

Scottish Centre for Japanese Studies

University of Stirling,
Stirling, FK9 4LA
Tel: 01786-466080   Fax: 01786-466088

Ms. Anne Goldie

The premier Centre in Scotland for the study of the Japanese language and of Japanese society, history and culture. *

Scottish Centre for Journalism Studies

(Strathclyde University and Glasgow
  Caledonian University),
University of Strathclyde,
26 Richmond Street,
Glasgow, G1 1XH
Tel: 0141-553-4166   Fax: 0141-552-3493

J. McKay

Training and education for postgraduates who want to enter journalism. Research centre for academic study of journalism. *

Scottish Centre for Pollen Studies

c/o Department of Biological Sciences,
Napier University,
10 Colinton Road,
Edinburgh, EH10 5DT
Tel: 0131-455-5014   Fax: 0131-455-2291

Eric Caulton, *Centre Director*

Scottish Centre for Post Qualification Pharmaceutical Education

University of Strathclyde,
Royal College Building,
204 George Street,
Glasgow, G1 1XW
Tel: 0141-548-4273   Fax: 0141-553-4102

Miss R.M. Parr, *Director*

The purpose of the Scottish Centre for Post Qualification Pharmaceutical Education is to maximise the contribution of community and hospital pharmacists in the NHS in Scotland through the provision of appropriate post qualification education and training. *

Scottish Centre for Studies in School Administration

Moray House Institute of Education,
Heriot-Watt University,
Holyrood Road,
Edinburgh, EH8 8AQ
Tel: 0131-558-6179   Fax: 0131-557-3458

Mr. J.E.A. Havard, *Director*

Scottish Centre for War Studies

Department of Modern History,
University of Glasgow,
Glasgow, G12 8QQ
Tel: 0141-339-8855   Fax: 0141-330-5000

Professor Hew Strachan

The Centre promotes the study of war in all its aspects both within the University of Glasgow and between the Armed Services and the academic community. *

Scottish Centre for the Book

Department of Print Media, Publishing &
  Communication,
Napier University,
Craighouse Campus,
Craighouse Road,
Edinburgh, EH10 5LG
Tel: 0131-455-6150   Fax: 0131-455-6193

Dr. David Finkelstein and Professor
  Alistair McCleery

*The Scottish Centre for the Book acts as a focus
for research into, scholarship in, and teaching
of print culture and the sociology of texts. It
hosts seminars and conferences and issues
publications relating to the past, present and
future of the printed word, its creation,
diffusion and reception. ***

Scottish Centre for the Education of the Deaf

Clerwood House,
Clermiston Road,
Edinburgh, EH12 6UT
Tel: 0131-314-6075   Fax: 0131-314-6077

Mrs L.Sutherland, *Administrator*

Scottish Chamber Choir

The Tanhouse,
Tanhouse Brae,
Culross,
Fife, KY12 8HY
Tel: 01383-880397

Mr. Adrian Coppolla, *Secretary*

Scottish Chamber Orchestra Chorus

4 Royal Terrace,
Edinburgh, EH7 5AB
Tel: 0131-557-6800   Fax: 0131-557-6933

Mr. James Waters, *Concerts Director*

Scottish Chamber of Safety

c/o Mr. J.K. Warden, Hon. Treasurer,
'Meadowview',
6 Glass Street,
Markinch,
Fife, KY7 6DP
Tel: 01592-758350

*Mr. McGinigal, the Honorary Secretary, can be
contacted at 27 Wallace Brae Crescent,
Danestone, Aberdeen, AB22 8YE. ***

Scottish Chambers of Commerce

Conference House,
The Exchange,
152 Morrison Street,
Edinburgh, EH3 8EB
Tel: 0131-477-8025   Fax: 0131-477-7002

Mr. Lex Gold, *Director*

Scottish Charities Office

Crown Office,
25 Chambers Street,
Edinburgh, EH1 1LA
Tel: 0131-226-2626   Fax: 0131-226-6912

B.M. Logan, *Director*

The Office is responsible for the supervision of the charitable sector with the aim to enhance public confidence in the integrity and effectiveness of charities. *

Scottish Charity Finance Directors' Group

Box SCFDG,
The Wise Group,
72 Charlotte Street,
Glasgow, G1 5DW
Tel: 0141-303-3131   Fax: 0141-303-0018

Mr. Martin Ogilvie, *Secretary*

SCFDG is a Scottish charity promoting and improving the standard of financial management in the charity sector in Scotland. *

Scottish Chess Association

26/5 Causewayside,
Edinburgh, EH9 1QB
Tel: 0131-667-0852

Frank Banaghan, *General Secretary*

Scottish Child Law Centre

4th floor,
Cranston House,
108 Argyle Street,
Glasgow, G2 8BH
Tel: 0141-226-3434   Fax: 0141-226-3043

Deirdre Watson, *Director*

Scottish Child and Family Alliance

55 Albany Street,
Edinburgh, EH1 3QY
Tel: 0131-557-2780

Anne Lancaster

Scottish Childminding Association

Room 7,
Stirling Business Centre,
Wellgreen,
Stirling, FK8 2DZ
Tel: 01786-445377   Fax: 01786-449062

Mrs. Anne McNellan, MBE, *Director*

Scottish Childminding Association exists to promote childminding as a quality childcare service by offering information and advice on what constitutes best practice and campaigning for the necessary resources for a high quality service. *

Scottish Children's Reporter Administration

Ochil House,
Springkerse Business Park,
Stirling, FK7 7XE
Tel: 01786-459500   Fax: 01786-459532

Mr. Alan D. Miller, *Principal Reporter*

SCRA took over management of the Children's Reporter Service throughout Scotland in 1996, and supports the Principal Reporter in performing the statutory functions of Reporters. *

Scottish China Association

see *The Scottish China Association*

Scottish Chiropodists Association

26 Dixon Avenue,
Crosshill,
Glasgow, G42 8EE
Tel: 0141-423-6976

E. Firestone

Scottish Chiropractic Association

Main Street,
St. Boswells,
Melrose,
Roxburghshire, TD6 0AP

Dr. Mark Cashley, *President*/Dr. Carla How, *Secretary* *

Scottish Chough Study Group

Department of Zoology,
University of Glasgow,
Glasgow, G12 8QQ
Tel: 0141-339-8855

Scottish Christian Alliance Limited

3 Nethercairn Place,
Newton Mearns,
Glasgow, G77 5SZ
Tel: 0141-616-0179   Fax: 0141-616-0179

Mr. N.D. McPhail-Smith

A Scottish charity which provides accommodation to different client groups at three locations, promoting the claims of Jesus Christ. *

Scottish Christian Benevolent Trust

19 Queen Street,
Glasgow, G1 3ED
Tel: 0141-221-4969

Scottish Church History Society

1 Denham Green Terrace,
Edinburgh, EH5 3PG
Tel: 0131-552-4059   Fax: 0131-552-4089

Rev. Dr. P.H. Donald, *Honorary Secretary*

Founded to promote the study of all aspects of Scottish Church history, the Society publishes the Records *annually to disseminate research papers. Conferences are also held periodically.* *

Scottish Churches Architectural Heritage Trust

15 North Bank Street,
Edinburgh, EH1 2LP
Tel: 0131-225-8644

Florence MacKenzie, *Director*

Scottish Churches China Group

121 George Street,
Edinburgh,
EH2 4YN
Tel: 0131-225-5722   Fax: 0131-226-6121

Jill Hughes

The SCCG has various programmes with both churches (Catholic and Protestant), secular colleges and universities in China. We send teachers of English and medical English each year and arrange study placements in Scotland for nurses, doctors and teachers from China.*

Scottish Churches Housing Agency

Walpole Hall,
Manor Place,
Edinburgh, EH3 7EB
Tel: 0131-226-2080   Fax: 0131-226-2190

Mr. Alastair Cameron

Supports and influences Scotland's churches in combating homelessness. Advisory service to local groups; learning materials; quarterly newsletter and regular gatherings. New members of Friends network welcome.*

Scottish Churches World Exchange

12 George Street,
Edinburgh, EH2 4YN
Tel: 0131-225-8115

Ms. Lynn Whitehead, *Adminstrative Officer*

Scottish Cinematograph Trade Benevolent Fund

c/o Ernst & Young,
George House,
George Square,
Glasgow, G2 1RR
Tel: 0141-552-3456

Scottish Circus Action Network

P.O. Box 248,
Aberdeen, AB25 1JE
Tel: 01224-690350   Fax: 01224-690350

Irene Boyne, *Coordinator*

Scottish Circus Action Network is a voluntary organisation which is campaigning through-out Scotland to end the use of animals in circuses.*

Scottish Civic Assembly

18 Claremont Crescent,
Edinburgh, EH7 4QD
Tel: 0131-556-3882

The Secretary

Scottish Civic Entertainment Association

North Lanarkshire Council,
Department of Leisure,
Buchanan Business Park,
Stepps,
Glasgow, G33 6HR
Tel: 0141-304-1924

Aileen Armstrong, *Secretary*

Scottish Civic Trust

see The Scottish Civic Trust

Scottish Civil Liberty Trust

146 Holland Street,
Glasgow, G2 2TU
Tel: 0141-332-5309

Scottish Civil Service Bowling Association

19 Muir Street,
Larkhall,
Lanarkshire, ML9 2BG
Tel: 01698-308684   Fax: 01698-308684

W. Lang

The competitions run by this Association are open to all CSSC members, i.e. both civil servants and affiliated fringe bodies. For more information, contact the above. *

Scottish Clay Target Association

10 Balgibbon Drive,
Callander,
Perthshire, FK17 8EU
Tel: 01877-331323

Mr. R.W. Forsyth, *Honorary Secretary*

Scottish Collaborative Initiative in Optoelectronic Sciences

Department of Physics,
Heriot Watt University,
Riccarton,
Edinburgh, EH14 4AS

Scottish College of Complementary Medicine

c/o The Complemetary Medicine Centre,
11 Park Circus,
Glasgow, G3 6AX
Tel: 0141-332-4924   Fax: 0141-353-3783

Mr. Brian Fleming

There is a range of complementary medicine available including acupuncture, Chinese herbal medicine, aromatherapy, osteopathy, allergy testing, homoeopathy, therapeutic counselling services and integrative arts counselling. *

Scottish College of Homoeopathy

11 Lynedoch Place,
Glasgow, G3 6AB
Tel: 0141-332-3917

Ms. Margaret Roy

The college offers professional training in homoeopathic medicine, four years part-time over 15 weekends/year. The ethos is team-work and hard work within a graduated programme. *

Scottish Collie Club

Roadside Cottage,
Roughrigg,
Longriggend,
by Airdrie, ML6 7RU
Tel: 01236-843315

Mrs. M. McCarte

Scottish Colportage Society

11 Newton Place,
Glasgow, G3 7PR
Tel: 0141-333-0546

Miss Margaret P. Milne

Scottish Committee of Optometrists

see The Scottish Committee of Optometrists

Scottish Community Care Forum

c/o 18/19 Claremont Crescent,
Edinburgh, EH7 4QD
Tel: 0131-557-2711   Fax: 0131-557-2711

Mrs. Karen Jackson

Scottish Community Care Forum is a national organisation that provides support, information and advice to all the Community Care Forums throughout Scotland. *

Scottish Community Development Centre

Suite 329,
Baltic Chambers,
50 Wellington Street,
Glasgow, G2 6HJ
Tel: 0141-248-1924   Fax: 0141-248-4938

Stuart Hashagen, *Director*

Scottish Community Diet

Royal Exchange House,
100 Queen Street,
Glasgow, G1 3ND
Tel: 0141-226-5261   Fax: 0141-221-0731

Ms. Jacqui MacIntyre

Scottish Community Drama Association

5 York Place,
Edinburgh, EH1 3EB
Tel: 0131-557-5552   Fax: 0131-557-5552

Ms. Maggie Gordon, *Secretary*

Website: http://www.btinternet.com/~scda, e-mail: scda@btinternet.com. *

Scottish Community Education Council (SCEC)

Rosebery House,
9 Haymarket Terrace,
Edinburgh, EH12 5EZ
Tel: 0131-313-2488   Fax: 0131-313-6800

Mr. Charlie McConnell, Chief Executive

*The SCEC is the Government's national agency
for adult education, community and youth
work. It is also the Occupational Training
Standards Council for this sector having
responsibility for advising the Government,
local authorities and other community
education providers.* *

Scottish Community Projects Fund

c/o RIAS,
15 Rutland Square,
Edinburgh, EH1 2BE
Tel: 0131-229-7545   Fax: 0131-228-2188

Mrs. June O'Hara

*The Scottish Community Projects Fund gives
grants to community let organisations who
want to produce a feasibility study for
building and environmental improvement
projects or employment initiatives.* *

Scottish Community Services Agency

52 St. Enoch Square,
Glasgow, G1 4DH
Tel: 0141-248-8587

Scottish Confederation of Trade & Industry

62 Kelvingrove Street,
Glasgow, G3 7SA
Tel: 0141-333-1980

Scottish Confocal Laser Scanning Microscope Facility

School of Biomedical Sciences,
University of St. Andrews,
St. Andrews, KY16 9TS
Tel: 01334-76161

Mr. John B. Mackie

*Biorad confocal laser scanning microscope two-
channel, fluorescein and rhodamine.* *

Scottish Congregational Church

P.O. Box 189,
Glasgow, G1 2BX
Tel: 0141-332-7667   Fax: 0141-332-8463

Rev. John Arthur, BA, *General Secretary* *

Scottish Congregational College

St Colms,
20 Inverleith Terrace,
Edinburgh, EH3 5NS
Tel: 0131-315-3595

Scottish Conservation Bureau

Historic Scotland,
Longmore House,
Salisbury Place,
Edinburgh, EH9 1SH
Tel: 0131-668-8668   Fax: 0131-668-8669

Carol E. Brown, *Conservation Bureau Manager*

The Scottish Conservation Bureau provides information, advice and support to all those concerned with the conservation of historic artefacts and buildings in Scotland. *

Scottish Conservation Partnership

Waterside Studios,
Coltbridge Avenue,
Edinburgh, EH12 6AH
Tel: 0131-346-1206

Scottish Conservation Projects Trust (SCP)

Balallan House,
24 Allan Park,
Stirling, FK8 2QG
Tel: 01786-479687   Fax: 01786-465359

Ms. Catherine Johnson, *Press & Publicity Officer*

Scottish Conservation Society

The Manse,
Dalry,
Kirkcudbrightshire

Scottish Conservative and Unionist Party

14 Links Place,
Edinburgh, EH6 7EZ
Tel: 0131-555-2900   Fax: 0131-555-2869

Scottish Consortium of Timber Frame Industries

TRADA Offices,
John Player Building,
Stirling Enterprise Park,
Stirling, FK7 7RS
Tel: 01786-445075   Fax: 01786-474412

Secretariat Coordinator

SCOTFI is an independently constituted company which represents the interests of member companies and customers. It has an elected chairman and secretariat based in Stirling. *

Scottish Constitutional Convention

c/o Rosebery House,
9 Haymarket Terrace,
Edinburgh, EH12 5XZ
Tel: 0131-474-9200   Fax: 0131-474-9292

Canon Kenyon Wright, *Chair of Executive Committee*

A broadly-based organisation to make plans for the future governance of Scotland and the establishment of a Scottish Parliament. *

Scottish Consultative Council on the Curriculum

Gardyne Road,
Broughty Ferry,
Dundee, DD5 1NY
Tel: 01382-455053

Cameron Harrison, *Director*

Scottish CCC is the principal adviser to the Secretary of State on the curriculum for 3–18 year olds. *

Scottish Consumer Council

Royal Exchange House,
100 Queen Street,
Glasgow, G1 3DN
Tel: 0141-226-5261   Fax: 0141-221-0731

Mr. Martyn Evans, *Director*

The Scottish Consumer Council (SCC) aims to promote the interests of Scottish consumers, with particular regard to those who experience disadvantage in society. The SCC researches and critically assesses the policies and practices of government, industry and the professions. *

Scottish Consumer Credit Association

33 Carmunnock Road,
Glasgow, G44 4TZ
Tel: 0141-649-6955

S. Green, *Chairman*

Scottish Consumers' Association for Natural Food

21 Clouston Street,
Glasgow, G20 8QR
Tel: 0141-334-4886   Fax: 0141-334-4886

Mr. George Stidolph, *Chairman*

A non-profit making association of individuals deeply concerned about the effects of genetic engineering on our health, on our environment and on the third world. *

Scottish Contaminated Land Forum (SCLF)

Envirocentre,
Wolfson Centre,
106 Rottenrow East,
Glasgow, G4 0NW
Tel: 0141-548-3168   Fax: 0141-552-0067

Ms. Susan Brack, *Secretary*

SCLF encourages and promotes effective and sustainable rehabilitation of contaminated land in Scotland and elsewhere through the knowledge and skills of Scottish-based professional services. *

Scottish Convention of Women

88 Main Street,
Davidson's Mains,
Edinburgh, EH4 5AB
Tel: 0131-336-3630

Scottish Conveyancing & Executry Services Board

Mulberry House,
16–22 Picardy Place,
Edinburgh, EH1 3YT
Tel: 0131-556-1945   Fax: 0131-556-8428

Mr. Robert H. Paterson, *Secretary*

The Board is responsible for registering and regulating the new professions of qualified conveyancer and executry practitioner. *

Scottish Cooperative Women's Guild

95 Morrison Street,
Glasgow, G5 8LP
Tel: 0141-429-1457

Morag Frame, *Secretary*

Scottish Cooperatives Development Company

Templeton Business Centre,
Templeton Street,
Bridgeton,
Glasgow, G40 1DA
Tel: 0141-554-3797

Scottish Corn Trade Association

8 Melville Crescent,
Edinburgh, EH3 7PQ
Tel: 0131-225-6834   Fax: 0131-225-4049

Nigel Cook

Scottish Corps of Retired Executives (SCORE)

c/o Scottish Business in the Community,
Romano House,
43 Station Road,
Edinburgh, EH12 7AF
Tel: 0131-334-9876   Fax: 0131-316-4521

Mr. Bob McCall, *Assistant Director*

Scottish Cot Death Trust

Royal Hospital for Sick Children,
Yorkhill,
Glasgow, G3 8SJ
Tel: 0141-357-3946   Fax: 0141-334-1376

Ms. Hazel Brooke, *Executive Director*

The Trust raises funds for research, provides support for bereaved families and offers education and advice to the public and health care professionals. *

Scottish Council Development and Industry

23 Chester Street,
Edinburgh, EH3 7ET
Tel: 0131-225-7911   Fax: 0131-220-2116

Ms. Penni McCallum

An independent, broadly-based membership organisation formed to influence and strengthen Scotland's economy through policy work and services for members. *

Scottish Council for Arbitration

55/57 Queen Street,
Edinburgh, EH2 3NS
Tel: 0131-220-4776

Scottish Council for Educational Technology (SCET)

74 Victoria Crescent Road,
Glasgow, G12 9JN
Tel: 0141-337-5000   Fax: 0141-337-5050

Mr. Nigel Paine, *Chief Executive*

Scottish Council for International Arbitration

27 Melville Street,
Edinburgh, EH3 7JF
Tel: 0131-220-4776   Fax: 0131-226-2501

J.M. Arnott, *Director*

Scottish Council for National Parks

15 Park Terrace,
Stirling, FK8 2JT
Tel: 01786-465714   Fax: 01786-473843

Mr. Brian K. Parnell, *Honorary Secretary*

A voluntary organisation which campaigned for National Parks in Scotland and – now government supports the principle – campaigns for appropriate legislation from the future Scottish Parliament. *

Scottish Council for Postgraduate Medical and Dental Education (SCPMDE)

4th floor,
Hobart House,
80 Hanover Street,
Edinburgh, EH2 1EL
Tel: 0131-225-4365   Fax: 0131-225-5891

Dr. G. Buckley/Mrs. H. Rippin/Mrs. K.P. Stiven

Special health board with responsibility for managing and funding postgraduate medical and dental education and training in Scotland. *

Scottish Council for Research in Education

15 St. John Street,
Edinburgh, EH8 8JR
Tel: 0131-557-2944   Fax: 0131-556-9454

Professor Wynne Harlen, OBE, *Director*

SCRE is an independent public sector body specialising in research relevant to policy and practice at all levels of education. It conducts research under contract and disseminates research findings and ideas. Website: http:// www.scre.ac.uk. *

Scottish Council for Single Homeless

9 Forrest Road,
Edinburgh, EH1 2QH
Tel: 0131-226-4382   Fax: 0131-220-3107

Mr. Laurie M. Naumann, *Director*

Scottish Council for Voluntary Organisations (SCVO)

18–19 Claremont Crescent,
Edinburgh, EH7 4QD
Tel: 0131-556-3882   Fax: 0131-556-0279

Ms Anne Boyle/Mr. Alistair Fergusson

Scottish Council of Independent Schools

21 Melville Street,
Edinburgh, EH3 7PE
Tel: 0131-220-2106   Fax: 0131-225-8594

Scottish Council of Law Reporting

Law Society,
26 Drumsheugh Gardens,
Edinburgh, EH3 7YR
Tel: 0131-226-7411   Fax: 0131-225-2934

Mr. David Cullen, *Deputy Secretary*

The Council is charged with the responsibility for publishing session cases – the authoritative case reports of the Supreme Courts of Scotland. *

Scottish Council of Physical Education

Physical Education,
Scottish Borders Council,
Education Department,
Newton St. Boswells, TD6 0SA
Tel: 01835-824000   Fax: 01835-822145

Mrs. E. Pearson, *Secretary**

Scottish Council on Alcohol

2nd floor,
166 Buchanan Street,
Glasgow, G1 2NH
Tel: 0141-333-9677   Fax: 0141-333-1606

Dr. Alan Foster, *Chief Executive*

The SCA aims to reduce alcohol misuse and to promote a resonsible approach to alcohol use and co-ordinates a network of 28 community-based counselling agencies throughout Scotland. *

Scottish Counties Evangelistic Movement

342 Argyle Street,
Glasgow, G2 8LT
Tel: 0141-248-5359

Mr Peter Sunderland, *Chairman*

Scottish Country Life Museums Trust

c/o National Museums of Scotland,
Chambers Street,
Edinburgh, EH1 1JF
Tel: 0131-247-4256   Fax: 0131-247-4312

Gavin Sprott, *Secretary*

The aims of SCLMT are the establishment of a Scottish national open-air museum of country life, to promote knowledge of the Scottish countryside and co-operation between national, regional and local museums of country life in Scotland. *

Scottish Countryside Activities Council

11 West Craigs Crescent,
Edinburgh, EH12 8NB
Tel: 0131-339-7014   Fax: 0131-339-7014

Mr. Robert Aitken, *Chairman*

Scottish Countryside Rangers Association

P.O. Box 37,
Stirling, FK8 2BL

Ms. Heather McLean

Scottish Courts Service

Hayweight House,
23 Lauriston Street,
Edinburgh, EH3 9DQ
Tel: 0131-229-9200

Mr. M. Ewart, *Chief Executive*

Scottish Crannog Centre

Croft-na-Caber,
Kenmore,
Loch Tay,
Perthshire, PH15 2HW
Tel: 01887-830583   Fax: 01887-830583

Ms. B.L.Andrian

Award-winning heritage attraction featuring Scotland's only authentic recreation of an Iron Age loch dwelling. Exhibits, video and ancient crafts bringthe past to life.

Scottish Cricket Union

Caledonia House,
South Gyle,
Edinburgh, EH12 9DQ
Tel: 0131-317-7247   Fax: 0131-317-7103

Mr. A.J. Ritchie, *Gen. Manager*/Mr. J.D. Love, *Director*

Governing body for cricket in Scotland. *

Scottish Crime Squad

50 Stewart Street,
Glasgow, G4 0HY
Tel: 0141-331-1881   Fax: 0141-331-1162

Det. Chief Supt. Grant Findlay, *Commander*

Scottish Criminal Record Office

173 Pitt Street,
Glasgow, G2 4JS
Tel: 0141-532-2504   Fax: 0141-532-2310

Chief Supt. Hugh Perry, *Officer in Charge*

Scottish Crofters Union (SCU)

Old Mill,
Broadford,
Isle of Skye, IV49 9AQ
Tel: 01471-822529   Fax: 01471-822799

Ms. F. Mandeville, *Crofting Adviser*/Mr. J. Toal, *Director.* *

Scottish Crop Research Institute

Mylnefield,
Invergowrie,
Dundee, DD2 5DA
Tel: 01382-562371   Fax: 01382-562426

Douglas L. Hood, *Secretary*

It is a major international centre for research on agricultural, horticultural and industrial crops and aims to increase knowledge of the basic biological sciences, improve crop quality and to develop environmentally benign methods of pest control. *

Scottish Croquet Association

2 Rannoch Drive,
Crossford,
Dunfermline, KY12 8XP
Tel: 01383-729289   Fax: 01383-729289

Mr. Nigel Gardner, *Honorary Secretary*

Promotes and administers the sport of croquet in Scotland. *

Scottish Crusaders

Challenge House,
29 Canal Street,
Glasgow, G4 0AD
Tel: 0141-331-2400   Fax: 0141-564-1211

Kevin Simpson, *Director*

A youth organisation operating 55 voluntary Christian youth groups throughout Scotland. Crusaders aims to reach unchurched young people aged 8–18 years. *

Scottish Cuba Defence Campaign

67 Cobbington Place,
Glasgow, G33 3UP

Scottish Cyclists' Union

The Velodrome,
Meadowbank Stadium,
London Road,
Edinburgh, EH7 6AD
Tel: 0131-652-0187   Fax: 0131-661-0474

Jim Riach, *Executive Officer*

The governing body for cycle sport in Scotland with over 100 affiliated clubs. There are over 300 events annually in mountain biking, road racing, track racing, time trialling and cyclo-cross, and we are responsible for the national cycling teams. *

Scottish Dachshund Club

Balgownie,
Ayr Road,
Irvine, KA11 5AB
Tel: 01294-311408

Mrs. J. McNaughton

Scottish Daily Newspaper Society

48 Palmerston Place,
Edinburgh, EH12 5DE
Tel: 0131-220-4353   Fax: 0131-220-4344

J.B. Raeburn, *Director*

The SDNS is the representative body for publishers of Scottish daily and Sunday newspapers. It represents the industry's interests to government and its activities include advertising agency recognition. *

Scottish Dairy Trade Federation

Phoenix House,
South Avenue,
Clydebank,
Glasgow,G81 2LG
Tel: 0141-951-1170   Fax: 0141-951-1129

Kirk Hunter

Scottish Dairymen's Association

Phoenix House,
South Avenue,
Clydebank,
Glasgow, G81 2LG
Tel: 0141-951-1170   Fax: 0141-951-1129

K.J. Hunter, *Secretary*

Scottish Dance Teachers' Alliance

339 North Woodside Road,
Glasgow, G20 6ND
Tel: 0141-339-8944   Fax: 0141-357-4994

Miss S. McDonald

We conduct amateur and professional dance examinations, also days of dance for both adults and children. We hold lists of names of dance teachers from all over the world, Scotland, England, Canada, South Africa, Japan, USA and Australia, etc. *

Scottish Dance Theatre

Dundee Rep Theatre,
Tay Square,
Dundee, DD1 1PB
Tel: 01382-229500   Fax: 01382-228609

Ms. Amanda Chinn, *Senior Administrator*

Scottish Dance Theatre is a contemporary dance company, based at Dundee Rep Theatre. Its work represents the best of Scotland's choreographic talent and emerging artists and offers a blend of maturity, imagination and confident flow of movement. *

Scottish Darts Association

213 Bonnyview Drive,
West Heathryfold,
Aberdeen, AB2 7EY
Tel: 01224-692535

Mr. L.A. Mutch, *General Secretary*

Scottish Decorators' Federation

222 Queensferry Road,
Edinburgh, EH4 2BN
Tel: 0131-343-3300   Fax: 0131-315-2289

Alan McKinney, *National Director*

*Also contact for Scottish Plastering and
Drylining Association and the Scottish section
of National Association of Scaffolding
Contractors; Stone Federation GB; National
Association of Roofing Contractors and
National Association of Specialist Contrac-
tors. **

Scottish Design Limited

Stock Exchange House,
7 Nelson Mandela Building,
Glasgow, G2 7JN
Tel: 0141-221-6121   Fax: 0141-221-8799

Mr. Andy Travers, *CEO*

*Offers services in design and product develop-
ment across all business sectors. Focused
towards improving competitiveness, from
initial innovation through product development, to manufacture and distribution. **

Scottish Development Education Centre

Old Playhouse Close,
Moray House Institute,
Holyrood Road,
Edinburgh, EH8 8AQ
Tel: 0131-557-3810   Fax: 0131-556-8239

Ms. Isabel Ross/Susan McIntosh

*Scottish DEC is an educational charity set up
to encourage the inclusion of global issues
within the school curriculum in Scotland.
We provide resources for teachers and try to
influence educational policy. **

Scottish Disabled Sailors Association

19 Dalmore Crescent,
Helensburgh, G84 8JP
Tel: 01436-675580

Mr. E. Chesher, *Honorary Secretary*

Scottish Disabled Sports Trust

7 Westerton of Mugdock,
Milngavie, G62 8LQ
Tel: 0141-956-6415

Mr. A.R. Mitchell

*The Trust invites donations and legacies to
grant aid projects for the promotion and
development of sport and physical recreation
for all disabled people. **

Scottish Distributive Industries Training Council

Beta Centre,
Innovation Park,
Stirling
Tel: 01786-451661

Scottish Dobermann Club

Hopeview,
Ballencrieff,
near Longniddry,
East Lothian, EH32 0PJ
Tel: 01875-870466

Mrs. J. Campbell

To foster and promote the Dobermann and to encourage examination for hereditary diseases and create opportunities for training including breed, obedience, shows and working trials. e-mail: DOBESCOT@AOL.com. *

Scottish Down's Syndrome Association (SDSA)

158–160 Balgreen Road,
Edinburgh, EH11 3AU
Tel: 0131-313-4225   Fax: 0131-313-4285

Mrs. Linda Dunion, *Director*

The Scottish Down's Syndrome Association (SDSA) is a membership organisation which works to improve the quality of life for everyone with DS in Scotland. *

Scottish Dowsing Association

68 Shakespeare Street,
Glasgow, G20 8TJ
Tel: 0141-954-5401   Fax: 0141-954-5401

Scottish Drugs Forum (SDF)

Shaftesbury House,
5 Waterloo Street,
Glasgow, G2 6AY
Tel: 0141-221-1175   Fax: 0141-248-6414

Ms. Irene Hendry, *Information Officer*

SDF is the national policy and information agency co-ordinating action on drug issues in Scotland. Publications include Monthly Bulletin, Where to get Help *– a directory of specialist drug services in Scotland and* Drugfax *– a reference guide on drugs commonly taken by drug users. **

Scottish Dyslexia Association

Unit 3,
Stirling Business Centre,
Wellgreen,
Stirling, FK8 2DZ
Tel: 01786-446650   Fax: 01786-471235

Mrs. Jean Traill, *Chairman*

Provide information on all aspects of dyslexia. The resource centre is open Monday to Friday, 9.00 am–5.00 pm. e-mail: Dyslexia.Scotland@Dial.Pipex.com. *

Scottish EDI Awareness Centre

14, 18 & 19 Hardengreen Business Centre,
Dalhousie Road,
Eskbank,
Edinburgh, EH22 3NX
Tel: 0131-654-1500   Fax: 0131-654-1510

Mr. John G. Henderson, *Chief Executive*

*This is a Scottish business organisation
promoting and supporting best practices of
supply-chain management. Particular focus
is given to logistic and operational matters
and how information and communications
technology can assist effective management.
One of three components of SPEED Ltd.
(Supply-chain Partnership Empowering
Economic Development). e-mail:
speed@speed.org.uk.* *

Scottish Early Music Consort

2 Port Dundas Road,
Glasgow, G2 3LD
Tel: 0141-335-1178   Fax: 0141-335-1179

Mary Carmichael, *Administrator*

Scottish Early Years and Family Network

Department of Social Science,
Glasgow Caledonian University,
Cowcaddens,
Glasgow, G4 0BA
Tel: 0141-353-1710   Fax: 0141-353-1443

Mr. Peter Lee, *Director*

Scottish Earth Mysteries Research

35 Fountain Road,
Bridge of Allan, FK9 4AU
Tel: 01786-832480

Mr. Ron Halliday, *Chairman*

*Investigates all aspects of the paranormal in
Scotland. Publishes a quarterly magazine
Phenomenal News (ed. Viv Alexander)
with research reports and articles (£5 pa).
Membership applications to above.* *

Scottish Ecological Design Association

c/o RIAS,
15 Rutland Square,
Edinburgh, EH1 2BE
Tel: 0131-229-7545   Fax: 0131-228-2188

George Grams, *Chairman*

*SEDA promotes and presents a range of
activities associated with the field of ecological design, including seminars, tours, a
technical information service, a newsletter,
networking and education.* *

Scottish Economic & Social History Society

c/o Department of History,
University of Strathclyde,
McCance Building,
Richmond Street,
Glasgow, G1 1XQ
Tel: 0141-552-4400

The Treasurer

Scottish Economic Society

c/o Department of Economics,
University of Glasgow,
Glasgow, G12 8QQ
Tel: 0141-330-5534   Fax: 0141-330-4047

Mr. F.G. Hay, *Secretary*

Advancing the study and teaching of economics,
facilitating discussion of Scottish economic
problems, through conferences, lectures,
research support and its publication, The
Scottish Journal of Political Economy. *

Scottish Education and Action for Development (Sead)

23 Castle Street,
Edinburgh, EH2 3DN
Tel: 0131-225-6550   Fax: 0131-226-6384

Ms. Liz Ferguson

Sead challenges poverty and social injustice,
working for sustainable development that
puts people at the heart of decision-making.
*e-mail: Sead@gn.apc.org. **

Scottish Education and Training

University of Glasgow,
Glasgow, G12 8QQ
Tel: 0141-330-5995   Fax: 0141-330-4947

Professor Sir Graeme Davies, *Principal*

Established to promote the Scottish education
capacity in international markets and to
increase overseas earnings. e-mail:
*gdavies@mis.gla.ac.uk. **

Scottish Educational Research Association

c/o 15 St. John Street,
Edinburgh, EH8 8JR
Tel: 0131-557-2944   Fax: 0131-556-9454

Ms. Christine Forde, *Honorary Secretary*

A membership association to promote research
in all sectors of education. The activities
include an annual conference, regular
*seminars on specific issues and a newsletter. **

Scottish Educational Trust for United Nations & International Affairs

Hopetown,
Charlotte Street,
Brightons,
Falkirk, FK2 0HP
Tel: 01324-715203

Mr. J. Harris

Scottish Egg Trade Association

North Bank Chambers,
26 West Nile Street,
Glasgow, G1 2PF
Tel: 0141-248-5117

Scottish Electro-Acoustic Music Association

Music Department,
University of Glasgow,
14 University Gardens,
Glasgow, G12 8QH
Tel: 0141-307-5509   Fax: 0141-307-8018

Steven Arnold, *Chairman*

Scottish Electronic Manufacturing Centre

Napier University,
219 Colinton Road,
Edinburgh, EH14 1DJ
Tel: 0131-455-4658

Scottish Employers' Council for the Clay Industries

c/o Giscol Brick,
Etna Works,
Lower Bathville,
Armadale,
West Lothian, EH48 2LZ
Tel: 01501-730671   Fax: 01501-733733

V.J. Burgoyne

Forum for companies in the clay industry in Scotland to meet and discuss topical issues. *

Scottish Employment Opportunities for People with Disabilities

5th floor,
Portcullis House,
21 India Street,
Glasgow, G2 4PZ
Tel: 0141-226-4544   Fax: 0141-248-5068

Mr. Rick Rennie, *Director Scotland*

Scottish Energy Efficiency Office

Scottish Office Education & Industry
    Department,
Floor 2F,
Victoria Quay,
Edinburgh, EH6 6QQ
Tel: 0131-244-1200   Fax: 0131-244-7145

Mr. J. Robertson, *Regional Officer*

Scottish Energy and Environment Centre

Dept of Mechanical, Manufacturing &
    Software Engineering,
Napier University,
10 Colinton Road,
Edinburgh, EH10 5DT
Tel: 0131-455-2672   Fax: 0131-455-2264

Mr. T.W. Summers

The Centre was established in 1982 to provide specialist services in energy conservation and environmental management. It utilises academic staff from a number of departments within Napier University as consultants and trainers. *

Scottish Engineering

105 West George Street,
Glasgow, G2 1QL
Tel: 0141-221-3181   Fax: 0141-204-1202

E.J.P. Smith

Successfully promotes the Scottish engineering industry and its interests in Scotland, the United Kingdom and Europe, and provides market-leader high quality practical support services in all aspects of employment. *

Scottish Ensemble

Millworks,
Field Road,
Busby,
Glasgow, G76 8SE
Tel: 0141-664-5055   Fax: 0141-644-2855

Roger Pollen, *Managing Director*

Scottish Enterprise

120 Bothwell Street,
Glasgow, G2 7JP
Tel: 0141-248-2700   Fax: 0141-221-3217

Mr. Crawford W. Beveridge, *Chief Executive*

Scottish Enterprise's purpose is to help generate jobs and prosperity for the people of Scotland. *

Scottish Enterprise Energy Group

10 Queens Road,
Aberdeen, AB15 4ZT
Tel: 01224-626310   Fax: 01224-627006

Ms. Kate Rottenburg

Scottish Environment Protection Agency – SEPA

Erskine Court,
The Castle Business Park,
Stirling, FK9 4TR
Tel: 01786-457700   Fax: 01786-446885

Ms. Rebecca Noon *

Scottish Environmental Education Council (SEEC)

Department of Environmental Science,
University of Stirling,
Stirling, FK9 4LA
Tel: 01786-467867   Fax: 01786-467864

Sheila Winstone, *Head of Communications*

Scottish Environmental Forum (SEF)

Bonnington Mill Business Centre,
72 Newhaven Road,
Edinburgh, EH6 5QG
Tel: 0131-554-9977   Fax: 0131-554-8656

Mr. Phillip Matthews, *Coordinator*

Scottish Environmental Industries Association

P.O. Box 15125,
Glasgow, G4 0LL
Tel: 01345-660137   Fax: 01345-660137

Scottish Environmental and Outdoor Centres Association Limited – Scottish Centres

Loaningdale House,
Carwood Road,
Biggar,
South Lanarkshire, ML12 6LX
Tel: 01899-221115   Fax: 01899-220644

Ms. Karen Lamb, *Administrative Officer*

Operates five residential outdoor education centres suitable for groups of 10+. Activities available, led by fully qualified staff with programmes tailored to meet individual needs. *

Scottish Episcopal Church

21 Grosvenor Crescent,
Edinburgh, EH12 5EE
Tel: 0131-225-6357   Fax: 0131-346-7247

Mr. John F. Stuart, *Secretary General* *

Scottish Episcopal Church – Social Responsibility Unit

5 St. Vincent Place,
Glasgow, G1 2DH
Tel: 0141-204-0955   Fax: 0141-221-7014

The Social Responsibility Officer

Help and support disadvantaged families, promote awareness of social responsibility throughout the diocese. *

Scottish Episcopal Renewal Fellowship

Rose Court,
Fortrose,
Ross-shire, IV10 8TN
Tel: 01381-20520

Mrs Mary McDonell, *Coordinator* *

Scottish Equality Awareness Trainers in Disability (SEATID)

c/o The Wise Group,
72 Charlotte Street,
Glasgow, G1 5DW

Scottish Esperanto Association

47 Airbles Crescent,
Motherwell, ML1 3AP
Tel: 01698-263199   Fax: 01698-286856

David W. Bisset, *Honorary Secretary*

The promotion and teaching of the international language, Esperanto. *

Scottish European Aid with Mercy Corps Europe

18 Hanover Street,
Edinburgh, EH2 2EN
Tel: 0131-225-4465   Fax: 0131-226-3106

Mr. Simon Sutt, *Fundraising Manager*

Scottish Evangelical Research Trust

17 Claremont Park,
Edinburgh, EH6 7PJ
Tel: 0131-554-1206   Fax: 0131-555 1002

Mr. David C. Searle

Rutherford House (owned by the SERT) is a residential theological study centre. It seeks to encourage effective ministry throughout Scotland by organising training courses and seminars, publishing, sponsoring study and reading groups and by its bi-annual conference. *

Scottish Evangelical Theology Society (SETS)

6 Frogston Grove,
Edinburgh, EH10 7AG
Tel: 0131-445-3673

The Rev. Angus Morrison, *Secretary*

Scottish Evangelistic Council

11 Newton Place,
Glasgow, G3 7PR
Tel: 0141-333-0546

Mr. B. McKenzie, *Chairman*

Scottish Ex-Services Charitable Organizations (SESCO)

New Haig House,
Logie Green Road,
Edinburgh, EH7 4HR
Tel: 0131-557-2782   Fax: 0131-557-5819

Ms. Deirdre Shandley

Umbrella organisation providing a forum for biannual discussion for ex-Services charitable organisations in Scotland. *

Scottish Export Association

13 Great King Street,
Edinburgh, EH3 6QW
Tel: 0131-558-1660   Fax: 0131-558-1635

Michael E L Weir, *Executive Director*

Scottish Family Planning Medical Society

9 Wyckliffe,
Dunfermline,
Fife, KY12 9BA
Tel: 01383-723259

Dr. S. Briggs, *Treasurer*

The Society welcomes medical practitioners with an interest in family planning, women's health and sexual medicine. Meetings are held twice yearly in central Scotland. *

Scottish Farm Venison

Balcormo Mains,
Leven,
Fife, KY8 5QF
Tel: 01333-360229   Fax: 01333-360540

Mr. John Gilmour, *Chairman*

Co-operative of Scottish venison farmers. *

Scottish Farm and Countryside Educational Trust

see The Scottish Farm and Countryside Educational Trust

Scottish Federation for Coarse Angling

13 Boghead Road,
Kirkintilloch, G66 4EG

Mr. James Brown, *Chairman*

Scottish Federation of Baton Twirling

55 Springkell Avenue,
Maxwell Park,
Glasgow, G41 1DP
Tel: 0141-424-0109

Mr. D. Wood, *President*

Scottish Federation of Egg Packers

Suite 101,
Albany House,
324–326 Regent Street,
London, W1R 5AA
Tel: 0171-580-7172   Fax: 0171-580-7082

M. Ring, *Secretary* *

Scottish Federation of Grocers' & Wine Merchants' Association

3 Loaning Road,
Edinburgh, EH7 6JE
Tel: 0131-652-2482   Fax: 0131-652-2896

L. Dewar, *Director*

Scottish Federation of Housing Associations (SFHA)

38 York Place,
Edinburgh, EH1 3HU
Tel: 0131-556-5777   Fax: 0131-557-6028

Mr. David Orr, *Director*

The representative body for Scottish housing associations and co-operatives. Its activities include training events; development of housing policy and legislation; campaigning; production of codes of practice; equal opportunities; information and advice to members. *

Scottish Federation of Meat Traders' Association

8 Needless Road,
Perth, PH2 0JW
Tel: 01738-37785   Fax: 01738-441059

Scottish Federation of Merchant Tailors

5 Portland Place,
London, W1N 3AA

Scottish Federation of Organists

7 Laird Street,
Coatbridge, ML5 3LJ
Tel: 01236-424553

Stewart Alston, *Secretary*

Scottish Federation of Sea Anglers

Caledonia House,
South Gyle,
Edinburgh, EH12 9DQ
Tel: 0131-317-7192   Fax: 0131-317-7192

Mr. David Wilkie, *Secretary/Administrator*

Recognised by the Scottish Sports Council as the governing body for the sport of sea angling in Scotland. *

Scottish Fencing

The Cockburn Centre,
40 Bogmoor Place,
Glasgow, G51 4TQ
Tel: 0141-445-1602   Fax: 0141-445-1602

Mr. C. Grahamslaw, *Administrator*

The national governing body for the sport of fencing in Scotland. *

Scottish Field Archery Association

125 Dewar Street,
Dunfermline,
Fife, KY12 8B
Tel: 01383-738561

Mrs. V. Catignani, *Secretary*

Scottish Field Studies Association

Kindrogan Field Centre,
Enochdhu,
Blairgowrie,
Perthshire, PH10 7PG
Tel: 01250-881286   Fax: 01250-881433

Ms. Alison Gimingham, *Director*

The Association provides facilities and training for anyone wanting to study anything to do with the countryside. Courses and conferences are based at Kindrogan Field Centre. e-mail: Kindrogan@btinternet.com. *

Scottish Financial Enterprise

94 George Street,
Edinburgh, EH2 3ES
Tel: 0131-225-6990   Fax: 0131-220-1353

James Scott, *Executive Director*

Scottish Fire Service Training School

Gullane,
East Lothian, EH31 2HG
Tel: 01620-842236   Fax: 01620-843045

D. Grant, *Commandant**

Scottish Fish Merchants Federation

South Esplanade West,
Aberdeen, AB9 2FJ
Tel: 01224-897744   Fax: 01224-871405

R. Grant *

Scottish Fisheries Museum

Harbourhead,
Anstruther,
Fife, KY10 3AB
Tel: 01333-310628

Scottish Fisheries Protection Agency

Pentland House,
47 Robb's Loan,
Edinburgh, EH14 1TY
Tel: 0131-556-8400

Capt. P.E. Du Vivier, *Chief Executive*

Scottish Fishermen's Federation

14 Regent Quay,
Aberdeen, AB1 2DE
Tel: 01224-582583   Fax: 01224-574958

Scottish Fishermen's Organisation

Braehead,
601 Queensferry Road,
Edinburgh, EH4 6EA
Tel: 0131-339-7972   Fax: 0131-339-6662

Mr. Eric Gibson, *Administration Officer*

Scottish Fishery Group

30/6 Elbe Street,
Edinburgh, EH6 7HN
Tel: 0131-555-0660   Fax: 0131-554-5902

Crick Carleton

Scottish Flour Millers Association

26 Newtyle Road,
Ralston,
Paisley, PA1 3JX
Tel: 0141-889-3660   Fax: 0141-887-3277

Maurice Crichton, *Secretary*

Scottish Food Studies Group

The Food Monitor,
24 Park Circus,
Glasgow, G3 6AP
Tel: 0141-331-1460   Fax: 0141-332-2460

Ms. Shona Hunter

Scottish Football Association

see The Scottish Football Association

Scottish Football League

see The Scottish Football League

Scottish Football Managers & Coaches Association

Raith Rovers Football Club,
Starks Park,
Pratt Street,
Kirkcaldy, KY1 1SA
Tel: 01592-263514   Fax: 01592-642833

Mr. Alex Smith, *Chairman*

Scottish Forestry Trust

5 Dublin Street Lane South,
Edinburgh, EH1 3PX
Tel: 0131-478-7044   Fax: 0131-538-7222

Dr. David A. Rook, *Director*

The Scottish Forestry Trust is a charitable trust established in 1983 to promote research, education and training in forestry. The Trust's primary objective is to support the British forestry industry which includes all aspects of forestry, timber production, marketing of wood, landscape, recreation, wildlife and the environment. *

Scottish Forum for Development Education in Schools

Old Playhouse Close,
Moray House Institute of Education,
Holyrood Road,
Edinburgh, EH8 8AQ
Tel: 0131-557-3810   Fax: 0131-556-8239

Robin Lloyd-Jones, *Coordinator*

SFDES is a network of organisations working to promote, in schools, global concerns and issues of justice and equality in an interdependent world. *

Scottish Forum for Graduate Education

Department of Social Anthropology,
University of Edinburgh,
Adam Ferguson Building,
George Square,
Edinburgh, EH8 9LL

Professor Anthony Cohen, *Convener*

Scottish Foundation

25–27 Elmbank Street,
Glasgow, G2 4PB
Tel: 0141-226-3431

Scottish Foundation for Kidney Disease

Eldon House,
74 Townhead,
Kirkintilloch,
Glasgow, G66 1NZ
Tel: 0141-777-7990   Fax: 0141-776-4720

Ms. Lynne Craig, *Director*

Scottish Foundation for Surgery in Nepal

University Department of Surgery,
Royal Infirmary,
Edinburgh, EH3 9YW
Tel: 0131-228-1783   Fax: 0131-228-2661

Professor Sir David Carter, *Chairman*

Our aims are to enable young Nepalese surgeons to come to this country for surgical training and to support the development of surgery in that country. *

Scottish Freshwater Group

Easter Cringate Cottage,
Stirling, FK7 9QX
Tel: 01786-451312

Dr. Peter Maitland, *Secretary*

Scottish Friends of Palestine

134 Ingleby Drive,
Glasgow, G31 2PP

Scottish Fuel Poverty Action Forum

26 Bridge Crescent,
Denny, FK6 6DO
Tel: 01324-824623

Scottish Furniture Manufacturers' Association

Merchants House Buildings,
30 George Square,
Glasgow, G2 1EG
Tel: 0141-248-2375   Fax: 0141-248-2362

A. Grahame Thomson

Scottish Furniture Trades Benevolent Association

30 George Square,
Glasgow, G2 1EQ

Scottish Further Education Guidance Association

Wester Hailes Opportunity Trust,
Unit 20D,
Wester Hailes Shopping Centre,
Edinburgh, EH14 2SW
Tel: 0131-442-4252

Evelyn Mills, *Secretary*

Scottish Further Education Unit

Argyll Court,
The Castle Business Park,
Stirling, FK9 4TY
Tel: 01786-892000   Fax: 01786-892001

Ms. Alison Reid, *Chief Executive*

SFEU, established in 1991, supports development in Scottish further education through key services, training, consultancy and advice, professional network operation, information processing and project management. Website is: http://www.sfeu.org.uk. *

Scottish Further and Higher Education Association

Gordon Chambers,
90 Mitchell Street,
Glasgow, G1 3NQ
Tel: 0141-221-0118   Fax: 0141-221-2583

Eric H. Smith, *General Secretary*

Scottish Gaelic Text Society

Department of Celtic,
University of Glasgow,
Glasgow, G12 8QQ
Tel: 0141-339-8855

Mr. J.W. Gleasure

Scottish Games Association

24 Florence Place,
Perth, PH1 5BH
Tel: 01738-627782   Fax: 01738-639622

Andrew Rettie, *Honorary Secretary*

The Scottish Games Association is the governing body for Highland and Border Games which are held throughout Scotland between May and September each year. *

Scottish Genealogy Society

Library and Family History Centre
15 Victoria Terrace,
Edinburgh, EH1 2JL
Tel: 0131-220-3677   Fax: 07070-713411

Honorary Secretary

Promotes research into Scottish family history. Publishes The Scottish Genealogist *quarterly and other material. Monthly meetings are held September to April.* *

Scottish Geotechnical Group

c/o 13 Eglinton Crescent,
Edinburgh, EH12 5DF
Tel: 0131-337-3213

I. McDonald

Scottish Glass Association

13 Woodside Crescent,
Glasgow, G3 7UP
Tel: 0141-332-7144   Fax: 0141-331-1684

Mr. J.A. Williams, *Secretary*

Scottish Glass Society

32 Farington Street,
Dundee, DD2 1PF
Tel: 01382-669864

Jack Searle

The SGS aims to develop the art and craft of glassmaking in Scotland. Its membership is open to all who have an interest in this objective. *

Scottish Gliding Association

Roselea,
Drum Road,
Keith, AB55 5ER
Tel: 01542-887585   Fax: 01358-789080

Mr. John Thomson, *Secretary*

Scottish Gliding Centre (SGU Limited)

see The Scottish Gliding Centre (SGU Limited)

Scottish Golf Course Wildlife Group

Scottish Natural Heritage,
Landscape & Restoration Branch,
2 Anderson Place,
Edinburgh, EH6 5NP

Scottish Golf Union

Scottish National Golf Centre,
Drumoig,
Leuchars,
St Andrews, KY16 0DW

Mr. E. Barnard, *President*

Scottish Golfers' Alliance

5 Deveron Avenue,
Giffnock,
Glasgow, G46 6NH
Tel: 0141-638-2066

Mrs. M.A. Caldwell, *Secretary & Treasurer*

The membership of the Scottish Golfers' Alliance comprises amateurs and professionals with other affiliated Alliances. *

Scottish Gospel Outreach

39 Meadowpark Street,
Glasgow, G31 2SA
Tel: 0141-554-0048

Scottish Great Dane Club

The Gables,
Bellevue Avenue,
Kirkintilloch,
Glasgow, G66 1AJ
Tel: 0141-776 3665/4390   Fax: 0141-776-3665

Mrs. J. Christie, *Secretary*

The object of the Club is to encourage and foster interest in the breed in Scotland and a free list of member/breeders resident in Scotland is available. One championship and two open shows are held annually. New members are welcome. *

Scottish Green Party

11 Greenbank Terrace,
Edinburgh, EH10 6ER
Tel: 0131-556-5160   Fax: 0131-447-1843

Mr. Robin Harper

The Scottish Green Party's purpose is to work to create a non-violent, democratic, just and sustainable society and contest elections to all levels of Government. We can also be contacted at P.O. Box 14080, Edinburgh, EH10 6YG. e-mail: scot.green@clan.com. *

Scottish Green Student Network

c/o Edinburgh University Green Society,
60 The Pleasance,
Edinburgh, EH8 9TG

Secretary

Scottish Grocers' Federation

Federation House,
3 Loaning Road,
Edinburgh, EH7 6JE
Tel: 0131-652-2482   Fax: 0131-652-2896

Lawrie Dewar, *Chief Executive*

Scottish Grocery Trade Employers' Association

3 Loaning Road,
Restalrig,
Edinburgh, EH7 6JE
Tel: 0131-652-2482

General Secretary

Scottish Gymnastics Association

8b Melville Street,
Falkirk, FK1 1HZ
Tel: 01324-612308   Fax: 01324-612309

Administration Manager

The governing body for gymnastics in Scotland. *

Scottish Gypsy/Traveller Association

Wilkie House,
37 Guthrie Street,
Edinburgh, EH1 1JG
Tel: 0131-650-6308   Fax: 0131-650-6310

Ms. Ruth Stewart, *Coordinator*

Scottish Handball Association

5 Skye Court,
Ravenswood,
Cumbernauld, G67 1PA
Tel: 01236-730720

Ms. Melanie Menzies, *Secretary*

Scottish Handmade Cheesemakers Association

Walston Braehead Farm,
Carnwath,
Lanarkshire, ML11 8NF
Tel: 01899-810257   Fax: 01899-810257

Humphrey Errington

Scottish Hang Gliding & Paragliding Federation

54 Culloden Road,
Balloch,
Inverness, IV1 2NH
Tel: 01463-793869

Mrs. I. Carson, *Secretary*

This is a federation of hang gliding and paragliding clubs in Scotland which aims to develop the sport in Scotland and support clubs and individuals. *

Scottish Hardwood Charter

Linwood Industrial Estate,
Linwood,
Renfrewshire, PA3 3BD
Tel: 01505-329124   Fax: 01505-328147

Mr. J. David Norman, *Co-Founder*

Environmental charity set up by David Norman and Professor David Bellamy in order to create more awareness of the problems surrounding tropical hardwood production. *

Scottish Health Advisory Service

Trinity Park House,
South Trinity Road,
Edinburgh, EH5 3SE
Tel: 0131-552-6255

Dr. S. Grant, *Director*

Scottish Health Education Board for Scotland

Woodburn House,
Canaan Lane,
Edinburgh, EH10 4SG
Tel: 0131-447-8044

Scottish Health Information Network (SHINE)

The Library,
The Development Group,
Scottish Health Service Centre,
Crewe Road South,
Edinburgh, EH4 2LF
Tel: 0131-623-2535

Maureen Thom, *President*

Scottish Health Visitors' Association

94 Constitution Street,
Leith,
Edinburgh, EH6 6AW
Tel: 0131-553-4061   Fax: 0131-553-4061

Mr. D.F. Forbes

Scottish Heart Valve Action Group

Flat 1/3,
197 Main Street,
Rutherglen,
Glasgow, G73 2HG
Tel: 0141-647-4509

Mrs. Susan Smith

Scottish Heart and Arterial Disease Risk Prevention (SHARP)

University Department of Medicine,
Ninewells Hospital & Medical School,
Dundee, DD1 9SY
Tel: 01382-660111   Fax: 01382-660675

Dr. Shirley McEwan, MBE

The aim of SHARP is to promote the prevention of cardiovascular disease in Scotland by education of health care professionals and by research. *

Scottish Higher Education Funding Council

Donaldson House,
97 Haymarket Terrace,
Edinburgh, EH12 5HD
Tel: 0131-313-6500   Fax: 0131-313-6501

Ms. Julia Amour, *Head of Corporate Affairs*

The Scottish Higher Education Funding Council was established in June, 1992 to provide financial support for teaching, research and associated activities in 21 Scottish higher education institutions. *

Scottish Hill Runners Association

3 Haywood Drive,
Galashiels,
Borders, TD1 3JB
Tel: 01896-58894

Mr. Alan Farningham, *Secretary*

Scottish Historic Buildings Trust

Saltcoats,
Gullane,
East Lothian, EH31 2AG
Tel: 01620-842757   Fax: 01620-842757

Mr. John Clare

A charitable trust which acquires, repairs and funds new uses for buildings of architectural or historic interest throughout Scotland. *

Scottish History Society

c/o Department of Scottish History,
University of Edinburgh,
17 Buccleuch Place,
Edinburgh, EH8 9LN
Tel: 0131-650-4035

Dr. S.I. Boardman, *Honorary Secretary**

Scottish Hockey Union

48 Pleasance,
Edinburgh, EH8 9TJ
Tel: 0131-650-8170   Fax: 0131-650-8169

Mrs. Lesley Giblin

Scottish Holstein Friesian Breeders' Club

7 Gallowhill Farm Cottages,
Lesmahagow Road,
Strathaven,
Lanarkshire, ML10 6BZ
Tel: 01357-523016

Ms. Aileen Neilson, *Secretary*

The Scottish Holstein Friesian Breeders' Club aims to promote agriculture by the encouragement, promotion and improvement of the breeding of Holstein Friesian cattle in the UK, Northern Ireland and Republic of Ireland with particular reference to Scotland. *

Scottish Homes

Thistle House,
91 Haymarket Terrace,
Edinburgh, EH12 5HE
Tel: 0131-313-0044   Fax: 0131-313-2680

Mr. Peter McKinlay, *Chief Executive*

Scottish Homes is the Government's National Housing Agency for Scotland, set up in 1989 to improve the quality and variety of housing in Scotland. *

Scottish Homing Union

231a Low Waters Road,
Hamilton, ML3 7QW
Tel: 01698-286983

Ms. Linda Brooks, *Secretary*

The governing body of racing pigeon fanciers in Scotland. *

Scottish Hospital Endowments Research Trust

16 Hope Street,
Edinburgh, EH2 4DB
Tel: 0131-226-2561

Scottish Hotel School

see The Scottish Hotel School

Scottish House Furnishers' Federation

203 Pitt Street,
Glasgow, G2 4DB
Tel: 0141-332-6381

Scottish House-Builders Association

Carron Grange,
Carrongrange Avenue,
Stenhousemuir, FK5 3BQ

Mr. S.C. Patten, *Director* *

Scottish Housing Associations Charitable Trust (SHACT)

38 York Place,
Edinburgh, EH1 3HU
Tel: 0131-556-5777   Fax: 0131-557-6028

Ms. Alison Rigg Campbell

SHACT is a fund-raising trust which supports housing-related projects in Scotland by making grants and interest-free loans to voluntary organisations and housing associations. *

Scottish Human Computer Interaction Centre

Department of Computer Science,
Heriot Watt University,
Riccarton,
Edinburgh, EH14 4AS

Professor A.C. Kilgour, *Director*

Scottish Human Rights Centre (SHRC)

146 Holland Street,
Glasgow, G2 4NG
Tel: 0141-332-5960   Fax: 0141-332-5309

Mr. Douglas Hamilton, *Administrator/Rights Officer*

Scottish Human Rights Centre promotes human rights in Scotland through advice and education, research, scrutiny of legislation and monitoring the application of international human rights treaties. *

Scottish Huntington's Association

Thistle House,
61 Main Road,
Elderslie,
Johnstone, PA5 9BA
Tel: 01505-322245   Fax: 01505-382980

Mrs. Ann Carruthers

To provide support to carers, sufferers and people 'at risk' of developing H.D. The aim is to provide H.D. advisory services throughout Scotland. *

Scottish Ice Hockey Association

Glenburn House,
21 Braeburn Drive,
Currie, EH14 6AQ
Tel: 0131-449-3163

Mrs. Aileen Robertson

Scottish Ice Skating Association

c/o The Ice Sports Centre,
Riversdale Crescent,
Edinburgh, EH12 5XN
Tel: 0131-337-3976

Mr. I. Mizen, *Administrator*

Scottish Independent Special Schools Group (SISSG)

Starley Hall School,
Aberdour Road,
Burntisland,
Fife, KY3 0AG
Tel: 01383-860314   Fax: 01383-860956

Mr. Phil Barton, *Chairman* *

Scottish Indoor Bowling Association

41 Montfode Court,
Ardrossan,
Strathclyde, KA22 7NJ
Tel: 01294-468372   Fax: 01294-605937

Mr. James Barclay, *Honorary Secretary*

Scottish Industrial Heritage Society

c/o Falkirk Museum Stores,
7/11 Abbotsinch Road,
Grangemouth, FK3 9UX

Ms. Carol Whittaker, *Chair*

The Society believes that Scotland's industrial heritage is important, not only historically but also because of its influence on the current industrial scene. e-mail: sihs@aol.com. Website: http://www.members.aol.com/sihs/. *

Scottish Industrial Sports Association

34 Caroline Terrace,
Edinburgh, EH12 8QX

Allan G. Shaw, *Secretary*

Scottish Inland Waterways Association (SIWA)

1 Craiglockhart Crescent,
Edinburgh, EH14 1EZ
Tel: 0131-443-2533

G.A. Hunter, *Secretary*

The Association co-ordinates the activities of all the Canal Societies in Scotland and organises 'clean ups' of the canal system. *

Scottish Institute for Wood Technology

University of Abertay Dundee,
Bell Street,
Dundee, DD1 1HG
Tel: 01382-308930   Fax: 01382-308663

Dr. Derek Sinclair, *Technical Director*

The SIWT provides research and technical services for producers and users of forest products. Services include management of forest and non-forest products-based scientific projects. *

Scottish Institute of Human Relations

56 Albany Street,
Edinburgh, EH1 3QR
Tel: 0131-556-0924   Fax: 0131-556-2612

Mr. A. Coyne, *Management Development Officer*

Scottish Institute of Maritime Studies

University of St. Andrews,
St. Andrews, KY16 9AJ
Tel: 01334-476161

Dr. C.J.M. Martin

Scottish Institute of Reflexology

15 Hazel Park,
Silverton Hill,
Hamilton,
Lanarkshire, ML3 7HH
Tel: 01698-427962   Fax: 01698-427962

Mrs. Ann L. McCaig, RGN, GSSR

*The Institute was established in 1987 to
provide a professional organisation for
qualified and student reflexologists, and to
promote, maintain and monitor the highest
standards among its members. **

Scottish Institute of Sports Medicine and Sports Science (SISMSS)

University of Strathclyde,
Jordanhill Campus,
76 Southbrae Drive,
Glasgow, G13 1PP
Tel: 0141-950-3189   Fax: 0141-950-3175

*The Institute's aim is to promote the quality of
sporting endeavour in Scotland through the
provision of the best available sports medicine
and sports science services. e-mail:
SISMSS@strath.ac.uk. Web site: http://
www.strath.ac.uk/Departments/SISMSS/. **

Scottish International Children's Festival

22 Laurie Street,
Edinburgh, EH6 7AB
Tel: 0131-554-6297   Fax: 0131-555-1304

Ms. Jayne Gross, *Development Manager*

*The most successful, unique, artistic event for
the under-15s in the UK. The best theatre
from all over the world plays yearly to an
average audience of 30,000 people. **

Scottish International Education Trust

22 Manor Place,
Edinburgh, EH3 7DS
Tel: 0131-225-1113

John F. McClellan

*To help fund the advanced education of
individual Scots and to support projects likely
to be of economic, social, cultural or environmental benefit to Scotland. **

Scottish International Foundation Programme

Hunter Hall East,
University of Glasgow,
Glasgow, G12 8QQ
Tel: 0141-330-5955   Fax: 0141-330-5558

Dr. A.J. Baker, *Director*

*The Scottish International Foundation
Programme, sponsored by the 13 Scottish
universities and Queen Margaret College,
provides pre-university courses of education to
'highers' standard for international students
wishing to enter university degree study. e-
mail: SIFP@gla.ac.uk. **

Scottish International Relief

Unit 9, 89 Vermont Street,
Glasgow, G41 1LU
Tel: 0141-429-1212   Fax: 0141-429-1212

Mr. Magnus MacFarlane-Barrow, *Director*

SIR is a registered charity which delivers aid to Bosnia, Croatia, Romania and Liberia to help those suffering the effects of war and poverty. *

Scottish International Resource Programme

British Council,
3 Bruntsfield Crescent,
Edinburgh, EH10 4HD
Tel: 0131-452-9789   Fax: 0131-452-9757

Mr. Mark Simmons, *Project Manager*

SIRP enables Scottish companies to work on projects with key future business contacts for mutual benefit, identify overseas managers currently in Scotland to undertake postgraduate work. *

Scottish Italian Association

804 Crow Road,
Glasgow, G13 1LY
Tel: 0141-959-9342

Scottish Jazz Network

18 Albion Street,
Glasgow, G1 1LH
Tel: 0141-552-3223

Ian Middleton

Scottish Jewish Archives Centre

Garnethill Synagogue
127 Hill Street,
Glasgow, G3 6UB
Tel: 0141-332-4911 and 0141-649-4526

Harvey Kaplan

Contains information, documents, photographs, literature, etc. pertaining to the history of the Jewish community in Scotland. *

Scottish Joint Action Group (SJAG)

Holyrood,
Innellan,
Dunoon,
Argyll, PA23 7SP
Tel: 01369-830429

Ms. Lorna Ahlquist, *Chairperson*

Scottish Joint Committee on Religious and Moral Education

Church of Scotland,
121 George Street,
Edinburgh, EH2 4YN
Tel: 0131-225-5722   Fax: 0131-220-3899

Rev. J. Stevenson, *Joint Secretary*

The Committee's aim and objective is the promotion of religious education, religious studies and moral education in schools and in further and higher education. *

Scottish Joint Consultative Committee for Building

Bush House,
Bush Estate,
Midlothian, EH26 0SB
Tel: 0131-445-5580

R.L. Dyer, *Scottish Secretary*

Scottish Joint Industry Board for the Electrical Contracting Industry

Bush House,
Bush Estate,
Midlothian, EH26 0SB
Tel: 0131-445-5577   Fax: 0131-445-5548

D.D.W. Montgomery

Scottish Joint Negotiating Committee for Teaching Staff in Further Education – Management Side

Rosebery House,
9 Haymarket Terrace,
Edinburgh, EH12 5XZ
Tel: 0131-346-1222

Scottish Joint Negotiating Committee for Teaching Staff in Further Education – Teachers' Side

46 Moray Place,
Edinburgh, EH3 6BH
Tel: 0131-225-6244

Scottish Ju-Jitsu Association

3 Dens Street,
Dundee, DD4 8BU
Tel: 01382-458262   Fax: 01382-458262

Robert G. Ross, *General Secretary*

The SJJA is the governing body for ju-jitsu in Scotland. It controls, regulates and promotes the sport and practice of ju-jitsu. *

Scottish Jubilee 2000 Campaign

Church of Scotland,
121 George Street,
Edinburgh, EH2 4YN
Tel: 0131-225-5722

Ms. Liz Hendry, *Scottish Coordinator*

Jubilee 2000 campaigns, both nationally and internationally, for the cancellation of the unpayable backlog of debt owed by the world's poorest countries by the end of the year 2000, under a clear, fair and transparent process on a case by case basis. *

Scottish Judo Federation

Caledonia House,
South Gyle,
Edinburgh, EH12 9DQ
Tel: 0131-317-7270   Fax: 0131-317-7050

Mr. C. McIver, *Chief Exeuctive*

Scottish Junior Football Association

46 St. Vincent Crescent,
Glasgow, G3 8NG
Tel: 0141-248-1095   Fax: 0141-248-1130 *

Scottish Karate Board

2 Strathdee Road,
Netherlee,
Glasgow, G44 3TJ
Tel: 0141-633-1116   Fax: 0141-633-1116

Mr. J.A. Miller, *Secretary*

Scottish Keep Fit Association

Caledonian House,
South Gyle Road,
Edinburgh, EH12 9DQ
Tel: 0131-317-7243

Scottish Kennel Club

3 Brunswick Place,
Edinburgh, EH7 5HP
Tel: 0131-557-2877   Fax: 0131-556-6784

Ian Allan Sim, *Secretary General*

Club with open membership, dedicated to promotion and encouragement of the improvement and well-being of dogs. Principal Scottish source of canine information through breeders' registers. *

Scottish Kippers and Herring Fishers Association

1 East Craibstone Street,
Aberdeen, AB9 1YH
Tel: 01224-581581

Scottish Knitwear Association

64 Toll Road,
Kincardine,
Alloa, FK10 4QZ
Tel: 01259-730357

Scottish Labour Action,

7 Burngreen,
Kilsyth, G65 0AG

Mr. Ian S. Smart, *Secretary*

Scottish Labour History Society

Department of Scottish History,
University of Glasgow,
9 University Gardens,
Glasgow, G12 8QH
Tel: 0141-339-8855

Ms. Irene Mavor, *Treasurer*

Scottish Labour Party

Delta House,
50 West Nile Street,
Glasgow, G1 iNA
Tel: 0141-572-6900   Fax: 0141-572-2566

The Scottish Labour Party is Scotland's largest political party with the highest lay member-ship; majority of MPs, MEPs and local councillors. *

Scottish Labour Women's Caucus

112 Camphill Avenue,
Glasgow, G41 3DU

Scottish Lace and Window Furnishings Association

1 Craigview Road,
Newmilns, KA16 9DQ
Tel: 01560-20041

Scottish Lacrosse Association

c/o St. Leonard's School,
St. Andrews, KY16 9QU
Tel: 01334-475149   Fax: 01334-4761512

Mrs. J. Caithness, *Secretary*

Scottish Ladies' Golfing Association – County Golf

Scottish National Golf Centre,
Drumoig,
Leuchars,
St. Andrews, KY16 0DW
Tel: 01382-549502   Fax: 01382-549512

Mrs. Susan Simpson, SLGA office

National organisation for ladies' amateur golf in Scotland. *

Scottish Land Court

1 Grosvenor Crescent,
Edinburgh, EH12 5ER
Tel: 0131-225-3595   Fax: 0131-226-4812

K.H.R. Graham, *Principal Clerk*

The Scottish Land Court has a variety of statutory jurisdictions to deal with disputes between landlords and tenants/crofters of agricultural holdings of various sizes through-out Scotland. *

Scottish Land Use Association

c/o Macaulay Land Use Research Institute,
Craigiebuckler,
Aberdeen, AB9 2QJ
Tel: 01224-318611   Fax: 01224-324880

Dr. P. Newbould, *Acting Chairman*

Scottish Landowners Federation

25 Maritime Street,
Leith,
Edinburgh, EH6 5PW
Tel: 0131-555-1031   Fax: 0131-555-1052

Dr. Maurice S. Hankey, *Director* *

Scottish Law Agents' Society

Signet Library,
Parliament Square,
Edinburgh, EH1 1RF
Tel: 0131-225-5051   Fax: 0131-225-5051

Mrs. J.H. Webster, *Secretary* *

Scottish Law Commission

140 Causewayside,
Edinburgh, EH9 1PR
Tel: 0131-668-2131   Fax: 0131-662-4900

Mr. W. Barclay, *Chief Clerk*

Scottish Law Librarians Group

c/o Royal Institution of Chartered Surveyors in Scotland,
9 Manor Place,
Edinburgh, EH3 7DN
Tel: 0131-225-7078   Fax: 0131-226-3599

Ms. Judith Lowe, *Secretary*

Membership consists of information professionals concerned with legal and commercial information provision, and are committed to promoting and advancing continuing professional development for their members, both in public and private practice. *

Scottish Lawn Tennis Association

177 Colinton Road,
Edinburgh, EH14 1BZ
Tel: 0131-444-1984   Fax: 0131-444-1973

Ms. Gloria Grosset, *Secretary*

Scottish League for Land Value Taxation

17 Elm Road,
Parkhall,
Clydebank, G81 3PW
Tel: 01389-875329   Fax: 0141-339 3911

Ian Sillars, *Secretary*

Ground rent/site value taxation campaign to secure for society unearned rents arising from public investment, subsidies, regulations and planning permission presently enjoyed exclusively by landowners. *

Scottish Learning Difficulties Association

53 Craw Road,
Paisley, PA2 6AE
Tel: 0141-889-7540

Mrs. I. Whyte, *Secretary*

Scottish Leather Producers' Association

c/o Anderson Fyfe,
90 St. Vincent Street,
Glasgow, G2 5UB
Tel: 0141-248-4381   Fax: 0141-204-1418

Scottish Legal Action Group (SCOLAG)

11th floor,
Fleming House,
134 Renfrew Street,
Glasgow, G3 6ST
Tel: 0141-353-3354   Fax: 0141-353-0354

Mr. Mike Dailly, *Editor*

Scottish Legal Aid Board

44 Drumsheugh Gardens,
Edinburgh, EH3 7SW
Tel: 0131-226-7061   Fax: 0131-220-4878

R. Scott, *Chief Executive*

The Scottish Legal Aid Board is responsible for ensuring that legal aid is made available to those who quality for it. *

Scottish Legal Education Trust

2 Abercromby Place,
Edinburgh, EH13 6JZ
Tel: 0131-556-4116   Fax: 0131-556-1624

Scottish Legal Services Ombudsman

2 Greenside Lane,
Edinburgh, EH1 3AH
Tel: 0131-556-5574   Fax: 0131-556-1519

Garry S. Watson, *Ombudsman*

The Scottish Legal Services Ombudsman investigates complaints about the way in which the professional legal bodies have handled the investigation of complaints against their members. *

Scottish Liberal Democrats

4 Clinton Terrace,
Edinburgh, EH12 5DR
Tel: 0131-337-2314

Scottish Library & Information Council

74 Victoria Crescent Road,
Glasgow, G12 9DE
Tel: 0141-357-5004

Scottish Library Association

1 John Street,
Hamilton, ML3 7EU
Tel: 01698-458888   Fax: 01698-458899

Robert Craig, *Director*

The SLA provides professional support for librarians/information officers in Scotland, including the development and promotion of standards and guidelines, continuing professional development, publications and advice to members.

Scottish Licensed Trade Association

10 Walker Street,
Edinburgh, EH3 7LA
Tel: 0131-225-5169   Fax: 0131-220-4057

Scottish Light Clothing Manufacturers' Association

Hargreaves Flooring,
Unit 13, Castleplace,
Bankside Industrial Estate,
Falkirk, FK2 7XB
Tel: 01324-611152

Scottish Liver Network

P.O. Box 14466,
Glenrothes,
Fife, KY7 6WA
Tel: 01573-470359   Fax: 01573-470359

Ms. Feyona McFarlane

Part of the British Liver Trust, this organisation aims to 'fight all liver disease'. Confidential information/support is offered and contact with nearest support group or help in starting group is available. *

Scottish Local Government Information Unit

Room 507,
Baltic Chambers,
50 Wellington Street,
Glasgow, G2 6HJ
Tel: 0141-226-4636   Fax: 0141-221-8786

Paolo Vestri, *Director*

SLGIU provides information and research services about local government issues. We publish a monthly bulletin, occasional guides and discussion papers and organise conferences and seminars. *

Scottish Local History Forum

128 Gowanbank,
Livingston,
Edinburgh, EH54 6EW
Tel: 01506-413554   Fax: 0131-225-8329

The Secretary

The Scottish Local History Forum is the umbrella organisation for local historians and local history societies in Scotland. *

Scottish Low Pay Unit

24 Sandyford Place,
Glasgow, G3 7NG
Tel: 0141-221-4491   Fax: 0141-221-6318

Ms. Morag Gillespie, *Director*

*Provides information and advice to low paid
workers and their advisers and training on
pay and employment rights. Conducts
research and campaign activities on low pay
issues.* *

Scottish Management Projects

Graham Hills Building,
University of Strathclyde,
40 George Sreet,
Glasgow, G1 1QE
Tel: 0141-552-1162   Fax: 0141-552-1331

Mr. Terry Lamb

*The leader in industry/university collaboration
for over 10 years. Visit our Web site to obtain
information on our collaborating marketing
scheme, training courses, consultancy and the
Scottish Marketing Awards. Website: http://
www.strath.ac.uk/org/SMP. e-mail:
t.lamb@strath.ac.uk.* *

Scottish Marine Trades' Association

18–20 Queens Road,
Aberdeen, AB15 4ZT
Tel: 01224-645454   Fax: 01224-644701

Iain Smith & Co., Solicitors, *Secretaries**

Scottish Maritime Museum Trust

Laird Forge Building,
Gottries Road,
Irvine, KA12 8QE
Tel: 01294-278283   Fax: 01294-313211

Jan Hay, *Customer Services Manager*

*The Trust is a company limited by guarantee,
which runs the Scottish Maritime Museum in
Irvine and outstation, Denny model ship
experiment tank, Dumbarton.* *

Scottish Marriage Care

50 Greenock Road,
Paisley, PA3 2LE
Tel: 0141-849-6183   Fax: 0141-849-6183

Mrs. Laura McGrath, *Executive Officer*

*An organisation whose purpose is to help people
prepare for, achieve and sustain successful
marriages and to support them if they break
down.* *

Scottish Marriage Guidance Council

58 Palmerston Place,
Edinburgh, EH12 5AZ
Tel: 0131-225-5006

Rev. J.G.M. Watt

Scottish Mask & Puppet Centre

8–10 Balcarres Avenue,
Kelvindale,
Glasgow, G12 0QF
Tel: 0141-339-6185   Fax: 0141-357-4484

Mr. Malcolm Yates Knight, *Honorary Secretary*

SMPC is the central information and advisory body for promotion of mask and puppet work in Scotland. It forms a link between professional puppeteers, educationalists, therapists and community arts workers. Charity no. SCO 14379. e-mail: sm010@post.almac.co.uk. *

Scottish Master Plasterers' Association

222 Queensferry Road,
Edinburgh, EH4 2BN
Tel: 0131-343-3300   Fax: 0131-315-2289

Mr. A. McKinney, *Secretary**

Scottish Master Slaters' & Roof Tilers' Association

13 Woodside Crescent,
Glasgow, G3 7UP
Tel: 0141-332-7144   Fax: 0141-331-1684

General Secretary

Scottish Master Wrights & Builders Association

26 West Nile Street,
Glasgow, G1 2PQ
Tel: 0141-221-0011   Fax: 0141-248-5117

John F. Lindsay, *Secretary*

Scottish Meat Wholesalers Association

Kinnaird Business and Consultancy
  Services,
The Old School House,
Kinnaird,
Perthshire, PH14 9QY
Tel: 01828-686116

Alan Stevenson, *Executive Manager*

Scottish Medical Aid for Cuba

7 Percy Street,
Glasgow, G51 1NZ

Jacki Kilpatrick

Scottish Medical Aid for Palestinians

73 Robertson Street,
Glasgow, G2 8DZ
Tel: 0141-204-1443

Scottish Medical Practices Committee

Room 023,
Trinity Park House,
South Trinity Road,
Edinburgh, EH5 3SE
Tel: 0131-551-8055

Mrs. Jean Crosbie, *Secretary*

Scottish Medical Research Fund

12 Hill Square,
Edinburgh, EH8 9DW
Tel: 0131-662-1084   Fax: 0131-662-4947

Scottish Meteorological Records

The Meteorological Office,
Saughton House,
Broomhouse Drive,
Edinburgh, EH11 3XQ
Tel: 0131-244-8368   Fax: 0131-244-8389

Mrs. E. Kerr

A collection of published literature and data on meteorology, climatology and atmospheric sciences. Also technical records of the weather in Scotland from 1857 to present. *

Scottish Militant Labour

P.O. Box 399,
Glasgow, G1 5BZ

Scottish Military History Society

4 Hillside Cottages,
Glenboig,
Lanarkshire, ML5 2QY

Thomas Moles, *Honorary Secretary* *

Scottish Milk Records Association

Underwood Road,
Paisley,
Renfrewshire, PA3 1TJ
Tel: 0141-848-0404   Fax: 0141-889-8819

Mr. Duncan Todd, *Director*

Scottish Milk Trade Federation

Thomson McLintock and Company,
Chartered Accountants,
216 West George Street,
Glasgow, G2 2PF
Tel: 0141-248-5181

Scottish Mining Disasters Relief Fund

c/o The Scottish Coal Co. Limited,
Castlebridge Colliery,
near Alloa, FK10 3PZ
Tel: 01259-730134   Fax: 01259-730351

Mr. Keith Donaldson, *Treasurer*

The Fund provides for relief of distress caused through accidents ocurring in the mining industry in Scotland. *

Scottish Mining Museum

Lady Victoria Colliery,
Newtongrange,
Midlothian, EH22 4QN
Tel: 0131-663-7519   Fax: 0131-654-1618

Ms. K. Lingstadt, *Curator**

Scottish Modern Pentathlon Association

10 (3F2) Montague Street,
Edinburgh, EH8 9QU
Tel: 0131-667-9945

Miss R. McFadden, *Secretary*

Scottish Mohair Producers Association

Mill of Thornton,
Old Meldrum,
Aberdeen
Tel: 01651-82253

Scottish Motor Neurone Disease Association

Unit 4,
76 Firhill Road,
Glasgow, G20 7BA
Tel: 0141-945-1077   Fax: 0141-945-2578

Ms. Jo Nimmo, *General Administrator*

Scottish Motor Racing Club

41 Fairfield Place,
East Kilbride, G74 5LP
Tel: 01355-265242

Scottish Motor Trade Association

3 Palmerston Place,
Edinburgh, EH12 5AF
Tel: 0131-225-3643   Fax: 0131-220-0446

D.R.W. Robertson, *Financial Manager/ Secretary*

Trade organisation representing the motor trade in Scotland.*

Scottish Mountain Leader Training Board

Glenmore,
Aviemore,
Inverness-shire, PH22 1QU
Tel: 01479-861248   Fax: 01479-861249

Mr. Allen Fyffe, *Secretary*

The SMLTB operates schemes of training and assessment for those engaged in leading others in the mountains of the UK in summer and winter.*

Scottish Mountaineering Club

4 Doune Terrace,
Edinburgh, EH3 6DY

Private mountaineering club with approximately 400 members and with extensive publications interest.*

Scottish Museums Council

County House,
20–22 Torphichen Street,
Edinburgh, EH3 8JB
Tel: 0131-229-7465   Fax: 0131-229-2728

Ms. Sarah Currier, *Librarian*

e-mail: inform@scottishmuseums.org.uk. *

Scottish Museums Federation

c/o Chatelherault,
Ferniegair,
by Hamilton,
Lanarkshire, ML3 7UE
Tel: 01698-894078

Mr. Robert Clark, *Secretary**

Scottish Music Education Forum

School of Music,
Northern College,
Hilton Place,
Aberdeen, AB24 4FA
Tel: 01224-283500   Fax: 01224-283900

Professor Jonathan Stephens

*A Forum for all societies/professional bodies
involved in aspects of music/music education
in Scotland. Its aims include information
exchange, promoting good practice and
enhancing its provision.* *

Scottish Music Hall Society

69 Langmuirhead Road,
Auchinloch,
Kirkintilloch, G66 5DS
Mr. Robert Bain

Tel: 0141-478-4108

*The Society exists to bring together people who
are interested in Scottish variety theatre past,
present and future.* *

Scottish Music Industry Association

P.O. Box 516,
Glasgow, G5 8PX
Tel: 0141-429-4174   Fax: 0141-420-1892

Scottish Music Information Centre

1 Bowmont Gardens,
Glasgow, G12 9LR
Tel: 0141-334-6393   Fax: 0141-337-1161

Kirsteen McCue

Scottish Music Therapy Council

c/o Music Therapy Department,
Herdmanflat Hospital,
Haddington,
East Lothian, EH41 3BU
Tel: 0131-536-8554

Ms. April Parkins, *Joint Coordinator*

*The Scottish branch of the Association of
Professional Music Therapists in Great
Britain provides a forum for sharing expertise
and promoting awareness of music therapy.* *

Scottish Musical Instrument Retailers' Association

M. & V. Taylor Music Shop,
212 Morrison Street,
Edinburgh, EH3 8EA
Tel: 0131-229-7454   Fax: 0141-353-3095

Scottish Musicians' Benevolent Fund

10 Manse Road,
Bearsden,
Glasgow, G61 3PT
Tel: 0141-942-1364   Fax: 0141-942-1364

Ms. Evelyn Bryson, *Honorary Secretary/ Treasurer*

Scottish National Association of Youth Theatres

Unit 106,
Stirling Enterprise Park,
John Player Building,
Stirling, FK7 7RP
Tel: 01786-449162

Gerry Ramage

A membership-led organisation committed to making drama accessible to all young people in Scotland regardless of geographic or economic circumstance. *

Scottish National Blood Transfusion Association (SNBTA)

2 Otterburn Park,
Edinburgh, EH14 1JX
Tel: 0131-443-7636

Mr. William Mack, *Secretary & Treasurer*

The Association protects the interest of voluntary donors of blood or bone marrow and ensures support and encouragement for Scottish National Blood Transfusion Service (SNBTS). *

Scottish National Blood Transfusion Service

Ellens Glen Road,
Edinburgh, EH17 7QT
Tel: 0131-664-2317

General Manager

Scottish National Camps Association

Dounans Outdoor Centre,
Aberfoyle,
Perthshire
Tel: 01877-382291

Scottish National Christian Endeavour Union

134 Wellington Street,
Glasgow, G2 2XL
Tel: 0141-332-1105

S

Scottish National Council of YMCAs

James Cove House,
11 Rutland Street,
Edinburgh, EH1 2AE
Tel: 0131-228-1464   Fax: 0131-228-5462

Mr. John Knox, *National General Secretary*

*A Christian organisation working throughout
Scotland providing a wide range of youth
work services including work with homelessness, drugs education, outdoor education,
creative arts and conference centres.* *

Scottish National Dictionary Association

27 George Square,
Edinburgh, EH8 9LD
Tel: 0131-650-4149   Fax: 0131-650-4149

Iseabail MacLeod, *Editorial Director*

*The Scottish National Dictionary Association
Limited was founded in 1929 to complete the
Scottish National Dictionary, since then it
has produced many other shorter dictionaries.
It also has a new research programme on the
Scots language.* *

Scottish National Federation for the Welfare of the Blind

P.O. Box 500,
Gillespie Crescent,
Edinburgh, EH10 4HZ
Tel: 0131-229-1456   Fax: 0131-229-4060

Mr. J.B.M. Munro, *Honorary Treasurer*

Scottish National Gallery of Modern Art

Belford Road,
Edinburgh, EH4 3DR
Tel: 0131-556-8921   Fax: 0131-343-2802

Mr. Richard Calvocoressi, *Keeper*

Scottish National Housing and Town Planning Council

62 Hawkhead Road,
Paisley, PA1 3NB
Tel: 0141-889-7056

J.M. Brown

Scottish National Institute for the War Blinded

P.O. Box 500,
Gillespie Crescent,
Edinburgh, EH10 4HZ
Tel: 0131-229-1456   Fax: 0131-229-4060

Mr. J.B.M. Munro

*Training, employment and aftercare for Scottish
ex-Services visually impaired.* *

Scottish National Party

6 North Charlotte Street,
Edinburgh, EH2 4JH
**Tel: 0131-226-3661   Fax: 0131-225-9397/
9774**

Michael Russell, *Chief Exec.*/Allison
Hunter, *Director*

*The Scottish National Party is a democratic
party which exists to benefit all the population of Scotland through the attainment of
independence.* *

Scottish National Portrait Gallery

1 Queen Street,
Edinburgh, EH2 1JD
Tel: 0131-556-8921 Fax: 0131-558-3691

Mr. Duncan Thomson, *Keeper*

Scottish National Ski Council (SNSC)

Caledonia House,
South Gyle,
Edinburgh, EH12 9DQ
Tel: 0131-317-7280 Fax: 0131-339-8602

Mr. Bruce Crawford, *Development Officer*

*SNSC is the national governing body for snowsports in Scotland. Membership is comprised of clubs, coaches, racers and individuals from all aspects of skiing and snowboarding. e-mail: admin@snsc.demon.co.uk. Web site: http:// www.snsc.demon.co.uk. ***

Scottish National Sweet Pea, Rose and Carnation Society

72 West George Street,
Coatbridge,
Lanarkshire, ML5 2DD

Scottish National Tribunal

22 Woodrow Road,
Glasgow, G41 5PN
Tel: 0141-427-3036

Rev. Dr. John Cunningham

Scottish National War Memorial

The Castle,
Edinburgh, EH1 2YT
Tel: 0131-226-7393

Scottish Natural Heritage

12 Hope Terrace,
Edinburgh, EH9 2AS
Tel: 0131-447-4784 Fax: 0131-446-2277

Mr. Roger Crofts, *Chief Executive*

Scottish Natural History Library

Foremount House,
Kilbarchan,
Renfrewshire, PA10 2EZ
Tel: 01505-702419

Dr. J.A. Gibson, *Chairman and Honorary Librarian*

Scottish Netball Association

Kelvin Hall,
Argyle Street,
Glasgow, G3 8AW
Tel: 0141-334-3650

Ms. Sharon McQueen, *Adminstrator*

Scottish Neuroscience Group

Gatty Marine Laboratories,
St. Andrew's University,
St. Andrews, KY16 9AJ
Tel: 01334-476161

Scottish Newspaper Publishers Association

48 Palmerston Place,
Edinburgh, EH12 5DE
Tel: 0131-220-4353   Fax: 0131-220-4344

J.B. Raeburn, *Director*

SNPA is the representative body for publishers of Scottish weekly newspapers. Its activities include marketing, representing the industry's interests to government and the provision of advisory services. *

Scottish Nursery Nurses' Examination Board

SQA,
Hanover House,
24 Douglas Street,
Glasgow, G2 7NQ
Tel: 0141-248-7900

Scottish Official Board of Highland Dancing

32 Grange Loan,
Edinburgh, EH9 2NR
Tel: 0131-668-3965   Fax: 0131-662-0404

Miss M. Rowan, *Director of Administration*

The world governing body for Highland dancing. *

Scottish Official Highland Dancing Association

36 High Street,
Dunbar,
East Lothian, EH42 1JH
Tel: 01368-863027

Mrs. Pauline Knox, *Secretary*

The SOHDA is a 'specialist' association which holds competitions, examinations, workshops, etc. Affiliated with many free-thinking dancing bodies worldwide, it is proud to welcome ALL dancers from every organisation without restrictions. *

Scottish Offshore Training Association Limited

Blackness Avenue,
Altens,
Aberdeen, AB1 4PG
Tel: 01224-899707   Fax: 01224-873221

N.G. Duggan, *Director*

Scottish Old Age Pensions Association (SOAPA)

c/o Age Concern Care & Repair,
54a Fountainbridge,
Edinburgh, EH3 9PT
Tel: 0131-229-1886

Mr. Jack Webster, *National Treasurer*

Scottish Old People's Welfare Council

113 Rose Street,
Edinburgh, EH2 3DT
Tel: 0131-220-3345

Scottish Opera for All

39 Elmbank Street,
Glasgow, G2 4PT
Tel: 0141-248-4567   Fax: 0141-221-8812

Jane Davidson

Scottish Opportunities

5th floor,
Portcullis House,
21 India Street,
Glasgow, G2 4PZ
Tel: 0141-226-4544   Fax: 0141-248-5068

Mr. Rick Rennie, *Director*

Scottish Orchid Society

20 Ancrum Road,
Dundee, DD2 2HZ
Tel: 01382-566953

Scottish Orienteering Association

Riversdale,
Slitrig Crescent,
Hawick, TD9 0EN
Tel: 01450-377383

Mrs. L. Knox, *Secretary*

Responsible for running and promoting the sport in Scotland. 20 clubs exist and details are available from the secretary. Fixture details available on the website: www.scottish_orienteering.org. *

Scottish Ornithologists' Club

21 Regent Terrace,
Edinburgh, EH7 5BT
Tel: 0131-556-6042   Fax: 0131-558-9947

Ms. Sylvia Laing, *Secretary*

The SOC has 14 branches and offers indoor meetings, field outings, and conferences. It also publishes Scottish Bird News, Scottish Birds, Scottish Bird Report *and* Raptor Roundup *and houses the best ornithological library in Scotland.* *

Scottish Out of School Care Network

Floor 9,
Fleming House,
134 Renfrew Street,
Glasgow, G3 6ST
Tel: 0141-331-1301   Fax: 0141-332-1206

Scottish Overseas Aid

35 Cedar Avenue,
Torbrex,
Stirling, FK8 2PQ
Tel: 01786-475989

Ms. Peggy Shatwell, *Secretary*

Scottish PAL ('Planning as Learning') Club

80 South Bridge,
Edinburgh, EH1 1HW
Tel: 0131-650-2732   Fax: 0131-650-6513

Howard Beck

Scottish Paragliding & Hang Gliding Federation

54 Culloden Road,
Balloch,
Inverness, IV1 2WH
Tel: 01463-793869

Mrs. I. Carson, *Secretary*

This is a federation of hang gliding and paragliding clubs in Scotland which aims to develop the sport and support clubs and individuals. *

Scottish Parent Teacher Council (SPTC)

63/65 Shandwick Place,
Edinburgh, EH2 4SD
Tel: 0131-228-5320/1   Fax: 0131-228-5320

Ms. Irene Ferguson, *Administrator*

SPTC is the national organisation for Parent and Parent Teacher Associations in Scotland. Over one thousand associations have membership. *

Scottish Partnership Agency for Palliative & Cancer Care

1a Cambridge Street,
Edinburgh, EH1 2DY
Tel: 0131-229-0538   Fax: 0131-228-2967

Mrs. M. Stevenson, *Director*

The Agency is a co-ordinating body which brings together voluntary and statutory organisations to work for improved palliative and cancer care services in Scotland. *

Scottish Passenger Agents Association

135 Wellington Street,
Glasgow, G2 2XE
Tel: 0141-248-3904   Fax: 0141-226-5047

L.J. McIntyre

Representing the retail travel industry in Scotland. *

Scottish Patriots

see The Scottish Patriots

Scottish Pekingese Association

154 Halbeath Road,
Dunfermline, KY11 4LB
Tel: 01383-724368

Mr. G.A.W. Baxter

Scottish Pelagic Fishermen's Association

21 Albert Street,
Aberdeen, AB25 1XX
Tel: 01224-632464   Fax: 01224-632184

James Slater or Denis Yule

To represent the interests of owners and share fishermen of pelagic fishing vessels in Scotland fishing principally for herring and mackerel. *

Scottish Pensioners' Forum

16 Woodlands Terrace,
Glasgow, G3 6DF
Tel: 0141-332-4946   Fax: 0141-332-4649

Ms. Ann Garscadden, *Administrator*

Scottish Permaculture

c/o Earthward,
Tweed Horizons,
Newton St. Boswells,
Roxburghshire, TD6 0SG
Tel: 01835-822122   Fax: 01835-822199

Graham Bell, *Director*

*Permaculture is a design system for creating
sustainable human settlements balancing
traditional knowledge and modern science.
Scottish Permaculture is a network of people
involved in projects implementing good design
to improve their land, garden, community or
business. **

Scottish Personnel Services

105 West George Street,
Glasgow, G2 1QL
Tel: 0141-221-4224   Fax: 0141-204-1202

E.J.P. Smith

*The non-engineering commercial arm of
Scottish Engineering, providing market-
leader high quality practical support services
in all aspects of employment. **

Scottish Pet Register

125 Kinnell Avenue,
Glasgow, G52 3RZ
Tel: 0141-883-0222

Scottish Petanque Association

1 Arbroath Crescent,
Causewayhead,
Stirling, FK9 5SQ
Tel: 01786-470619

Bob Boyle, *Secretary*

Scottish Pharmaceutical Federation

135 Wellington Street,
Glasgow, G2 2XD
Tel: 0141-221-1235   Fax: 0141-248-5892

F.E.J. McCrossin, *Secretary*

*SPF looks after the interests of 550 members
who own approximately 1,050 pharmacies
in Scotland. The SPF is affiliated to the
National Pharmaceutical Association. e-
mail: secretary@spf.netkonect.co.uk. **

Scottish Pharmaceutical General Council

34 York Place,
Edinburgh, EH1 3HU
Tel: 0131-556-2076

Dr. C. Virden

Scottish Pharmaceutical Sciences Group

Flat 21/4C Western Court,
Western Infirmary,
Dumbarton Road,
Glasgow, G11 6NT

Mrs. I. Cooper, *Honorary Secretary*

Scottish Pharmaceutical Standing Committee

42 Queen Street,
Edinburgh, EH2 3NH
Tel: 0131-467-7766   Fax: 0131-467-7767

Dr. C. Virden, *Secretary*

Scottish Philatelic Society

160 Muir Wood Road,
Currie,
Midlothian, EH14 5HQ
Tel: 0131-449-2345

H.J. Revell, *Secretary*

Scottish Physical Education Association

c/o Faculty of Education,
University of Strathclyde,
Jordanhill,
Glasgow, G13 1PP
Tel: 0141-959-1232

Scottish Pig Industry Initiative

Rural Centre,
West Mains,
Ingliston,
Midlothian, EH28 8NZ
Tel: 0131-335-3111   Fax: 0131-335-3800

Peter Brown, *Managing Director*

Scottish Pipers' Association

5 Barrington Drive,
Glasgow, G4 9DS

Miss B. MacDougall

Scottish Pistol Association

Sandhole,
Furnace,
Inveraray,
Argyll, PA32 8XU
Tel: 01499-500640   Fax: 01499-500640

Mr. & Mrs. McCarthy, *Joint Secretaries*

Scottish Plastering and Drylining Association

see Scottish Decorators' Federation

Scottish Plant Owners Association

see The Scottish Plant Owners Association

Scottish Poetry Library

Tweeddale Court,
14 High Street,
Edinburgh, EH1 1TE
Tel: 0131-557-2876

Ms. Tessa Ransford, *Director*

Free lending and reference library specialising in mainly 20th century Scottish and international poetry – books, magazines, tapes, newscuttings. Information service, van visits, computer indexes to poetry. *

Scottish Poisons Information Bureau

Royal Infirmary,
Edinburgh, EH3 9YW
Tel: 0131-536-2298   Fax: 0131-536-2304

Mrs. A.M. Good, *Information Officer*

The Scottish Poisons Information Bureau provides information on overdose and accidental poisoning, to medical professionals ONLY. *

Scottish Police College

Tulliallan Castle,
Kincardine,
Alloa,
Clackmannanshire, FK10 4BE
Tel: 01259-732000   Fax: 01259-732100

Mr. Hugh I. Watson, *Commandant*

Scottish Police Federation

5 Woodside Place,
Glasgow, G3 7QF
Tel: 0141-332-5234   Fax: 0141-331-2436

Scottish Polo Association

The Grange,
Cupar,
Fife, KY15 4QH
Tel: 01382-624234   Fax: 01382-330497

Captain M. Fox-Pitt, *Secretary*

Scottish Pomeranian Club

Hailstonemyre Cottage,
Ayr Road,
Larkhall,
Lanarkshire, ML9 3DW
Tel: 01698-791467

Miss C.M. McDowall

Club for supporters of Pomeranian breed of toy dogs; responsible for organisation of shows for the breed. *

Scottish Pool Association

3 Strath Gardens,
Dores,
Inverness, IV1 2TT
Tel: 01463-751282

Mr. N.A. Donald, *Honorary General Secretary*

Recognized by the Scottish Sports Council as the governing body of the sport in Scotland. A member of the European and United Kingdom Pool Association. *

Scottish Poppy Appeal

New Haig House,
Logie Green Road,
Edinburgh, EH7 4HR
Tel: 0131-557-2782   Fax: 0131-557-5819

Cameron Whyte

The Scottish Poppy Appeal is the fund-raising arm of the Earl Haig Fund Scotland, a benevolent charity serving the needs of Scotland's ex-Armed Services veterans. *

Scottish Post-Qualifying Consortium

117 Brook Street,
Glasgow, G40 3AP
Tel: 0141-550-7729

Ms. Ruby McCallum, *Development Officer*

Scottish Postal History Society

32 Bryan Street,
Whitehill,
Hamilton, ML3 0JW
Tel: 01698-283067

T.J. Woods, *Secretary*

Scottish Potato Trade Association

25 South Methven Street,
Perth, PH1 5ES
Tel: 01738-620451   Fax: 01738-631155

David Hunter, *Secretary*

Scottish Potters' Association

The Adam Pottery,
76 Henderson Row,
Edinburgh, EH3 5BJ
Tel: 0131-557-3978

Janet Adam

Scottish Prayer Book Society

32 Crompton Avenue,
Glasgow, G44 5TH
Tel: 0141-637-8309

Mrs. P.R. Fleetwood, *Secretary**

Scottish Pre-Cast Concrete Manufacturers' Association

9 Princes Street,
Falkirk, FK1 1LS
Tel: 01324-622088

General Secretary

Scottish Pre-Retirement Council

Alexandra House,
204 Bath Street,
Glasgow, G2 4HL
Tel: 0141-332-9427

Mr. Archie M. McGown, *Director*

*To promote education for retirement by provision of pre-retirement courses and seminars, exhibitions and meetings. **

Scottish Pre-School Play Association (SPPA)

SPPA Centre,
14 Elliot Place,
Glasgow, G3 8EP
Tel: 0141-221-4148   Fax: 0141-221 6043

Ms. Mary Wales, *Development Manager*

*A voluntary organisation providing support and advice to parents and pre-school groups (throughout Scotland) providing education and care for children under five. **

Scottish Print Employers Federation

48 Palmerston Place,
Edinburgh, EH12 5DE
Tel: 0131-220-4353 Fax: 0131-220-4344

J.B. Raeburn, *Director*

The Federation is the employers' association for the Scottish printing industry providing its members with a range of advisory services in employment, training, health and safety matters, etc. *

Scottish Printing Archival Trust

5 Abercorn Avenue,
Edinburgh, EH8 7HP
Tel: 0131-661-3791

Mr. J.C. Keppie, *Honorary Secretary* *

Scottish Prison Complaints Commission

Government Buildings,
Broomhouse Drive,
Edinburgh, EH11 3XA
Tel: 0131-244-8423 Fax: 0131-244-8430

Jim McManus, *Commissioner*

An independent body established by the Secretary of State to review complaints by prisoners about any aspect of their treatment by the Scottish Prison Service. *

Scottish Prison Officers' Association (SPOA)

21 Calder Road,
Saughton,
Edinburgh, EH11 3PF
Tel: 0131-443-8175 Fax: 0131-444-0657

Mr. D. Turner

Scottish Prison Service

Calton House,
5 Redheughs Rigg,
Edinburgh, EH12 9HW
Tel: 0131-244-8699 Fax: 0131-244-8774

Mrs. Ruth Sutherland

An executive agency within the Scottish Office Home Department, existing to help those in secure custody for whom the courts consider appropriate such a disposal. *

Scottish Property Network

University of Paisley,
Paisley, PA1 2BE
Tel: 0141-561-7300 Fax: 0141-561-7319

Ms. Anne Neilson

Scottish Property Network is an independent database of commercial and industrial property whether owner-occupied, let or vacant. Further information is available on www.scottishproperty.co.uk. *

Scottish Prostitutes Education Project (SCOT-PEP)

77 The Shore,
Leith, EH6 6RG
Tel: 0131-555-3453

Ms. Ruth Morgan Thomas, *Coordinator*

Scottish Provision Trade Association

George House,
36 North Hanover Street,
Glasgow, G1 2AD
Tel: 0141-552-3422   Fax: 0141-552-2935

Eric H. Webster

Scottish Public Relations Consultants Association

Barkers Scotland,
234 West George Street,
Glasgow, G2 4QY
Tel: 0141-248-5030   Fax: 0141-204-0033

Mr. Nevin McGhee, *Chairman*

The professional association for accredited public relations consultants in Scotland. *

Scottish Publishers Association

Scottish Book Centre,
137 Dundee Street,
Edinburgh, EH11 1BG
Tel: 0131-228-6866   Fax: 0131-228 3220

Mrs. Lorraine Fannin, *Director*

The Scottish Publishers Association aims to help publishing concerns in Scotland to conduct their book publishing businesses in a professional manner, to market their output to the widest possible readership within Scotland, the UK and overseas and to encourage the development of a literary culture in Scotland. *

Scottish Pug Dog Club

Castledene,
Innerwick,
Dunbar,
East Lothian, EH42 1QT
Tel: 01368-840244

Mrs. T. Greenhill Reid

Scottish Pure Water Association

108 Millfield Hill,
Erskine,
Renfrewshire, PA8 6JJ
Tel: 0141-812-0768

Mrs. Marion Munro, *Secretary*

To oppose the use of public water supplies for the purpose of mass medication and, in particular, to oppose the fluoridation of such supplies. *

Scottish Qualifications Authority

Hanover House,
24 Douglas Street,
Glasgow, G2 7NQ
Tel: 0141-242-2214   Fax: 0141-248-2244

Mr. David Miller, *Chairman*

The SQA is responsible for most academic and vocational qualifications available in Scotland's schools, colleges, training centres and in the workplace.*

Scottish Quality Beef and Lamb Association

Rural Centre,
West Mains,
Ingliston,
Newbridge, EH26 0SB
Tel: 0131-333-5335   Fax: 0131-333-2935

Scottish Railway Preservation Society

Bo'ness Station,
Union Street,
Bo'ness,
West Lothian, EH51 9AQ
Tel: 01506-822298

David Morrison, *Marketing Manager*

Scottish Record Fish Committee (Saltwater)

8 Burt Avenue,
Kinghorn,
Fife, KY3 9XB
Tel: 01592-890055

G.T. Morris

Scottish Record Industry Association

P.O. Box 516,
Glasgow, G5 8PZ
Tel: 0141-429-4174

Ronnie Simpson, *Chairman*

Scottish Record Office

H.M. General Register House,
Princes Street,
Edinburgh, EH1 3YY
Tel: 0131-535-1314   Fax: 0131-535-1360

Mr. P.M. Cadell, *Keeper of the Records of Scotland*

To select, preserve and make available the national archives of Scotland to the highest standards; to promote the growth and maintenance of proper archive provision throughout the country; and to lead the development of archival practice in Scotland.*

Scottish Record Society

c/o Scottish History Department,
University of Glasgow,
Glasgow, G12 8QQ
Tel: 0141-339-3355

Dr. James Kirk, *Honorary Secretary*

The Scottish Record Society was founded in 1897 and has published many volumes of calendars and indices of public records relating to Scotland which are of particular value to historians and genealogists.*

Scottish Records Advisory Council

c/o Scottish Record Office,
H.M. General Register House,
Edinburgh, EH1 3YY
Tel: 0131-535-1314   Fax: 0131-535-1360

Dr. Donald Abbott, *Secretary*

*SRAC is a statutory body reporting to the
Secretary of State on the care of, and public
access to, the historical records of Scotland.* *

Scottish Records Association

Mitchell Library,
North Street,
Glasgow, G3 7DN

Membership Secretary

Scottish Recreational Land Association

18 Abercromby Place,
Edinburgh, EH3 6TU
Tel: 0131-556-4466

Scottish Reformation Society

The Magdalen Chapel,
41 Cowgate,
Edinburgh, EH1 1JZ
Tel: 0131-220-1450

Scottish Reformed Church

5 Prince Edward Street,
Glasgow, G42 8LU
Tel: 0141-423-8188

Scottish Refugee Council (SRC)

43 Broughton Street,
Edinburgh, EH1 3JU
Tel: 0131-557-8083   Fax: 0131-556-7617

Mr. Raymond Albeson, *Manager*

*SRC provides advice, support and practical
help to asylum seekers, refugees and their
families. We also campaign on issues which
affect them.* *

Scottish Regional Committee of the National Joint Council for the Building Industry

13 Woodside Crescent,
Glasgow, G3 7RL
Tel: 0141-332-7144

Mr. S.C. Patten, *Secretary*

Scottish Republican Forum

133 London Road,
Glasgow, G1 5BS

Scottish Republican Socialist Party

133 London Road,
Glasgow, G1 5BS

Scottish Retired Teachers' Association

129 Mayfield Road,
Edinburgh, EH9 3AN
Tel: 0131-667-6494

Mr. Douglas N. Currie, *National Secretary*

This Association, affiliated to the Public Services Pensioners Council in London, exists to protect the living conditions and pensions of retired teachers in Scotland. *

Scottish Rifle Association

1 Mortonhall Park Terrace,
Edinburgh, EH17 8SU
Tel: 0131-664-9674

Mr. C. Aitken, *Honorary Secretary*

The governing body for fullbore target rifle shooting in Scotland. Responsible for principal championship events and the selection of athletes for the Commonwealth Games and other national competitions. *

Scottish Rights of Way Society

John Cotton Business Centre,
10 Sunnyside,
Edinburgh, EH7 5RA
Tel: 0131-652-2937

Judith Lewis, *Secretary*

Safeguarding rights of way in Scotland; answering queries about rights of way problems and principles of law and practice. *

Scottish Road Safety Campaign

Heriot-Watt Research Park (North),
Riccarton,
Currie,
Edinburgh, EH14 4AP
Tel: 0131-472-9200 Fax: 0131-472-9201

Director/Assistant Director

The SRSC is the main co-ordinating body for road safety encouragement activities in Scotland. It is mainly funded by The Scottish Office. *

Scottish Rock Garden Club

P.O. Box 14063,
Edinburgh, EH10 4YE

Membership Secretary

Scottish Rottweiler Club

7 Hallside Village,
Cambuslang,
Glasgow, G72 7XD
Tel: 0141-641-8690

Mrs. S. Brown

Help and advice given on owning a Rottweiler (breed club). *

Scottish Rugby League Development Association

26 Hunters Avenue,
Dumbarton, G82 2RZ

Graham Watson, *Secretary*

Scottish Rugby Referees Association

Winning, Megson & Co.,
1 Grindlay Street Court,
Edinburgh, EH9 3AR
Tel: 0131-228-2501   Fax: 0131-228-5554

Mr. Ray Megson, *Chairman*

Scottish Rugby Union

Murrayfield,
Roseburn Street,
Edinburgh, EH12 5PJ
Tel: 0131-346-5000   Fax: 0131-346-5001

W.S. Watson, *Chief Executive**

Scottish Salmon Board

Drummond House,
Scott Street,
Perth, PH1 5EJ
Tel: 01738-635973   Fax: 01738-621454

Mr. Michael A. Lloyd, *Marketing Manager*

*The Scottish Salmon Board is the marketing
arm of the Scottish salmon industry. It
markets salmon carrying the Tartan quality
mark in the UK and Label Rouge in
France. **

Scottish Salmon Growers Association

Drummond House,
Scott Street,
Perth, PH1 5EJ
Tel: 01738-635420   Fax: 01738-621454

W.J.J. Crowe, *Chief Executive*

Scottish Salmon Information Service

18 Rutland Square,
Edinburgh, EH1 2BJ
Tel: 0131-229-8411   Fax: 0131-228-1644

*For advice on all aspects of preparing and
cooking tartan quality mark Scottish salmon,
nutritional information and free Scottish
salmon factsheets and recipe leaflets. **

Scottish Salmon Smokers Association

163c Cargo Terminal,
Turnhouse Road,
Edinburgh, EH12 0AL
Tel: 0131-317-7329   Fax: 0131-317-7196

Norman Maclean, *Secretary*

Scottish Samaritan Trust

40 Drummond Place,
Gargunnock,
Stirling, FK8 3BZ
Tel: 01786-860317

R.M. Clark, *Treasurer*

*A Trust set up to provide financial assistance to
all Samaritan branches in Scotland. **

Scottish Scenic Trust

Greenacres,
Logiealmond,
Perth, PH1 3TQ
Tel: 01738-88302   Fax: 01738-88416

Scottish School of Forestry

Inverness College,
3 Longman Road,
Inverness, IV1 1SA
Tel: 01463-790431   Fax: 01463-792497

Mr. Jim McDougall

Serving the forest industry with courses from craft level to degrees on forestry, arboriculture, horticulture, rural skills and conservation. Short, full-time courses are available in all disciplines. For further information please contact us. *

Scottish School of Reflexology

2 Wheatfield Road,
Ayr, KA7 2XB
Tel: 01292-287142   Fax: 01292-287142

Dr. W. Douglas Bell

Courses are conducted in Aberdeen, Dundee, Edinburgh, Motherwell, Glasgow and Newcastle-on-Tyne. Free prospectus sent on request. Accredited by the Scottish Institute of Reflexology. *

Scottish Schoolgirls and Youth Hockey Association

Strathallan School,
Forgandenny,
Perth, PH2 9EG
Tel: 01738-812614

Ms. L. Smith *

Scottish Schools Ethos Network

Moray House Institute of Education,
Edinburgh University,
Holyrood Road,
Edinburgh, EH8 8AQ
Tel: 0131-558-6378   Fax: 0131-558-6978

Ms. Gina Reddie, *Administrator*

School ethos is centrally concerned with people and relationships, with the human side of learning. It lies at the heart of quality in Scottish schools. It involves pupils, parents and school staff working in partnership to make schools the best they can be. The Network supports this. *

Scottish Schools' Athletic Association

11 Muirfield Street,
Kirkcaldy, KY2 6SY
Tel: 01592-260168

A.Jack

Scottish Schools' Badminton Association

Caledonia House,
South Gyle,
Edinburgh, EH12 9DQ
Tel: 0131-317-7260   Fax: 0131-317-7489

Scottish Schools' Badminton Union

35 Swisscot Walk,
Hamilton,
Midlothian, ML3 8DX
Tel: 01698-322874

Mr. Murray Carr, *Secretary*

Scottish Schools' Basketball Association

Caledonia House,
South Gyle,
Edinburgh, EH12 9DQ
Tel: 0131-317-7260   Fax: 0131-317-7489

Mr. T. Hardie, *Chairman*

*The Scottish Schools' Basketball Association
develops and promotes basketball competitions in Scottish secondary schools.* *

Scottish Schools' Equipment Research Centre

St. Mary's Building,
23 Holyrood Road,
Edinburgh, EH8 8AE
Tel: 0131-558-8180   Fax: 0131-558-8191

J. Richardson, *Executive Director*

*The trading name of SSERC Limited which
also includes STS Support Services and
SSERC Soft. An agency which provides
advice, information, consultancy and training
on science and technology education equipment and facilities.* *

Scottish Schools' Football Association

6 Park Gardens,
Glasgow, G3 7YF
Tel: 0141-353-3215   Fax: 0141-353-3815

Mr. J.C. Watson, *General Secretary*

*The organising body for football played in
schools.* *

Scottish Schools' Golf Association

16 Windsor Gardens,
St. Andrews, KY16 8XL
Tel: 01334-475681

Ms. Dorothy Scott, *Secretary*

Scottish Schools' Orienteering Association

159 Warriston Street,
Carntyne,
Glasgow, G33 2LA
Tel: 0141-770-7618

Mr. Terry O'Brien, *Secretary*

*Responsible for promoting the sport in Scottish
schools and organising the annual schools'
orienteering festival.* *

Scottish Schools' Rowing Council

1 Kirkhill Gardens,
Edinburgh, EH16 5DF
Tel: 0131-667-5389

Mr. R.H.C. Neil, *Secretary*

Scottish Schools' Rugby Union

59 Lochinver Crescent,
Dundee, DD2 4TY
Tel: 01382-660907   Fax: 01382-435701

Mr. D. Stibbles, *Honorary Secretary*

*The object of the Scottish Schools' Rugby Union
is to foster the game of rugby union in schools
in Scotland.* *

Scottish Schools' Sailing Association

c/o RYA Scotland,
Caledonia House,
South Gyle,
Edinburgh, EH12 9DQ
Tel: 0131-317-8566

Secretary *

Scottish Schools' Ski Association

Lasswade High School Centre,
Eskdale Drive,
Bonnyrigg,
Edinburgh, EH19 2LA
Tel: 0131-663-7171   Fax: 0131-663-6634

Miss S. Outerson, *Chairman*

Scottish Schools' Swimming Association

16 Craigleith Crescent,
Edinburgh, EH4 3JL
Tel: 0131-332-5397

Mrs. R. Brockie, *Secretary*

Scottish Schools' Table Tennis Association

7(b) Bonaly Grove,
Edinburgh, EH13 0QD
Tel: 0131-441-6004

Mr. Ralph Knowles *

Scottish Science & Technology Forum

University of Strathclyde,
George Street,
Glasgow, G1 1XQ
Tel: 0141-552-4400

Dr. Robert Nuttall, *Director*

Scottish Science Library

National Library of Scotland,
33 Salisbury Place,
Edinburgh, EH9 1SL
Tel: 0131-226-4531   Fax: 0131-662-3810

Head of the Scottish Science Library

*Part of the National Library of Scotland, the
Scottish Science Library is a reference only
library catering for the needs of science,
industry and business.* *

Scottish Scrap Association

112 West George Street,
Glasgow, G2 1QF
Tel: 0141-332-7484   Fax: 0141-333-0581

George Ross

Scottish Screen

74 Victoria Crescent Road,
Dowanhill,
Glasgow, G12 9JN
Tel: 0141-302-1700   Fax: 0141-302-1711

Mr. John Archer, *Chief Executive*

Scottish Screen was created in April, 1997 by the Secretary of State for Scotland to stimulate the film and television industry through production and development, finance, training, education, marketing, archive and promoting Scotland as a location. *

Scottish Sculpture Trust (SST)

6 Darnaway Street,
Edinburgh, EH3 6BG
Tel: 0131-220-4788   Fax: 0131-220-4787

Mr. Andrew Guest, *Director*

The SST promotes new opportunities and new audiences for contemporary sculpture in Scotland. It provides information and advice, produces publications, conferences and meetings and develops special projects. *

Scottish Sculpture Workshop

1 Main Street,
Lumsden,
Aberdeenshire, AB54 4JN
Tel: 01464-861372   Fax: 01464-861550

Mr. Christopher Fremantle

The Scottish Sculpture Workshop provides the location, facilities and help to anyone interested in pursuing their sculptural practice. It manages the commissioning of all forms of visual art, mounts exhibitions and hosts international residencies. *

Scottish Secondary Teachers' Association

15 Dundas Street,
Edinburgh, EH3 6QG
Tel: 0131-556-5919   Fax: 0131-556-1419

D.H. Eaglesham, *General Secretary*

Professional association and trade union for secondary teachers in Scotland. Recognized by SOEID and all local authorities. Represents members in all Scottish secondary schools. *

Scottish Security Association

P.O. Box 308,
Glasgow, G44 4BH
Tel: 0141-649-3233

The Scottish Security Association is an organisation established to provide, and encourage, the science and professional practices of industrial and commercial security. The Association has no political or trade union connections or aspirations. *

Scottish Sensory Centre

Moray House Institute of Education,
Heriot-Watt University,
Holyrood Road,
Edinburgh, EH8 8AQ
Tel: 0131-558-6501

Marianna Buultjens

Scottish Sheet Metal Workers' (Employers') Association

180 St. Vincent Street,
Glasgow, G2 5SJ
Tel: 0141-221-1211

Scottish Shetland Sheepdog Club

Vaila,
Ayr Road,
Irvine,
Ayrshire, KA11 5AB
Tel: 01294-311447

Mrs. M.K.G. Anderson

Scottish Ship Chandlers Association

18–20 Queen's Road,
Aberdeen, AB1 6YT
Tel: 01224-633926   Fax: 01224-644701

Iain Smith & Co., *Secretary*

Scottish Shooting Council

39 Pelstream Avenue,
Stirling, FK7 0BG
Tel: 01786-75769

Scottish Siberian Husky Club

Achagavel,
by Ardgour,
Fort William,
Inverness-shire, PH33 7AF
Tel: 01967-411231   Fax: 01967-411231

Ms. H.M. Fielden

A canine club promoting the Siberian Husky in ownership and welfare, responsible breeding, exhibition and rallying. Various events are organised throughout the year and advice is freely given. *

Scottish Ski Club

Muircambus,
Elie,
Fife, KY9 1HD

Scottish Small-Bore Rifle Association

1 Cherry Lane,
Dumfries, DG1 4SE
Tel: 01387-268795

Mr. C.G. De Jonckheere

Scottish Snowboard Association

'Nostra Casa',
Buckler Burn Road,
Petercutler,
Aberdeen, AB1 0NN
Tel: 01224-252067   Fax: 01224-212931

Mr. G. Henderson, *Chairman*

Scottish Society for Autistic Children (SSAC)

see The Scottish Society for Autistic Children

Scottish Society for Conservation & Restoration

The Glasite Meeting House,
33 Barony Street,
Edinburgh, EH3 6NX
Tel: 0131-556-8417   Fax: 0131-557-0049

The Secretary

SSCR is an independent organisation promoting the conservation and restoration of Scotland's historic, scientific and artistic materials. *

Scottish Society for Crop Research

c/o Scottish Crop Research Institute,
Mylnefield,
Invergowrie,
Dundee, DD2 5DA
Tel: 01382-562371   Fax: 01382-562426

Douglas L. Hood, *Secretary*

The Society provides a link between the Scottish Crop Research Institute and farmers, processors and other interested bodies by organising field walks and meetings, financing publications and through the formation of sub-committees on specialised topics. e-mail: lhood@SCRI.SARI.ac.uk. *

Scottish Society for Employment of Ex-Regular Sailors, Soldiers & Airmen

New Haig House,
Logie Green Road,
Edinburgh, EH7 4HR
Tel: 0131-557-1747   Fax: 0131-557-5819

Mr. Frank McGuinness

Scottish Society for Northern Studies

c/o School of Scottish Studies,
University of Edinburgh,
27 George Square,
Edinburgh, EH8 9LD
Tel: 0131-650-4162   Fax: 0131-650-4163

Mr I.A. Fraser

The Society provides a Scottish meeting ground for papers and informal discussion in various fields concerned with Scandinavian and related cultures. *

Scottish Society for Psychical Research

131 Stirling Drive,
Bishopbriggs,
Glasgow, G64 3AX
Tel: 0141-772-4588

Mrs. D. Plowman, *Secretary*

The Society was founded in 1987 to investigate all types of paranormal phenomena. Monthly lectures are held, September to April. A public helpline is also available. *

S

Scottish Society for the History of Photography

Scottish National Gallery,
The Mound,
Edinburgh, EH2 2HR
Tel: 0131-556-8921

Scottish Society for the Mentally Handicapped

13 Elmbank Street,
Glasgow, G2 4QA
Tel: 0141-226-4541

N. Dunning, *Director*

Scottish Society for the Preservation of Historical Machinery

c/o Mechanical Engineering Research,
Annexe,
49 Spencer Street,
Glasgow, G13 1DZ

Scottish Society for the Prevention of Cruelty to Animals (Scottish SPCA)

Braehead Mains,
603 Queensferry Road,
Edinburgh, EH4 6EA
Tel: 0131-339-0222   Fax: 0131-339-4777

Mrs. Diana Allen, *Public Relations Director*

*The Scottish SPCA exists to protect all animals
at risk from cruelty, neglect or accidental
injury in Scotland, backed up by 50 Inspec-
tors, 14 animal homes and an education
unit.* *

Scottish Society for the Protection of Wild Birds

Foremount House,
Kilbarchan,
Renfrewshire, PA10 2EZ
Tel: 01505-702419

Dr. J.A. Gibson, *Honorary Secretary &
Treasurer*

Scottish Society of Composers

see The Scottish Society of Composers

Scottish Society of Playwrights

c/o Drama Department,
Queen Margaret College,
Clerwood Terrace,
Edinburgh, EH12 8TS
Tel: 0131-317-3000

Professor Ian Brown, *Chairman*

*Founded in 1973 to foster the interests of
playwrights living and working in Scotland.
Areas of special interest are contracts,
conditions, publishing, promotion, support
and dispute mediation.* *

Scottish Society of the History of Medicine

Department of History,
University of Stirling,
Stirling, FK9 4LA

Mrs. B.M. White, *Honorary Secretary*

Scottish Software Federation

Livingston Software Innovation Centre,
1 Michaelson Square,
Kirkton Campus,
Livingston, EH54 7DP
Tel: 01506-472200   Fax: 01506-472201

Polly Purvis, *Operations Manager*

Scottish Solar Energy Group

c/o Dept. of Mechanical Engineering,
Napier University,
Colinton Road,
Edinburgh, EH10 5DT
Tel: 0131-455-2660   Fax: 0131-455-2264

Mr. Kerr MacGregor, *Chairman*

*Our aim is to promote solar energy in Scotland.
We have a membership of about 50 and
organise lectures, visits, conferences and field
trips. New members are welcome. e-mail:
K.macgregor@napier.ac.uk.* *

Scottish Solicitors' Discipline Tribunal

22 Rutland Square,
Edinburgh, EH1 2BB
Tel: 0131-229-5860   Fax: 0131-229-0255

John M. Barton, *Clerk to the Tribunal**

Scottish Solicitors' Guarantee Fund

The Law Society of Scotland,
Law Society's Hall,
26 Drumsheugh Gardens,
Edinburgh, EH3 7YR
Tel: 0131-226-7411   Fax: 0131-225-2934 *

Scottish Somali Action

Edinburgh University Settlement,
Wilkie House,
37 Guthrie Street,
Edinburgh, EH1 1JG
Tel: 0131-650-6314   Fax: 0131-650-6328

Ms. Sarah Bayne, *Coordinator*

*Scottish Somali Action, in partnership with
Somalis in the UK, brings together people
and groups to promote peace, reconciliation
and reconstruction in Somalia.* *

Scottish Speed Skating Union

Hartley House,
22, Racecourse View,
Ayr, KA7 2TX
Tel: 01292-610888

Mr. G. Henderson, *Secretary*

Scottish Spina Bifida Association

190 Queensferry Road,
Edinburgh, EH4 2BW
Tel: 0131-332-0743   Fax: 0131-343-3651

Mr. A.H.D. Wynd, *General Secretary*

*We seek to increase public awareness and
understanding of spina bifida and hydro-
cephalus and to provide for the special needs
of individuals and their families.* *

Scottish Spinal Cord Injury Association

Unit 22,
100 Elderpark Street,
Glasgow, G51 3TR
Tel: 0141-440-0960

Scottish Sport Parachute Association

Strathallan Airfield,
Auchterarder,
Perthshire, PH3 1LA
Tel: 01764-662572

Miss A.E. Johnson, *Secretary*

*The governing body of sport parachuting in
Scotland, with the aim of promoting and
developing the sport in Scotland.* *

Scottish Sporting Car Club

75 Lanfine Road,
Paisley, PA1 3NJ

James Sime, *Secretary*

Scottish Sports Aid Foundation

76 Constitution Street,
Edinburgh, EH6 6RP
Tel: 0131-555-4584

Scottish Sports Association for People with Disabilities (SSAD)

Fife Inst. of Physical & Rec. Education,
Viewfield Road,
Glenrothes,
Fife, KY6 2RB
Tel: 01592-415700   Fax: 01592-415710

Mrs. Margaret MacPhee, *Administrator*

Scottish Sports Council

Caledonia House,
South Gyle,
Edinburgh, EH12 9DQ
Tel: 0131-317-7200   Fax: 0131-317-7202

Ms. Kate Vincent

*The Scottish Sports Council is a government-
funded agency for developing sport in
Scotland. Established by Royal Charter in
1972, the Council's current priorities are in
the areas of youth sport and elite level sport.
In addition, the Council is responsible for the
administration of the Lottery Sports Fund in
Scotland.* *

Scottish Squash

Caledonia House,
South Gyle,
Edinburgh, EH12 9DQ
Tel: 0131-317-7343   Fax: 0131-317-7734

Mr. F.N. Brydon, *Chief Executive*

Scottish Staffordshire Bull Terrier Club

5 Marlage,
Ashgill,
Larkhall,
Strathclyde, ML9 3DJ
Tel: 01698-887696

Mrs. Y. Hedges

Scottish Steel Founders' Association

Glencast Ltd,
Kirkland Works,
Leven, KY8 2LE
Tel: 01333-23641   Fax: 01333-25734

P.T. Hughes

Scottish Steel Stockholders' Association

4 Orr Square,
Paisley, PA1 2DL
Tel: 0141-849-1133   Fax: 0141-848-5670

D.P. MacLean, *Secretary* *

Scottish Storytellers' Forum

Netherbow Arts Centre,
43–45 High Street,
Edinburgh, EH1 1SR
Tel: 0131-556-9579

Donald Smith

Scottish Storytelling Centre

The Netherbow,
43–45 High Street,
Edinburgh, EH1 1SR
Tel: 0131-557-5724

Scottish Sub-Aqua Club

The Cockburn Centre,
40 Bogmoor Place,
Glasgow, G51 4TQ
Tel: 0141-425-1021   Fax: 0141-425-1021

Mrs. A. Bannon, *Administrative Secretary*

*Scot SAC is the governing body of sport diving
(SCUBA) in Scotland and has 70 branches.
A magazine and yearbook are published.
Website: http://www.ssac.demon.co.uk.
e-mail: ab@hqssac.demon.co.uk.* *

Scottish Subsea Technology Group

The Innovation Centre,
Exploration Drive,
Offshore Technology Park,
Bridge of Don,
Aberdeen, AB23 8GX
Tel: 01224-706323   Fax: 01224-820236

J.T.C. Hay, *Chairman*

*SSTG was formed to promote the creation and
development of high technology subsea and
ocean-related industries in Scotland. The
ultimate goal is to create a pre-eminent
resource committed to innovation in the
development of ocean technologies.* *

Scottish Sunday School Union for Christian Education

1 Evelyn Villas,
Holehouse Road,
Kilmarnock, KA3 7AX
Tel: 01563-22278

Rev. Ada V. Mcleod, *General Secretary*

Scottish Surfing Federation

20 Strichen Road,
Fraserburgh, AB43 5QZ
Tel: 01346-516451   Fax: 01346-515902

Mr. Chris Noble, *Secretary*

Scottish Swimming

Holmhills Farm,
Greenlees Road,
Cambuslang,
Glasgow, G72 8DT
Tel: 0141-641-8818

Ms. Elaine Mackenzie, *Administration Manager*

The Scottish Amateur Swimming Association is the governing body for swimming, diving, water polo, open water swimming, masters and synchro. *

Scottish Swimming Awards

44 Frederick Street,
Edinburgh, EH2 1EX
Tel: 0131-225-7271   Fax: 0131-225-7271

Miss J. Gallagher, *Awards Manager*

Provides swimming awards to encourage people of all ages and abilities to swim. *

Scottish Table Tennis Association

Caledonia House,
South Gyle,
Edinburgh, EH12 9DQ
Tel: 0131-317-8077   Fax: 0131-317-8224

Mr. A. Elrick, *Chairman*

Scottish Talking Newspaper Group

177 Broomfield Crescent,
Edinburgh, EH12 7NH

Mr. Brian D. West, *Secretary*

Scottish Target Shooting Federation

1 Mortonhall Park Terrace,
Edinburgh, EH17 8SU
Tel: 0131-664-9674

Mr. Colin R. Aitken, *Honorary Secretary*

The federated representative body of the four Target Shooting Sports in Scotland. The formal link between the Sports and the Scottish Sports Council, Commonwealth Games Council, etc. *

Scottish Tartans Society

Hall of Records,
Port-na-Craig Road,
Pitlochry, PH16 5ND
Tel: 01796-474079   Fax: 01796-474090

Mr. & Mrs. Keith Lumsden

The register of all publicly known tartans and the conservation store for the museum. Scottish Tartans Museum at Edinburgh has an archive of tartans and a library. *

Scottish Teacher Researcher Support Network

SCRE Information Services,
15 St John Street,
Edinburgh, EH8 8JR
Tel: 0131-557-2944   Fax: 0131-556-9454

Meg Cowie, *Network Coordinator*

The STRSN sets out to bring together practitioners in education who wish to do research and experienced researchers willing to help. The Network offers members information and contact with other teachers interested in education research and experienced researchers. Web site: http://www.scre.ac.uk/tpr. *

Scottish Technology & Management Programmes (STAMP)

3 Woodside Place,
Glasgow, G3 7Q
Tel: 0141-353-5230

Scottish Temperance Alliance

St. George's Building,
5 St. Vincent Place,
Glasgow, G1 2DH
Tel: 0141-221-4616

Scottish Tenants Organisation (STO)

c/o TPAS,
20/24 St. Andrews Street,
Glasgow, G1 5PD
Tel: 0141-552-3633

Mr. John Carracher, *Secretary*

Scottish Tenpin Bowling Association

17E Hughenden Road,
Glasgow, G12 9XP
Tel: 0141-334-9989

Mr. Derek Brooker, *Secretary*

Scottish Terrier Club (Scotland)

2 Smiths Croft,
Auldgirth,
Dumfries, DG2 0XG
Tel: 01387-74420

Mrs. M. Plunkett

Scottish Texel Sheep Breeders Club

22 Hardacres,
Lanark,
Strathclyde, ML11 7QP
Tel: 01555-663228

Mr. Brian R. Ross, *Secretary*

The club is an affiliated member of the British Texel Sheep Society and is actively involved in the promotion of the Texel sheep. *

Scottish Text Society

27 George Square,
Edinburgh, EH8 9LD

Miss L. Pike, *Honorary Secretary*

The Society is the major publisher of texts from Scotland's rich literary history. Publications cover poetry, drama and prose from the 14th to 18th centuries.
e-mail: lorna.pike@ed.ac.uk. *

Scottish Textile Association

91 Mitchell Street,
Glasgow, G1 3LN
Tel: 0141-226-3262   Fax: 0141-226-3264

Dr. Alastair Alexander, *Chief Executive*

Scottish Theatre Marketing

MacRobert Arts Centre,
University of Stirling,
Stirling, FK9 4LA

Scottish Timber Trade Association

Office 14,
John Player Building,
Stirling Enterprise Park,
Springbank Road,
Stirling, FK7 7RP
Tel: 01786-451623   Fax: 01786-473112

David J. Sulman

Trade Association representing Scottish timber importers and merchants. An Area Association of the Timber Trade Federation. *

Scottish Tory Reform Group

26 Cramond Avenue,
Edinburgh, EH4 6NE
Tel: 0131-312-7803

Mr. Gilmour W. Parvin, *Chairman*

The STRG exists to support the Scottish Tory Party through the generation of innovative, progressive, policy ideas for the benefit of Scottish people.
e-mail: Cramond@compuserve.com. *

Scottish Tourette Syndrome Support Group

41 Carron Street,
Springburn,
Glasgow, G22 6BB
Tel: 0141-557-1979

Mrs. McKay

Scottish Tourist Board

23 Ravelston Terrace,
Edinburgh, EH14 3EU
Tel: 0131-332-2433   Fax: 0131-343-1513

Mr. Tom Buncle, *Chief Executive*

Scottish Tourist Guides Association (STGA)

Great Hill House,
by Cambusbarron,
Stirling, FK7 9QS
Tel: 01786-447784   Fax: 01786-447784

Morag Holdsworth

Highly-trained, professional guides based throughout Scotland to guide groups of any size, on foot, by coach or by car. 17 languages available. *

Scottish Trade International

120 Bothwell Street,
Glasgow, G2 7JP
Tel: 0141-228-2869   Fax: 0141-221-3712

Scottish Trades Union Congress

333 Woodlands Road,
Glasgow, G3 6NG
Tel: 0141-337-8100   Fax: 0141-337-8101

Scottish Trades Union Congress – Women's Committee

333 Woodlands Road,
Glasgow, G3 6NG
Tel: 0141-337-8100   Fax: 0141-337-8101

Ms. Ronnie McDonald

To promote equality for women and fairness at work. To develop campaigns with women's/voluntary organisations on key issues (e.g. family policy, women's representation, poverty, health, economic and employment strategies). *

Scottish Traditional Karate Federation

Westbourne Centre,
Barrhead,
Renfrewshire
Tel: 0141-880-8898

Scottish Traditions of Dance Trust

see The Scottish Traditions of Dance Trust

Scottish Traffic Area Office

J Floor,
Argyle House,
3 Lady Lawson Street,
Edinburgh, EH3 9SE
Tel: 0131-529-8500   Fax: 0131-529-8501

Scottish Training Advisory Service (STAS)

Thistle Foundation,
Niddrie Mains Road,
Edinburgh, EH16 4EA
Tel: 0131-661-3366   Fax: 0131-661-4897

Ms. Jeannie Rocks, *Training Coordinator*

STAS (Scottish Training Advisory Service) is a training consortium of three national voluntary organisations who each provide services for people with physical difficulties. *

Scottish Training Foundation

Block 5, Unit 5,
Templeton Business Centre,
62 Templeton Street,
Glasgow, G40 1DA
Tel: 0141-554-2127   Fax: 0141-554-2803

Scottish Trampoline Association

90 Paradise Road,
Kemnay,
Near Inverurie, AB51 5ST
Tel: 01467-642045

Mr. J. Morrison, *Secretary*

Scottish Tramway and Transport Society

P.O. Box 78,
Glasgow, G3 6ER

Mr. Stuart Little, *Honorary General Secretary*

Formed in 1951 as the Scottish Tramway Museum Society, the STTS publishes historical details of Scottish tramway fleets and assists professional organisations preserving Scottish transport. *

Scottish Transport Group

8 Hope Street,
Edinburgh, EH2 4DB
Tel: 0131-226-7491

Scottish Transport Studies Group

Centre for Business History,
4 University Gardens,
Glasgow, G12 8QQ
Tel: 0141-339-8855   Fax: 0141-330-4889

Thomas Hart, *Secretary*

Scottish Transputer Centre

University of Strathclyde,
Royal College Building,
204 George Street,
Glasgow, G1 1XN

Professor T. Durrani, *Director*

Scottish Traveller Education Programme

Moray House Institute of Education,
Holyrood Road,
Edinburgh, EH8 8AQ
Tel: 0131-558-6371

Ms. Elizabeth Jordan, *Programme Director*

STEP is funded by the SOEID to promote positive change in schools to ensure an inclusive educational experience for all travellers throughout Scotland. *

Scottish Tree Trust

30 Edgemont Street,
Glasgow, G41 3EL
Tel: 0141-649-2462

Greer Hart, *President*

A group dedicated to protecting and creating Scottish native woodlands and forming close connnections with Eastern/Central/Baltic European countries for environmental projects. *

Scottish Triathlon Association

15 New Ardreck Road,
Killearn,
Glasgow, G63 9AD
Tel: 01360-550692

Dr. A.C. Fisher, *President*

Scottish Tribunal

Erskine House,
68 Queen Street,
Edinburgh, EH2 4NN
Tel: 0131-226-6541   Fax: 0131-226-3156

D. Granger Brash, *Clerk*

Scottish Trust for Underwater Archaeology (STUA)

c/o Department of Archaeology,
University of Edinburgh,
Old High School,
Infirmary Street,
Edinburgh, EH1 1LT
Tel: 0131-650-2368

Dr. Nicholas Dixon

The STUA promotes the research, recording and preservation of Scotland's underwater heritage through education and training, survey and excavation, experimental projects and public exhibitions. e-mail: tndixon@hsy1.ssc.ed.ac.uk. *

Scottish Trust for the Physically Disabled

77 Craigmount Brae,
Edinburgh, EH12 8YL
Tel: 0131-317-7227   Fax: 0131-317-7294

Mr. Richard Gregory

Provides grants to people who have physical disabilities in relation to accommodation and transport. Grants are only made to meet needs consequent upon the person's disability. *

Scottish Tug of War Association

2 Davaar Avenue,
Craigens,
Cumnock, KA18 3BB
Tel: 01290-420493   Fax: 01290-420493

Mrs. F.J. Shankland, *Secretary*

Scottish USSR Society

8 Belmont Crescent,
Glasgow, G12 8EU
Tel: 0141-339-9706

Scottish Union of Power Loom Overlookers (SUPLO)

3 Napier Terrace,
Dundee, DD2 2SL
Tel: 01382-612196   Fax: 01382-612196

Mr. Jim Reilly, *General Secretary**

Scottish Unionist and Conservative Party

see Scottish Conservative and Unionist Party

Scottish United Services Museum

Edinburgh Castle,
Edinburgh, EH1 2NG
Tel: 0131-225-7534   Fax: 0131-225-3848

S.C. Wood, *Keeper*

Scottish Universities Council on Entrance

12 The Links,
St. Andrews, KY16 9JB
Tel: 01334-72406

A.D. Mackintosh

Scottish Universities Physical Education Association

Department of Physical Education,
University of Aberdeen,
Butchart Recreation Centre,
University Road,
Old Aberdeen, AB9 2UW
Tel: 01224-272318   Fax: 01224-272315

Fraser McGlynn, *President*

The Scottish Universities Physical Education Association (SUPEA) is the professional organisation representing those working in sport, physical education, recreation and associated disciplines within Scottish Higher Education.*

Scottish Universities' Research and Reactor Centre

Rankine Avenue,
Scottish Enterprise Technology Park,
East Kilbride, G75 0QF
Tel: 01355-223332   Fax: 01355-229898

Professor R.D. Scott

Research centre supported by Glasgow, Edinburgh and Strathclyde Universities. Areas of expertise are mass spectrometry and nuclear radiation detection.*

Scottish Urban Archaeological Trust

55 South Methven Street,
Perth, PH1 5NX
Tel: 01738-622393   Fax: 01738-631626

Mr. David Bowler, *Director*

We investigate the origins and development of Scotland's historic towns and their hinterlands, through excavation, survey and historical research. *

Scottish Urban Regeneration Forum (SURF)

1st floor,
Broomloan House,
170 Edmiston Drive,
Glasgow, G51 2YS
Tel: 0141-427-6066   Fax: 0141-427-7242

Mr. Colin Armstrong, *Chief Executive*

Scottish Users Network (SUN)

c/o SCVO,
18–19 Claremont Crescent,
Edinburgh, EH7 4DQ
Tel: 0131-556-3882   Fax: 0131-557-4969

Ms. Carena Brogan, *Coordinator*

Scottish Vernacular Buildings Working Group

c/o Arbroath Museum,
Signal Tower,
Ladyloan,
Arbroath, DD11 1PU
Tel: 01241-875598

Ms. Margaret H. King, *Secretary*

We exist to foster interest in Scotland's traditional buildings by publishing our journal and monographs and by two annual conferences including site visits and lectures throughout Scotland. *

Scottish Veterans' Garden City Association

New Haig House,
Logie Green Road,
Edinburgh, EH7 4HQ
Tel: 0131-557-1188   Fax: 0131-557-5819

Mr P. H. Baker, *General Secretary*

Scottish Veterans' Harriers Club

46 Riverside Gardens,
Clarkston,
Glasgow, G76 8EP
Tel: 0141-664-5448

Alex Muir

Scottish Veterans' Residences

53 Canongate,
Edinburgh, EH8 8BS
Tel: 0131-556-0091   Fax: 0131-557-8734

Lt. Col. I. Ballantyne, FIMgt, *General Secretary*

The Scottish Veterans' Residences is a charitable organisation, formed in 1910, which provides accommodation at Whitefoord House, Rosendael and the Murray Home for former members of the Armed Forces who are in necessitous circumstances. *

Scottish Vintage Bus Museum

M90 Commerce Park,
Lathalmond,
by Dunfermline, KY12 0SD
Tel: 01383-623380

Scottish Volleyball Association

48 The Pleasance,
Edinburgh, EH8 9TJ
Tel: 0131-556-4633   Fax: 0131-557-4314

Miss Gillian Anderson, *Executive Officer**

Scottish Voluntary HIV and AIDS Forum

c/o SCVO,
18–19 Claremont Crescent,
Edinburgh, EH7 4QD
Tel: 0131-556-3882   Fax: 0131-556-0279

Mr. Roy Kilpatrick, *Coordinator*

Scottish Water Ski Association

Scottish Water Ski Centre,
Town Loch,
Town Hill,
Dunfermline, KY12 0HT
Tel: 01383-620123   Fax: 01383-620122

Alan Murray, *Development Officer*

Our organisation's remit is to promote the sport of water skiing to all in a friendly and safe environment through established clubs. *

Scottish Water and Sewerage Customers' Council

Ochil House,
Springkerse Business Park,
Stirling, FK7 7XE
Tel: 01786-430200   Fax: 01786-430218

The Customers' Council is the industry watchdog which looks after the interests of customers of the three Scottish water and sewerage authorities. *

Scottish Wheelchair Dance Association

Din-Arch,
5 Seath Avenue,
Langbank, PA14 6PD
Tel: 01475-540469   Fax: 01505-337033

Ms. Cath Douglas, *Chairperson*

Scottish White Fish Producers' Association Limited

18–20 Queen's Road,
Aberdeen, AB1 6YT
Tel: 01224-633926   Fax: 01224-644701

R. McColl

Scottish Wider Access Programme (West)

Charles Oakley Building,
300 Cathedral Street,
Glasgow, G1 2TA
Tel: 0141-553-2471   Fax: 0141-552-6090

Ms. Myra Duffy, *Director*

The Scottish Wider Access Programme in the west of Scotland is a consortium of further and higher education institutes set up to create access opportunities for adults with few, or no, qualifications. *

Scottish Wild Land Group

8 Hartington Place,
Edinburgh, EH10 4LE
Tel: 0131-229-2094

Alistair Cant, *Team Coordinator*

A small campaigning body, run by volunteers, to protect wild land and ensure only sensitive development. Publishes Wild Land News *three times a year.* *

Scottish Wildlife Trust

Cramond House,
Kirk Cramond,
Cramond Glebe Road,
Edinburgh, EH4 6NS
Tel: 0131-312-7765   Fax: 0131-312-8705

Mr. Stan Blackley

Scotland's leading body concerned with the protection of all forms of Scottish wildlife and Scotland's natural environment. *

Scottish Wildlife and Countryside Link (SWCL)

P.O. Box 64,
Perth, PH2 0TF
Tel: 01738-630804   Fax: 01738-643290

Jennifer Anderson, *Coordinator*

Scottish Windsurfing Association

c/o RYA Scotland,
Caledonia House,
South Gyle,
Edinburgh, EH12 9DQ
Tel: 0131-317-7388   Fax: 0131-317-8566

Secretary *

Scottish Wirework Manufacturers' Association

William Reid and Sons,
162 Glenpark Street,
Glasgow, G31 1PG
Tel: 0141-554-7081   Fax: 0141-554-7162

I.W. Reid

Scottish Women's Aid (SWA)

12 Torphichen Street,
Edinburgh, EH3 8JQ
Tel: 0131-221-0401   Fax: 0131-221-0402

Any staff member

Supports the work of the 39 local women's aid groups, who provide information, support and refuge for abused women, children and young people. Provides training for a wide variety of agencies about the abuse of women. *

Scottish Women's Bowling Association

Kingston House,
3 Jamaica Street,
Greenock, PA15 1XX
Tel: 01475-724676   Fax: 01475-724676

Mrs. E. Allan, *Secretary* *

Scottish Women's Football Association

4 Park Gardens,
Glasgow, G3 7YE
Tel: 0141-353-1162   Fax: 0141-353-1823

Ms. M. McGonigle, *Executive Administrator* *

Scottish Women's Indoor Bowling Association

39/7 Murrayburn Park,
Edinburgh, EH14 2PQ
Tel: 0131-453-2305   Fax: 0131-453-2305

Mrs. Muriel Old, *Honorary Secretary*

The objects of SWIBA are to promote and foster indoor bowling for women in Scotland and to act in the best interests of its member clubs; to enforce the rules and regulations of indoor bowling as laid down by the World Indoor Bowls Council. *

Scottish Women's Land Army Welfare & Benevolent Fund

Ingliston,
Edinburgh, EH8 8NB
Tel: 0131-333-1023

Scottish Women's Rugby Union

11 Bavelaw Crescent,
Penicuik,
Midlothian, EH26 9AX
Tel: 01968-673355   Fax: 01968-673355

Mrs. M. Sharp, *Secretary*

Scottish Women's Rural Institutes

42 Heriot Row,
Edinburgh, EH3 6ES
Tel: 0131-225-1724   Fax: 0131-225-8129

Ms. Anne Peacock, *General Secretary*

*Aims to advance education and training of those who live and work in the country; promote preservation of Scotland's rural traditions; social welfare and recreation.**

Scottish Woodland History Discussion Group

c/o Institute for Environmental History,
St. Andrew's University,
St. John's House,
St. Andrews, KY16 9QW
Tel: 01334-463300   Fax: 01333-311193

T.C. Smout

*Run jointly by the Universities of Stirling and St. Andrews, the Group publishes an annual newsletter and holds an annual meeting to discuss woodland history.**

Scottish Woodland Owners Association

6 Chester Street,
Edinburgh, EH3 7RD
Tel: 0131-226-3475

Scottish Woollen Trade Mark Association

45 Moray Place,
Edinburgh, EH3 6EQ
Tel: 0131-225-3149   Fax: 0131-220-4942

Margaret S. Duncan

Scottish Working People's History Trust

21 Liberton Brae,
Edinburgh, EH16 6AQ
Tel: 0131-664-2436

Ian MacDougall, *Secretary and Research Worker*

*Seeks out, lists and encourages deposit in public repositories of all documentary sources, and records working people's recollections of work, housing, etc. Charity no. SCO 20357.**

Scottish Working Trials Society

Ballagan Farm Cottage,
Campsie Road,
Strathblane,
Stirlingshire, G63 9AG
Tel: 01360-770285

Mrs. C. Russell

*Our Society organises two championship and three open trials a year. These are as far apart as the Borders and Ballater in Aberdeenshire. Our aim is to encourage all breeds of dogs to compete in K.C. working trials.**

Scottish Workshop Publications

c/o Donaldson's College for the Deaf,
West Coates,
Edinburgh, EH12 5JJ
Tel: 0131-337-9911

Ms. Susan Napier, *Secretary*

Scottish Workshop Publications provides work experience and employment for deaf people in writing, typesetting, printing, graphics, publishing and selling books. *

Scottish Youth Dance Festival

86 Brunswick Street,
Edinburgh, EH7 5HU
Tel: 0131-557-3072   Fax: 0131-557-3072

Judy Adams, *Administrative Director*

SYDF offers young people aged 14–21 a week of classes and performances every July. SYDF also runs dance workshops and youth leaders training throughout Scotland. *

Scottish Youth Hockey Board

'Marrald',
Brabloch Crescent,
Paisley, PA3 4RG
Tel: 0141-887-9731   Fax: 0141-882-6455

Mr. G. Ralph, *Chairman*

Scottish Youth Hostels Association (SYHA)

7 Glebe Crescent,
Stirling, FK8 2JA
Tel: 01786-891400   Fax: 01786-891333

Mr. W.B. Forsyth, *General Secretary*

Scottish Youth Hostels offer young people the opportunity to see Scotland by providing a chain of almost 80 low cost, safe, comfortable and friendly youth hostels. *

Scottish Youth Theatre

6th floor,
Gordon Chambers,
90 Mitchell Street,
Glasgow, G1 3NQ
Tel: 0141-221-5127   Fax: 0141-221-9123

Ms. Carolyn Lappin, *Manager*

Scottish Youth Theatre provides participatory and performance-based drama activities for children and young people throughout Scotland. *

Scottish and Northern Ireland Plumbing Employers' Federation (SNIPEF)

2 Walker Street,
Edinburgh, EH3 7LB
Tel: 0131-225-2255   Fax: 0131-226-7638

Mr. Robert D. Burgon, *Director & Secretary*

The Scottish and Northern Ireland Plumbing Employers' Federation is the national trade association for all types of firms involved in the plumbing and domestic heating industry in Scotland and Northern Ireland. *

Scout Association, The Scottish Council

Fordell Firs,
Hillend,
Dunfermline, KY11 5HQ
Tel: 01383-419073   Tel: 01383-414892

Mr. James A. Duffy, *Chief Executive*

The Association has c.50,000 members in Scotland. It aims to promote the development of young people in achieving their full physical, intellectual, social and spiritual potential. *

Scripture Union Scotland (SU)

9 Canal Street,
Glasgow, G4 0AB
Tel: 0141-332-1162   Fax: 0141-352-7600

Mrs. Mary Bonham, *PA to the Director*

Scripture Union Scotland aims to bring the message of Jesus Christ to young people and to encourage all people in daily Bible reading and prayer. e-mail: postmaster@scriptureunionscotland.org.uk. *

Sea Cadets

see The Sea Cadets

Sea Fish Industry Authority

18 Logie Mill,
Logie Green Road,
Edinburgh, EH7 4HG
Tel: 0131-558-3331   Fax: 0131-558-1442

Duncan Robertson, *Secretary*

A statutory body set up to assist the fish industry through marketing research and development, training and aquaculture. *

Seagull Trust

Princes House,
5 Shandwick Place,
Edinburgh, EH2 4RG
Tel: 0131-229-1789   Fax: 0131-229-1789

Mr. Frank Coutts

The Seagull Trust provides free canal cruising in Scotland for disabled and disadvantaged people. *

Seal Network

Broadford,
Isle of Skye, IV49 9AQ
Tel: 01471-822487   Fax: 01471-822487

Ms. Grace Yoxon

To act as a co-ordinated network for all organisations concerned with the welfare of seals. *

Search and Rescue Dogs Association

Highland SARDA,
Toux Croft,
Fetterangus,
Mintlaw, AB42 4LX
Tel: 01771-622002

Mr. A. Jones, *Secretary*

A voluntary organisation for training search dogs and handlers for mainly mountain rescue work. *

Secretary of Commissions for Scotland

St. Andrew's House,
Edinburgh, EH1 3DG
Tel: 0131-244-2691   Fax: 0131-244-2683

Mrs. J. Richardson, *Secretary of Commissions*

Securities Institute

c/o Bell Lawrie, White & Co. Limited,
Morloch House,
36 King's Stables Road,
Edinburgh, EH1 2EU
Tel: 0131-225-2566   Fax: 0131-529-0199

Alex Lyall, *Scottish Branch President*

Sense Scotland

5/2, 8 Elliot Place,
Clydeway Centre,
Glasgow, G3 8EP
Tel: 0141-221-7577   Fax: 0141-204-2797

Mr. John Calder/Ms. Linda Long

Servite Housing (Scotland) Charitable Trust

118 Strathern Road,
Broughty Ferry,
Dundee, DD5 1JW
Tel: 01382-480915   Fax: 01382-480151

Ms. Sheila Campbell, *Secretary*

To promote and assist in the provision of housing and related amenities for those in need by reason of age, infirmity, disablement or handicap, etc. *

Seventh Day Adventist Church (Scottish Mission)

'Maylea',
5 Ochilview Gardens,
Crieff,
Perthshire, PH7 3EJ
Tel: 01764-653090

A. R. Rodd, *President*

The SDA Church is a Protestant, Evangelical church found in over 205 countries with over 10,000,000 members. *

Shared Care Scotland

123 Duncan Crescent,
Dunfermline, KY11 4DA
Tel: 01383-622462   Fax: 01383-622813

John Leggate, *National Development Officer*

Shelter Scotland

4th floor,
Scotia Bank House,
6 South Charlotte Street,
Edinburgh, EH2 4AW
Tel: 0131-473-7170   Fax: 0131-473-7199

Ms. Liz Nicholson, *Director*

*Shelter, the Scottish campaign for homeless
people, runs housing aid centres throughout
Scotland to help those in housing need, and
campaigns to change the system that causes
homelessness.* *

Sheltered Housing Owners' Confederation of Scotland

170–173 Comely Bank Road,
Edinburgh, EH4 1DH
Tel: 0131-343-6100

Miss Malloch, *Secretary*

Shen Therapy Association UK

26 Inverleith Row,
Edinburgh, EH3 5QH
Tel: 0131-551-5091   Fax: 0131-478-7035

Ms. Catherine Leishman

Shetland Cattle Herd Book Society

Hogan,
Bridge of Walls,
Shetland, ZE2 9NT
Tel: 01595-809375   Fax: 01595-809475

Mrs. J. Evelyn Leask, *Secretary* *

Shih Tzu Club of Scotland

Friarside,
Cessnock Road,
Galston,
Ayrshire, KA4 8LR
Tel: 01563-820247

Mrs. V. Grugan

*The Club is an organization to promote the
welfare of the Shih Tzu dog.* *

Show Business Benevolent Fund

12 St Vincent Street,
Glasgow, G1 2EQ
Tel: 0141-248-3434   Fax: 0141-221-0432

T. Davies Brock, *Secretary*

Sight Savers International (Scottish Office)

2 Torphichen Place,
Haymarket,
Edinburgh, EH3 8DU
Tel: 0131-228-8920   Fax: 0131-228-8920

Silicone Support UK

3 Cherrybank Road,
Merrylee,
Glasgow, G43 2PQ
Tel: 0141-637-8450   Fax: 0141-637-8450

Ms. Margot Cameron

Sino Scottish Institute

University of Abertay Dundee,
Bell Street,
Dundee, DD1 1HG
Tel: 01382-308933   Fax: 01382-308990

Dr. Ray Higgins

*The Sino Scottish Institute aims to promote
economic, cultural, business and educational
links and the expansion of trade between
Scotland and China.* *

Six Circle Group

Block 5, Unit C,
Templeton Business Centre,
Bridgeton,
Glasgow

Tina Cunningham, *Chairperson*

Skill: National Bureau for Students with Disabilities, Scottish Branch

North Glasgow College,
110 Flemington Street,
Springburn,
Glasgow, G21 4BX
Tel: 0141-558-9001

Ms. Sue Brogan

Smokeline

Network Scotland,
57 Ruthven Lane,
Glasgow, G12 9JG
Tel: 0800-848484

Mr. David Dougan, *Information Officer*

*We have a telephone helpline offering advice,
support and information on the giving up of
smoking.* *

Social Credit International

8 Baileyfield Road,
Portobello,
Edinburgh, EH15 1DL
Tel: 0131-669-5275

Mr. Iain McGregor, *Secretary*

*Non-party and non-class, it continues the policy
of the original Social Credit Secretariat,
founded by Scottish Christian economic
reformer and engineer, C.H. Douglas in
1933.* *

Social Iceberg Foundation (Scotland)

14 Albany Street,
Edinburgh, EH1 3QB
Tel: 0131-467-0467   Fax: 0131-467-3467

Ms. Carol Rankin, *PA to Director*

*The charity of Big Issue in Scotland which
helps vendors move back into society through
housing resettlement and training projects.* *

Social Security Commissioners

23 Melville Street,
Edinburgh, EH3 7PW
Tel: 0131-225-2201   Fax: 0131-220-6782

Richard Lindsay, *Secretary*

Social Work Services Inspectorate

The Scottish Office Home Department,
St. Andrews House,
Edinburgh, EH1 3DG
Tel: 0131-244-5542

A. Skinner, *Chief Inspector*

We provide professional advice on social work policy and practice to the Secretary of State, his ministers and officials. Our advice is based on research and professional experience. *

Socialist Educational Association

74 Terregles Avenue,
Glasgow, G41 4LX
Tel: 0141-423-8353

Mr. David Watt, *Secretary*

The SEA is the educational affiliate for the Scottish Labour Party. The SEA seeks to influence the Scottish Labour Party and promote comprehensive education. *

Society for Back Pain Research

Department of Orthopaedic Surgery,
University of Aberdeen,
Polwarth Building,
Foresterhill,
Aberdeen, AB9 2ZD
Tel: 01224-681818   Fax: 01224-685373

Dr. R.M. Aspden, *Honorary Secretary*

Society for Companion Animal Studies (SCAS)

10b Leny Road,
Callander, FK17 8BA
Tel: 01877-330996   Fax: 01877-330996

Anne Docherty, *Secretary*

A membership organisation which promotes the importance of human-companion animal relationship through publications, training, conferences and information and referral service. *

Society for Computers and Law

50 Blacket Place,
Edinburgh, EH9 1RJ
Tel: 0131-668-3474   Fax: 0131-667-8152

Mr. John A. Sibald, *Chairman, Scottish Branch*

Society for Counselling & Information on Miscarriage

12 Renfield Street,
Glasgow, G2 5AL
Tel: 0141-221-1586

Society for the Advancement of Brain Injured Children (SABIC)

The David Elder Centre,
503 Langlands Road,
Govan,
Glasgow, G51 4JY
Tel: 0141-445-5141   Fax: 0141-445-2372

Ms. Phyllis Smith, *Administrator*

Society for the History of Natural History – Scottish Branch

Scottish Natural History Library,
Foremount House,
Kilbarchan,
Renfrewshire, PA10 2EZ
Tel: 01505-702419

Dr. J.A. Gibson, *Scottish Representative*

Society for the Protection of Unborn Children (SPUC)

see The Society for the Protection of Unborn Children (SPUC)

Society of Antiquaries of Scotland

Royal Museum of Scotland,
1 Chambers Street,
Edinburgh, EH1 1JF
Tel: 0131-225-7534

Mrs. Fionna Ashmore, *Director*

The Society organises lectures, conferences, seminars and excursions, publishes an annual Proceedings, *a twice-yearly newsletter and a monograph series and grant-aids research, into all aspects of Scottish history and archaeology.* *

Society of Authors in Scotland

24 March Hall Crescent,
Edinburgh, EH16 5HL
Tel: 0131-667-5230

Ms. Alanna Knight, *Secretary*

Bookshop, library and social events for Scottish members. All legal and contract matters are handled by the London office, 84 Drayton Gardens, SW10 9SB, tel: 0171-373-6642. *

Society of Chief Officers of Trading Standards in Scotland (SCOTSS)

Environmental and Consumer Protection
  Department,
Municipal Buildings,
Castle Street,
Forfar, DD8 3AF
Tel: 01307-473310   Fax: 01307-467158

J. Matthew

*The Society is a section of ITSA (Institute of
  Trading Standards Administration), and the
  Scottish liaison group for LACOTS (Local
  Authority Coordinating Body on Food and
  Trading Standards). It is also the discussion
  and action forum for Chief Officers.* *

Society of Directors of Personnel in Scotland

31 Court Street,
Haddington,
East Lothian, EH41 3AE
Tel: 01620-827259   Fax: 01620-827612

*The Society represents the personnel function in
  Scottish local government.* *

Society of Hospital Linen Service & Laundry Managers

c/o Ninewells Hospital & Medical School,
Dundee, DD1 9SY
Tel: 01382-632104

G. Nixon, *Chairman*

Society of Indexers (Scottish Group)

'Bentfield',
3 Marine Terrace,
Gullane,
East Lothian, EH31 2AY
Tel: 01620-842247   Fax: 01620-842247

Mrs. Anne McCarthy

*The Society of Indexers aims to safeguard and
  improve indexing standards and to promote
  professional indexing. It provides training
  and produces a directory of indexers available.* *

Society of Law Accountants in Scotland

see The Society of Law Accountants in Scotland

Society of Local Authority Chief Executives

c/o Aberdeenshire Council,
Woodhill House,
Westburn Road,
Aberdeen, AB16 5GB
Tel: 01467-620981

Mr. Alan Campbell *

Society of Messengers-at-Arms and Sheriff Officers

21 Ainslie Place,
Edinburgh, EH3 6AJ
Tel: 0131-225-9110   Fax: 0131-220-3468

Mr. Alan Hogg, *Administrative Secretary* *

Society of One-Armed Golfers

11 Campbell Place,
Torrance,
Glasgow, G64 4HR
Tel: 01360-622476

Mr. Hugh F. Ross, *Honorary Secretary*

Since its inception in 1932, the Society has organised competitions to foster goodwill and fellowship among people who play golf despite the loss of one arm. *

Society of Scottish Anaesthetists

Department of Anaesthetics,
Royal Infirmary of Edinburgh,
Edinburgh, EH3 9YW
Tel: 0131-536-1000 *

Society of Scottish Artists

11a Leslie Place,
Edinburgh, EH4 1NF
Tel: 0131-332-2041

Ms. Susan Cornish, *Secretary*

An artist-run organisation focusing on the annual exhibition held in Edinburgh at the RSA. Other exhibitions take place during the year. Membership is open to all. *

Society of Solicitors in the Supreme Courts of Scotland

Parliament House,
11 Parliament Square,
Edinburgh, EH1 1RF
Tel: 0131-225-6268   Fax: 0131-225-2270

Mr. Ian L.S. Balfour, MA, LLB, SSC

A body of practising solicitors founded in 1784, incorporated by Royal Charter and a member of the College of Justice in Scotland. *

Society of St. Vincent de Paul

546 Sauchiehall Street,
Glasgow, G2 3NG
Tel: 0141-332-7752   Fax: 0141-332-6775

The National Secretary

Society of Writers to H.M. Signet

Signet Library,
Parliament Square,
Edinburgh, EH1 1RF
Tel: 0131-225-4923

Andrew M. Kerr, *Clerk*

Society of the Innocents

272 St. Vincent Street,
Glasgow, G2 5RL
Tel: 0141-221-3700   Fax: 0141-221-3773

Mr. John McGrory, *General Manager*

Pregnancy care/pregnancy advice/pregnancy testing centre. *

Soft UK Trisomy 13/18 and Related Disorders

11 Newlands Road,
Uddingston,
Glasgow, G71 5QP
Tel: 01698-818380

Ms. Liz Egan

*Soft provides support, assistance and informa-
tion for families: after a prenatal diagnosis;
with a newly-diagnosed baby; caring for a
surviving child and experiencing the loss of a
child.* *

Soldiers' & Airmen's Scripture Readers Association

23 Curriehill Castle Drive,
Balerno,
Midlothian, EH14 5TA
Tel: 0131-449-5928   Fax: 0131-449-5928

Mr. N.M.D. Innes, *Area Representative*

*Since 1838 we have been sharing the Christian
faith with men, women and families of the
Army and Royal Air Force in major Scottish
locations as well as throughout the UK and
in overseas stations.* *

Soldiers' Sailors' & Airmen's Families Association Forces Help

New Haig House,
Logie Green Road,
Edinburgh, EH7 4HR
Tel: 0131-557-1697   Fax: 0131-557-5819

Ms. Jennifer Spence, *Branch Secretary*

*SSAFA Forces Help objectives are to look after
the welfare of Service and ex-Service families.
To act as advisers and to assist in obtaining
grants for those in need.* *

Sonic Arts Network

Department of Aesthetic Education,
Northern College,
Aberdeen, AB24 4FP
Tel: 01224-283601   Fax: 01224-283900

Dr. Pete Stollery, *Scottish Representative*

*Sonic Arts Network is a UK body which
represents interests in the area of music
technology. There is a strong emphasis on
composition and education.* *

Special Needs Information Point (SNIP)

Room 7,
14 Rillbank Terrace,
Royal Hospital for Sick Children,
Edinburgh, EH9 1LN
Tel: 0131-536-0583   Fax: 0131-536-0001

Ms. Shirley Young, *Information Officer
Coordinator*

S

Spinal Injuries Scotland (SIS)

Festival Business Centre,
150 Brand Street,
Glasgow, G51 1DH
Tel: 0141-314-0056   Fax: 0141-314-0056

The Administrator

The SIS is concerned with all spinal cord injured, their families and friends. We offer an information service, talkline, legal advice service, welfare rights adviser, spinal unit visits and sports division. *

Sportability Scotland

221 St. Vincent Street,
Glasgow, G2 5QY
Tel: 0141-248-3363   Fax: 0141-248-3232

Mr. Colin Cox

Sports Aid Foundation

76 Constitution Street,
Leith,
Edinburgh, EH6 6RP

Mr. George Bowmaker

St Andrew Animal Fund

Queensferry Chambers,
10 Queensferry Street,
Edinburgh, EH2 4PG
Tel: 0131-225-6039   Fax: 0131-220-6377

Mr. Les Ward, *Secretary*

The St Andrew Animal Fund was formed in 1969 for the protection of animals from cruelty and the prevention of the infliction of suffering on animals throughout Scotland and elsewhere. *

St Andrew's Ambulance Association

St. Andrew's House,
48 Milton Street,
Glasgow, G4 0HR
Tel: 0141-332-4031   Fax: 0141-332-6582

Mr. Brendan Healy, *Chief Executive*

St Andrew's Children's Society Limited

Gillis Centre,
113 Whitehouse Loan,
Edinburgh, EH9 1BB
Tel: 0131-452-8248   Fax: 0131-452-9153

Mr. Stephen J. Small

We are a voluntary adoption agency in existence for 75 years. We recruit, assess and approve adoptive parents and foster carers for all ages of children. *

St Bernard Club of Scotland

77 Perveril Rise,
Deadridge,
Livingston,
Lothian, EH54 6NX
Tel: 01506-413548

Mr. C. Fisher

St Margaret of Scotland Adoption Society (SMAS)

274 Bath Street,
Glasgow, G2 4JR
Tel: 0141-332-8371   Fax: 0141-332-8393

Ms. Margaret Campbell, *Director*

The Society is a voluntary adoption agency offering a full range of pre- and post-adoption services. We work within a child-centred and anti-discriminatory framework reflecting the Society's Christian values and beliefs. *

State Hospitals Board for Scotland

State Hospital,
Carstairs,
Lanark, ML11 8RP
Tel: 01555-840293   Fax: 01555-840024

Mr. Dick Manson, *General Manager*

The State Hospital provides high quality psychiatric care in a secure setting for the whole of Scotland and Northern Ireland. *

Stationery Office – Scotland

South Gyle Crescent,
Edinburgh, EH12 9EB
Tel: 0131-479-9000

Mr. John Falconer *

Stepfamily Scotland

5 Coates Place,
Edinburgh, EH3 7AA
Tel: 0131-225-5800   Fax: 0131-225-3514

Ms. Nora Rundell, *Director*

Stepfamily Scotland's prime service is to the helpline operated by a team of trained volunteers. Stepfamily Scotland works to provide support and information for members of stepfamilies and those who work with them. *

Stepping Stones in Scotland

55 Renfrew Street,
Glasgow, G2 3BD
Tel: 0141-331-2828   Fax: 0141-331-1991

Mr. Gordon Henry, *Policy and Information Officer*

Stepping Stones in Scotland – where families come first. The organisation provides services through four family centres, an anti-poverty and a contact centre. *

Stone Federation GB

see Scottish Decorators' Federation

StressWatch Scotland

The Barn,
42 Barnweil Road,
Kilmarnock, KA1 4JF
Tel: 01563-574144   Fax: 01563-574144

Ms. Eileen Wilson, *Administrator*

The aims of StressWatch are to provide support, information and advice to those suffering from stress, anxiety, phobias and panic attacks. *

S

Student Awards Agency for Scotland

Gyleview House,
3 Redheughs Rigg,
South Gyle,
Edinburgh, EH12 9HH
Tel: 0131-244-5823   Fax: 0131-244-5887

Ken MacRae, *Chief Executive*

SAAS provide financial support and other related services for Scottish domiciled students undertaking full time courses of higher education throughout the United Kingdom. *

Sue Ryder Foundation (Scotland)

General Office,
Unit 23,
Thistle Business Park,
Broxburn,
West Lothian, EH52 5AS
Tel: 01506-852183   Fax: 01506-852183

Mr. Robert McDonald *

Sustrans Scotland

53 Cochrane Street,
Glasgow, G1 1HL
Tel: 0141-572-0234   Fax: 0141-552-3599

Mr. Les Tombs, *Office Manager*

Promotion of the national cycle network in Scotland. Promotion and building of links to schools and train stations and promoting sustainable transport. *

Swimming Teachers Association (Scottish Division)

4 Delfie Drive,
Greenock, PA16 9EN

Mrs. C. Paul, ASTA

Synod of the Methodist Church in Scotland

21 Queen Street,
Stirling, FK8 1HL
Tel: 01786-474601

Rev. W. Attwood, *Secretary*

Tak Tent Cancer Support Scotland

Block C20,
Western Court,
100 University Place,
Glasgow, G12 6SQ
Tel: 0141-211-1930   Fax: 0141-211 1879

Mrs. Carol Horne, *Manager*

A network of 17 self-help groups, the resource centre, helpline and youth project provide support and information for cancer patients, their relatives and friends. *

Tangents

8–10 Lauriston Street,
West Port,
Edinburgh, EH3 9DJ
Tel: 0131-229-1950   Fax: 0131-229-1992

Ms. Una Murray, *Development Worker*

Tangents is a national youth organisation for 16–25 year olds, run by young people for young people, using peer education methods to promote young people's issues. *

Taste of Scotland Scheme

33 Melville Street,
Edinburgh, EH3 7JF
Tel: 0131-220-1900   Fax: 0131-220-6102

Taste of Scotland publish the Guide to Good Eating Places in Scotland. *All establishments listed have received a thorough inspection on the quality of food, preparation and presentation with particular emphasis given to Scottish ingredients.* *

Tear Fund

Challenge House,
29 Canal Street,
Glasgow, G4 0AD
Tel: 0141-332-3621   Fax: 0141-332-3621

Peter Chirnside, *Secretary*

Tenant Participation Advisory Service (TPAS)

74–78 Saltmarket,
Glasgow, G1 5LD
Tel: 0141-552-3633   Fax: 0141-552-0073

Ms. Marjorie Bain, *Director*

TPAS is an independent organisation run by its membership of tenants and landlords and offers advice, information, training and practical support to both tenants and landlords. *

Tenants Information Service

Unit 16,
Meadow Mill,
West Hendersons Wynd,
Dundee, DD1 5BY
Tel: 01382-225012

Mr. Greg Brown

Tenovus – Scotland

234 St. Vincent Street,
Glasgow, G2 5RJ
Tel: 0141-221-6268   Fax: 01292-311433

Mr. E. R. Read, *General Secretary*

Terra Nova

Ancaster Business Centre,
Cross Street,
Callander,
Perthshire, FK17 8AS
Tel: 01877-331666 Fax: 01877-331678

Mr. Philip Roycroft

*Terra Nova designs and delivers training and
development programmes which promote
learning within organisations. It specialises
in leadership, teamwork and culture change.* *

The Association of Managers in General Practice

Netherwyndings Mill,
Stonehaven,
Kincardineshire, AB39 3UU
Tel: 01569-764284 Fax: 01569-767458

Ms. Debbie Thomson, *Administrator*

*AMGP's purpose is to enhance and promote the
standard of professional management's
contribution to patient care by the provision
of continuing professional development and
quality services.* *

The Association of Scottish Police Superintendents

173 Pitt Street,
Glasgow, G2 4JS
Tel: 0141-221-5796 Fax: 0141-532-2489

Chief Supt. A. Forrest, *Honorary Secretary*

*The Association exists to consider and bring to
the notice of Chief Constables, the Secretary
of State for Scotland and the Police Negotiating Board for the United Kingdom, matters
affecting the welfare and efficiency of the
police service.* *

The Boys' Brigade (BB)Scottish Headquarters

Carronvale House,
Carronvale Road,
Larbert, FK5 3LH
Tel: 01324-562008 Fax: 01324-552323

Mr. Ian McLaughlan, *Secretary for Scotland*

*The Boys' Brigade is a Christian voluntary
youth organisation with 36,000 members
and volunteers in 800 companies in Scotland. It provides activities for the educational, physical and spiritual development of
young people between 6 and 18 years.* *

The Chartered Institute of Arbitrators (Arbiters), Scottish Branch

Whittinghame House,
1099 Great Western Road,
Glasgow, G12 0AA
Tel: 0141-334-7222 Fax: 0141-334-7700

B.L. Smith, *Honorary Secretary and Treasurer* *

The Child Psychotherapy Trust in Scotland

13 Park Terrace,
Glasgow, G3 6BY
Tel: 0141-353-3399 Fax: 0141-332-3999

Mrs. C.M. Fife, *Administrator*

*We promote training in therapeutic work with
children, young people and families and we
offer advice to families seeking therapeutic
help.* *

The Church of Scotland Guild

121 George Street,
Edinburgh, EH2 4YN
Tel: 0131-225-5722   Fax: 0131-220-3113

Mrs. Lorna M. Paterson, *General Secretary*

The Guild invites and encourages women to commit their lives to Christ and to enable them to express their faith in worship, prayer and action. *

The Educational Institute of Scotland

46 Moray Place,
Edinburgh, EH3 6BH
Tel: 0131-225-6244   Fax: 0131-220-3151

Mr. R. Smith, *General Secretary*

The EIS is a trade union which represents teachers and lecturers in all sectors of education in Scotland. *

The European Movement (Scottish Council)

9 Alva Street,
Edinburgh, EH2 4PH
Tel: 0131-220-0377   Fax: 0131-226-4105

Ms. Barbara MacLeod

Independent, non-profit-making organisation which provides information to members on the European Union through education, debate and discussion. Close links with sister organisation in London and International E.M. Councils. Supports activities of youth branch, Young European Movement. *

The Gaelic Books Council

see Comhairle nan Leabhraichean

The Game Conservancy Trust

Couston,
Newtyle,
Perthshire, PH12 8UT
Tel: 01828-650543   Fax: 01828-650560

I. Johnston, *Secretary*

A registered charity, The Game Conservancy Trust is a research organisation whose primary objective is the conservation and study of game species and their habitats. *

The General Assembly of the Church of Scotland

121 George Street,
Edinburgh, EH2 4YN
Tel: 0131-240-2240   Fax: 0131-240-2239

The Rev. Finlay A.J. Macdonald, *Principal Clerk*

The Church of Scotland is the national church. It is presbyterian in government with a membership of 700,000 communicants. It also has congregations in England and continental Europe. *

The Girls' Brigade in Scotland

Boys' Brigade House,
168 Bath Street,
Glasgow, G2 4TQ
Tel: 0141-332-1765

Mrs. A. Webster, *Brigade Secretary*

A Christian uniformed organisation for girls which offers fun, friendship and a range of exciting activities to suit girls from Primary 1–Secondary 6. *

The Institute of Chartered Accountants of Scotland

27 Queen Street,
Edinburgh, EH2 1LA
Tel: 0131-225-5673   Fax: 0131-225-3813

Peter W. Johnston, *Chief Exectuve & Secretary*

The Institute's corporate objective is to uphold the integrity and standing of the profession of chartered accountancy in the interests of society and the membership, through excellence in education, development of accountancy, service to members and enforcement of professional standards. *

The Lawyers Christian Fellowship

20 Waterside Drive,
Mearns Park,
Newton Mearns,
Glasgow, G77 6TL
Tel: 0141-616-0522

Alan & Joyce Holloway, *Treasurer and Secretary*

UK-wide fellowship of Christian law students and lawyers from every age, stage and branch of the legal profession united in prayer, support, service and witness. *

The Malt Distillers Association of Scotland

1 North Street,
Elgin, IV30 1UA
Tel: 01343-544077   Fax: 01343-548523

W.P. Mennie, of Grigor & Young, *Secretaries* *

The Maritime and Coastguard Agency (MCA)

Scotland & N. Ireland Region,
Marine Office,
Marine House,
Blaikies Quay,
Aberdeen, AB11 5EZ
Tel: 01224-574122   Fax: 01224-573725

Captain F. Duffin, *Regional Chief Surveyor*

An Executive Agency of the Department of Environment, Transport and the Regions (DETR) whose overall aims are to develop, promote and enforce high standards of maritime safety and pollution prevention; to minimise loss of life amongst seafarers and coastal users and to minimise pollution from ships to sea and coast line. *

The National Youth Orchestra of Scotland

13 Somerset Place,
Glasgow, G3 7JT
Tel: 0141-332-8311   Fax: 0141-332-3915

Ms. Lesley Paterson

The National Youth Orchestra of Scotland provides residential orchestral training for hundreds of young Scots musicians, aged 8 to 28 years, with professional soloists and conductors. e-mail: nyos@cqm.co.uk. *

The Post Office

Scottish Post Office Board,
102 West Port,
Edinburgh, EH3 9HS
Tel: 0131-228-7300   Fax: 0131-228-7218

Mr. Martin Cummins, *Secretary to Board*

The Post Office is a public sector group required by government to operate its services commercially. It also has a long tradition of strong social commitment, particularly to rural areas. The group is organised as a holding company with four wholly owned businesses: Royal Mail, Post Office Counters Ltd., Parcelforce Worldwide and Subscription Services. *

The Poverty Alliance

Scottish Anti Poverty Network,
162 Buchanan Street,
Glasgow, G1 2LL
Tel: 0141-353-0440   Fax: 0141-353 0686

Mr. Damian Killeen

The Poverty Alliance is a network of voluntary, statutory and other organisations working together to combat poverty. The Poverty Alliance is the Scottish representative organisation on the European Anti Poverty Network (EAPN). *

The Prince's Trust – Action in Scotland

7th floor,
Fleming House,
134 Renfrew Street,
Glasgow, G3 6ST
Tel: 0141-331-0212   Fax: 0141-331-0210

Ms. Liz Byrne, *Network Development Officer*

The Prince's Trust – Action in Scotland supports the most disadvantaged young people aged 14–25 years through a variety of programmes including grant giving, study support and residential courses. *

The Prince's Trust Volunteers

7th floor,
Fleming House,
134 Renfrew Street,
Glasgow, G3 6ST
Tel: 0141-331-0211   Fax: 0141-331-0210

Ms. Yvonne Murphy, *Office Manager*

The Prince's Trust Volunteers aims to provide a personal development programme of the highest quality for teams of young people from diverse backgrounds through working in the community. *

The Princess Royal Trust for Carers

Kirkstane House,
139 St. Vincent Street,
Glasgow, G2 5JF
Tel: 0141-221-5066   Fax: 0141-221-4623

Mr. Colin Williams, *Director, Carer Support*

The Trust aims to provide, through its network of carers' centres, the help and support that carers need in ways that they most want. *

The Royal Institution of Chartered Surveyors in Scotland

7&9 Manor Place,
Edinburgh, EH3 7DN
Tel: 0131-225-7078   Fax: 0131-226-3599

Ms. Eileen Masterman, *Director*

The RICS in Scotland is the professional body representing all chartered surveyors living and working in Scotland. A self-regulatory body, developing and promoting chartered surveyors' skills. *

The Royal Scottish Agricultural Benevolent Institution (RSABI)

Ingliston,
Edinburgh, EH28 8NB
Tel: 0131-333-1023   Fax: 0131-333-1027

Mr. I.C. Purves-Hume, *Director*

Entirely supported by voluntary contributions. Provides direct financial and in-kind help to anyone in distress who is or has been in farming, forestry, horticulture, fish farming and rural estate work in Scotland and their dependants. A welfare advice service is also available. *

The Royal Scottish Automobile Club (Motor Sport) Limited

11 Blythswood Square,
Glasgow, G2 4AG
Tel: 0141-204-4999 Fax: 0141-204 4949

Mr. J.C. Lord, *Secretary*

Motor Sport in Scotland is recognized by the Scottish Sports Council and the RAC Motor Sports Association and is the organiser of international motor sport events.*

The Royal Scottish Pipe Band Association

45 Washington Street,
Glasgow, G3 8AZ
Tel: 0141-221-5414 Fax: 0141-221-1561

Mr. Iain M. White, *Executive Officer*

The Association has twelve UK branches and maintains a bond of fellowship with pipe band personnel worldwide. It organises all major UK pipe band championships.*

The Royal Society for the Relief of Indigent Gentlewomen of Scotland

14 Rutland Square,
Edinburgh, EH1 2BD
Tel: 0131-229-2308 Fax: 0131-229-0956

George F. Goddard, MBE, CA, *Secretary & Cashier*

Assisting ladies of Scottish birth or education with professional or business backgrounds, over 50, existing on low incomes and limited savings. Charitable grants payable.*

The Royal Zoological Society of Scotland

Edinburgh Zoo,
134 Corstorphine Road,
Edinburgh, EH12 6TS
Tel: 0131-334-9171 Fax: 0131-316-4050

Professor R.J. Wheater, OBE, *Director*

The mission of the Royal Zoological Society of Scotland is to promote, through the presentation of our living collections, the conservation of animal species and wild places by captive breeding, environmental education and scientific research.*

The St Andrew Animal Fund

Queensferry Chambers,
10 Queensferry Street,
Edinburgh, EH2 4PG
Tel: 0131-225-6039 Fax: 0131-220-6377

Mr. Les Ward, *Secretary*

The St Andrew Animal Fund was formed in 1969 to carry out the purely charitable activities formerly carried out by Advocates for Animals, namely the protection of animals from cruelty and suffering.*

The Salmon and Trout Association

10 Great Stuart Street,
Edinburgh, EH3 7TN
Tel: 0131-225-2417 Fax: 0131-225-2417

Ms. Mary Brown, *Administrator*

We exist to safeguard the salmon and trout fisheries of the UK and the interests of those who fish for them by rod and line.*

The Scottish Agricultural College

West Mains Road,
Edinburgh, EH9 3JG
Tel: 0131-535-4078

Mr. Barry Sheppard, *Marketing Department*

Throughout Scotland SAC offers research, education, training and consultancy in the fields of food, land and the environment. Website: http://www.sac.ac.uk. *

The Scottish Assessors' Association

Chesser House,
500 Gorgie Road,
Edinburgh, EH11 3YJ
Tel: 0131-469-5589   Fax: 0131-469-5599

Mr. John A. Cardwell, *Vice President*

The Scottish Assessors' Association promotes uniformity in the operation of valuation and electoral registration legislation and acts as a consultative and advisory body in these areas. *

The Scottish China Association

10 Queen's Crescent,
Edinburgh, EH9 2AZ
Tel: 0131-667-9369   Fax: 0131-556-9065

Dale Finlayson, *Membership Secretary*

The Association's aim is to foster friendship and understanding between the people of Scotland and China. Meetings in Edinburgh and Glasgow and there is a quarterly magazine. *

The Scottish Civic Trust

The Tobacco Merchants House,
42 Miller Street,
Glasgow, G1 1DT
Tel: 0141-221-1466   Fax: 0141-248-6952

Mr. J.N.P. Ford, *Administration and Finance Director*

The Trust is concerned with Scotland's built environment and heritage, by encouraging public interest in the quality of architecture and planning. *

The Scottish Committee of Optometrists

7 Queens Buildings,
Queensferry Road,
Rosyth,
Fife, KY11 2RA
Tel: 01383-419444   Fax: 01383-416778

David S. Hutton, CA, *Secretary/Treasurer*

To confer on and/or promote matters affecting optometrists practising or resident in Scotland. To run conferences and seminars to educate students, optometrists and further research. *

The Scottish Farm and Countryside Educational Trust

Royal Highland Centre,
Ingliston,
Edinburgh, EH28 8NF
Tel: 0131-333-3805   Fax: 0131-333-5236

Ms. Dorothy Amyes, *Director*

An independent organisation providing information, teaching resources and other activities about agriculture and the countryside in Scotland. *

The Scottish Football Association

6 Park Gardens,
Glasgow, G3 7YF
Tel: 0141-332-6372   Fax: 0141-332-7559

J. Farry, *Chief Executive*

The governing body for football in Scotland, formed in 1873 with a principal object of promoting, fostering and developing the game of Association football. *

The Scottish Football League

188 West Regent Street,
Glasgow, G2 4RY
Tel: 0141-248-3844   Fax: 0141-221-7450

Peter Donald, *Secretary*

The League promotes and extends the game of association football and provides league championship and cup competitions for clubs and concludes commercial contracts on their behalf. *

The Scottish Gliding Centre (SGU Limited)

Portmoak Airfield,
Scotlandwell,
by Kinross, KY13 7JJ
Tel: 01592-84543

A. Bauld, *Chairman*/J. Provan, *Secretary*

The Centre provides a glider launching and pilot training service for members and visitors. Members of the public can arrange for a trial flight. *

The Scottish Hotel School

University of Strathclyde,
94 Cathedral Street,
Glasgow, G4 0LG
Tel: 0141-548-3941   Fax: 0141-552-2870

Ms. Sandra Miller

The Scottish Hotel School is an international leader in hotel, hospitality and tourism education offering undergraduate and postgraduate programmes in hospitality management and tourism. *

The Scottish Office

St. Andrew's House,
Edinburgh, EH1 1DG
Tel: 0131-556-8400   Fax: 0131-244-2683

Mr. C.C. MacDonald, *Principal Establishment Officer*

The Scottish Office Agriculture, Environment and Fisheries Department

Pentland House,
47 Robb's Loan,
Edinburgh, EH14 1TY
Tel: 0131-556-8400   Fax: 0131-224-6000

Mr. A.M. Russell, *Secretary*

The Scottish Office Department of Health

St. Andrew's House,
Regent Road,
Edinburgh, EH1 3DG
Tel: 0131-556-8400

Mr. G.R. Scaife, *Chief Executive*

The Scottish Office Development Department

Local Government Group,
Victoria Quay,
Edinburgh, EH6 6QQ
Tel: 0131-244-7037   Fax: 0131-244-7058

Mr. Ted Davison

The Scottish Office Education and Industry Department

Victoria Quay,
Edinburgh, EH6 6QQ
Tel: 0131-556-8400   Fax: 0131-244-7122

Mr. G.R. Wilson, *Secretary*

The Department (SOEID) administers Government policy for education and training, and advises Secretary of State on industrial and economic development in Scotland. It also oversees policy on the arts and cultural heritage. *

The Scottish Office Home Department

St. Andrew's House,
Edinburgh, EH1 3DG
Tel: 0131-556-8400

Mr. J. Hamil, *Secretary*

The Scottish Office Pension Agency

St. Margaret's House,
151 London Road,
Edinburgh, EH8 7TG
Tel: 0131-244-3211   Fax: 0131-244-3579

Mr. R. Garden, *Chief Executive*

The Agency is responsible for administering the pension arrangements of 330,000 people, mainly teachers and employees of the NHS in Scotland. *

The Scottish Office, Solicitor's Office

Victoria Quay,
Edinburgh, EH6 6QQ
Tel: 0131-556-8400   Fax: 0131-244-0508

R. Brodie, *Solicitor*

The Scottish Patriots

8 Baileyfield Road,
Portobello,
Edinburgh, EH15 1DL
Tel: 0131-669-5275

Mr. Iain McGregor, *Administrator*

*Founded by Wendy Wood, it has sought
Scotland's political independence for over 50
years including 25 years opposed to European
union. Promotes heritage and culture.* *

The Scottish Plant Owners Association

302 St. Vincent Street,
Glasgow, G2 5RZ
Tel: 0141-248-3434   Fax: 0141-221-1226

Campbell White, *Secretary* *

The Scottish Society for Autistic Children (SSAC)

Hilton House,
Alloa Business Park,
The Whins,
Alloa, FK10 3SA
Tel: 01259-720044   Fax: 01259-720051

Ms. Helen Petrie

*The leading service provider for autism in
Scotland, including a residential school, day
services and accommodation for adults,
respite care, family support, advice, information and training.* *

The Scottish Society of Composers

c/o 'Mazagon',
4 Glen Road,
Lennoxtown, G65 7JX
Tel: 01360-313217   Fax: 01360-319020

Derek Ball, *Secretary*/Neil Butterworth,
Chairman

*Promoting wider knowledge of contemporary
music in Scotland through international and
local liaison, annual awards to musicians,
distribution of catalogues and sponsorship of
new music recording.* *

The Scottish Traditions of Dance Trust

54 Blackfriars Street,
Edinburgh, EH1 1NE
Tel: 0131-558-8737   Fax: 0131-558-8737

Ms. Jennifer Swanson

*The national organisation with a remit to
research, conserve, foster and promote ALL of
Scotland's dance traditions.* *

T

The Sea Cadets

Northern Area HQ,
HMS Caledonia,
Rosyth,
Fife, KY11 2XH
Tel: 01383-416300   Fax: 01383-419772

Area Officer

The Sea Cadets is a national youth organisation for boys and girls aged 10–18 offering many adventurous activities which develop personal qualities using a nautical theme. *

The Society for the Protection of Unborn Children (SPUC)

5 St. Vincent Place,
Glasgow, G1 2DH
Tel: 0141-221-2094   Fax: 0141-248-2105

Mr. John F. Crabbe, *Manager Scotland*

Through education and political work, our mission is to defend human life with love from conception until natural death. *

The Society of Law Accountants in Scotland

17 Golden Square,
Aberdeen, AB10 1NY
Tel: 01224-408408   Fax: 01224-408400

Mrs. Carol A. Pike, *General Secretary*

The Society encourages and promotes law accounting in Scottish Law Offices by providing a two year course run jointly with The Law Society of Scotland, and seminars and branch meetings in Aberdeen, Dundee, Edinburgh, Glasgow and Inverness. *

The Whole Works Complementary Therapy and Counselling Centre

Jacksons Close,
209 Royal Mile,
Edinburgh, EH1 1PZ
Tel: 0131-225-8092

The Administrator

Established in 1992 with 30 therapists offering a full range of skills and expertise. Over 400 clients a week enjoy our friendly, imaginative and professional service. *

The Woodland Trust

Glenruthven Mill,
Abbey Road,
Auchterarder,
Perthshire, PH3 1DP
Tel: 01764-662554   Fax: 01764-662553

Mr. Douglas Orr, *Operations Director Scotland*

Thistle Foundation

27a Walker Street,
Edinburgh, EH3 7HX
Tel: 0131-225-7282

Mr. Philip Croft, *Director*

Tibetan Spaniel Club of Scotland

Stables House,
Pavilion Estate,
Melrose,
Roxburghshire, TD6 9BN
Tel: 01896-823642

Mrs. C. Rankin

Breed club with facilities to advise on the breed. *

Timber Growers Association

5 Dublin Street Lane South,
Edinburgh, EH1 3PX
Tel: 0131-538-7111   Fax: 0131-538-7222

Mr. Peter Wilson, *Chief Executive*

Timber Growers Association is Great Britiain's leading association for all those involved in woodlands. It is recognised by government as the voice of the timber growing sector, aiming that it can operate effectively, responsibly and profitably. TGA provides effective support to the membership through a range of member services. *

Time Out Scotland

c/o GCUS,
11 Queen's Crescent,
Glasgow, G4 9AS
Tel: 0141-332-2444

Mr. Gordon MacNicol

A self-help group for past and present sufferers of depression which meets every Wednesday evening. Time Out Scotland is a registered charity. *

Torch Trust for the Blind

26 Talbot Drive,
Glasgow, G13 3RR
Tel: 01324-624325

Mr. Alec Cordiner

Town and Country Planning Association Scotland

Wellknowe Place,
Thornton Hall,
Lanarkshire, G74 5AX
Tel: 0141-644-1255

Richard W Colwell, *Chairman*

Traditional Music and Song Association of Scotland

95-97 St. Leonard's Street,
Edinburgh, EH8 9QY
Tel: 0131-667-5587   Fax: 0131-662-9153

Lindsey Lewis, *National Organiser*

Training 2000

Dalian House,
350 St Vincent Street,
Glasgow, G3 8XQ
Tel: 0141-248-4486   Fax: 0141-248-4489

Mr. Loie Larkin, *Administrator*

Tranquilliser Addiction

Solicitors' Group

Lomond House,
Beveridge Square,
Livingston, EH54 6QR
Tel: 01506-419999 Fax: 01506-410099

Mr. K.R.W. Hogg

Transport & General Workers Union

21 Logie Mill,
Unit 11,
Beaverbank Business Park,
Edinburgh, EH7 4HG
Tel: 0131-556-9676 Fax: 0131-558-1027

Mr. Ripley, *Regional Industrial Organiser*

Transport Salaried Staffs' Association

180 Hope Street,
Glasgow, G2 2UE
Tel: 0141-332-4698 Fax: 0141-332-9879

Mr. R.S. King, *Secretary*

Trekking and Riding Society of Scotland

Boreland,
Fearnan,
Aberfeldy,
Perthshire, PH15 2PG
Tel: 01887-830274 Fax: 01887-830606

Ms. Liz Menzies, *Secretary*

Trekking and Riding Society of Scotland specialises in looking after the interests of all those seeking a riding or pony trekking holiday in Scotland. It operates an inspection scheme to monitor and maintain standards and provides appropriate training courses. *

Tuberous Sclerosis Association of Great Britain

7 Bent Road,
Hamilton,
Lanarkshire, ML3 6QB
Tel: 01698-427998

Mrs. Nessie Garrett, *Scottish Organiser*

National organisation founded in 1977, financed by fundraising and donations with over 110 families in Scotland as members. Provides support, advice, information, help and promotes research into the disease. *

Turning Point Scotland

121 West Street,
Glasgow, G5 8BA
Tel: 0141-418-0882   Fax: 0141-420-6170

Ms. Netta Maciver, *Director*

Turning Point Scotland runs services for people who are extremely vulnerable and the nature of their behaviour focuses media attention on them and their carers. Specifically we provide services for drugs, alcohol, mental health and learning disabilites. *

Twins and Multiple Births Association (TAMBA) Regional

22 Mansewood Road,
Glasgow, G43 1TN
Tel: 0141-571-2319

Mrs. Joy McCormack

U

UNICEF in Scotland

43 Aytoun Road,
Glasgow, G41 5HW
Tel: 0141-422-1662   Fax: 0141-424-1881

Mrs. Anne Forrester, *Scottish Officer*

UNICEF is primarily concerned with long-term programmes to benefit children in health, education, water and sanitation. Nonetheless, UNICEF responds immediately to emergency situations. *

UNISON Scotland

Unison House,
14 West Campbell Street,
Glasgow, G2 6RX
Tel: 0141-332-0006   Fax: 0141-331-1203

Mr. Chris Bartter, *Communications Officer*

UNISON is Scotland's largest trade union. We represent 150,000 members in the public services. Committed to equality, we are member-centred, and have a large network of local stewards. *

Unemployed Voluntary Action Fund

Comely Park House,
80 New Row,
Dunfermline, KY12 7EJ
Tel: 01383-620780

Ms. Sandra Carter

The Unemployed Voluntary Action Fund assists the development of volunteering projects by creating opportunities for unemployed people to be involved in meeting local community needs. *

Union of Catholic Mothers (Scottish National Council)

34 Kirkwood Avenue,
Clydebank, G81 2SX
Tel: 0141-952-1570

Mrs. M Lyden

Union of Construction, Allied Trades & Technicians

6 Fitzroy Place,
Glasgow, G3 7RL
Tel: 0141-221-4893   Fax: 0141-221-2297

Mr. A. Ritchie, *Secretary*

Union of Shop, Distributive & Allied Workers

'Muirfield',
342 Albert Drive,
Glasgow, G41 5PG
Tel: 0141-427-6561   Fax: 0141-427-3155

Mr. P. McCormick, *Divisional Officer*

Unit for the Study of Government in Scotland

University of Edinburgh,
Chisholm House,
High School Yards,
Edinburgh, EH1 1LZ
Tel: 0131-650-2456   Fax: 0131-650-6345

Lindsay Adams

Publishers of a quarterly journal, Scottish Affairs, *and other major reports on Scottish politics and society. Deails of publications, conferences and other activities from Lindsay Adams. e-mail: Ladams@ed.ac.uk.* *

Unitarian Historical Society

6 Ventnor Terrace,
Edinburgh, EH9 2BL
Tel: 0131-667-4360

Rev. A.M. Hill, *Secretary*

United Free Church of Scotland

11 Newton Place,
Glasgow, G3 7PR
Tel: 0141-332-3435   Fax: 0141-333-1973

Rev. John Fulton, *General Secretary*

A small Presbyterian denomination with almost 6000 members in 70 congregations served by 45 ministers and pastors. *

United Kingdom Environmental Law Association, Scottish Branch

c/o Biggart, Baillie and Gifford,
11 Glenfilas Street,
Edinburgh, EH3 6YY
Tel: 0131-226-5541   Fax: 0131-226-2278

Dr. Norman Oliver, *Secretary*

United Kingdom Men's Movement (Scotland)

P.O. Box 16168,
Glasgow
Tel: 0141-959-4194

Mr. George McAulay, *Chairman* *

United Kingdom Shareholders' Association (Scotland)

The Maples,
Kinlochard,
Aberfoyle,
Stirling, FK8 3TL
Tel: 01877-387285   Fax: 01877-387285

Mr. William MacLean, *Chairman*

UKSA (Scotland), a voluntary organisation, holds regular meetings on investment matters, campaigns for shareholders' rights, and provides a forum where investors can share views and concerns. *

V

Valuation Office Agency (Scotland)

Meldrum House,
15 Drumsheugh Gardens,
Edinburgh, EH3 7UN
Tel: 0131-225-4938   Fax: 0131-220-4384

Mr. A. MacLaren, *Chief Valuer*

Values into Action Scotland (VIA)

1F3, 21 Iona Street,
Edinburgh, EH6 8SP
Tel: 01524-389705   Fax: 01524-389705

Ms. Liz Henderson, *Development Worker*

VIA offers education/training events for people with and without learning difficulties. It also campaigns on rights and opportunities available to people with learning difficulties. *

Variety Club of Great Britain

437 Crow Road,
Glasgow, G11 7DZ
Tel: 0141-357-4411

Venture Scotland

Bonnington Mill,
72 Newhaven Road,
Edinburgh, EH6 5QG
Tel: 0131-553-5333   Fax: 0131-553-5333

Mr. Rob Bushby, *Coordinator*

Victim Support Scotland

14 Frederick Street,
Edinburgh, EH2 2HB
Tel: 0131-225-7779   Fax: 0131-225-8456

Ms. Alison Paterson

Victoria League in Scotland

22 Hanover Street,
Edinburgh, EH2 2EP
Tel: 0131-220-2336   Fax: 0131-220-4842

Mrs. Elizabeth Best

Our charity promotes international friendship. We arrange hospitality for international students with local families; outings and social events. We have no political or religious affiliations. *

Vincent Wildlife Trust – Scottish Branch

Barjarg,
Barrhill,
Girvan,
Ayrshire, KA26 0RB
Tel: 01465-821225

Jim & Rosemary Green, *Ecologists*

Vision 21 – Action for Sustainable Communities

The Rectory,
Glencarse,
Perth, PH2 7LX
Tel: 01738-860386

Canon Kenyon Wright

Viva: Young Volunteers in Action

c/o SCEC,
Rosebery House,
9 Haymarket Terrace,
Edinburgh, EH12 5EZ
Tel: 0131-313-2488   Fax: 0131-313-6600

Ms. Louise MacDonald, *Development Officer*

National focus for youth volunteering in Scotland. Aims to promote volunteering to young people aged 15–25; provide information about voluntary work and to show positive examples of young people volunteering. *

Vocal Re-Entry Group

13 Cowgate,
Dundee, DD1 2HS
Tel: 01382-201016   Fax: 01382-204584

Rusty Murray

Voluntary Association for Mental Welfare (VAMW)

VAMW House,
150 Gavin Street,
Motherwell, ML1 2RJ
Tel: 01698-259291   Fax: 01698-259754

Mr. John Thomson, *Director*

Voluntary Euthanasia Society of Scotland (VESS)

17 Hart Street,
Edinburgh, EH1 3RN
Tel: 0131-556-4404   Fax: 0131-557-4403

Mr. Christopher Docker, *Executive Secretary*

VESS exists to campaign for greater choice at the end of life, and is a leading source of information on right-to-die issues and living wills. *

Voluntary Service Overseas (VSO)

9 Minto Street,
Edinburgh, EH9 1RG
Tel: 0131-667-3073   Fax: 0131-667-3073

Ms. Kate O'Brien, *Scottish Representative*

Volunteer Development Scotland (VDS)

72–80 Murray Place,
Stirling, FK8 2BX
Tel: 01786-479593   Fax: 01786-447148

Ms. Irene Hendry, *Information Officer*

WEA Scotland (Workers' Educational Association) Scottish Association

Riddle's Court,
322 Lawnmarket,
Edinburgh, EH1 2PG
Tel: 0131-226-3456   Fax: 0131-220-0306

Joyce Connon, *Scottish Secretary*

*A democratic organisation which provides
adults with access to organised learning.
Priority is given to the needs of disadvantaged
groups and overcoming barriers to learning.* *

WWF Scotland (World Wide Fund for Nature)

8 The Square,
Aberfeldy,
Perthshire, PH15 2DD
Tel: 01887-820449   Fax: 01887-829453

Ms. Dorothy Rodger, *Public Support Officer*

*WWF works to influence policymakers on
environmental issues of concern in Scotland.
People can support WWF by becoming
members or volunteering locally.* *

Wallace Clan Trust for Scotland

Braveheart Centre,
Craig House,
64 Darney Street,
Glasgow, G41 2SE
Tel: 0141-429-6915   Fax: 0141-429-6968

Mr. T.C. MacLucas, *Training Manager*

*A Scottish charity promoting and researching
histories and cultures of the people of
Scotland. Partaking in the image of Scotland
on film, wardrobe/weaponry supply.* *

War Widows Association of Great Britain

Flat G2,
271 Crow Road,
Broomhill,
Glasgow, G11 7BG
Tel: 0141-334-4972

Mrs. H. Murphy, MBE, *Secretary*

*The Secretary can be contacted at 52 West
Street, Gorseinon, Swansea, SA4 2AF.* *

WaterAid

419 Balmore Road,
Glasgow, G22 6NU
Tel: 0141-355-5321   Fax: 0141-355-5154

Ms. Sarah Hunter, *Regional Fundraising
Assistant*

*WaterAid's aim is to help some of the poorest
communities in Africa and Asia provide
themselves with a safe water supply close to
home.* *

Weimaraner Club of Scotland

Actim,
8 Powburn Crescent,
Kylepark,
Uddingston,
Glasgow, G71 7SS
Tel: 01698-813817

Mr. A. Kousourou

Wheelchair Loan Service Scotland (WLSS)

3 Greenfern Avenue,
Mastrick,
Aberdeen, AB16 6QR
Tel: 01224-663180

Peter or Irene Houston

We operate a manual wheelchair loan service on a short term basis. There is no charge but donations gratefully received. Anyone can contact us. Charity no. SCO 23629. *

Whippet Club of Scotland

26 High Street,
Lochwinnoch,
Renfrewshire, PA12 4DB
Tel: 01505-842123

Mrs. A. Skelley, *Honorary Secretary*

The Whippet Club of Scotland holds two shows annually. For information on the Pedigree Whippet Racing Club, contact Mr. D.F. Lindsay, 07868-70352. *

Who Cares? Scotland

Block 4, Unit C3,
Templeton Business Centre,
Templeton Street,
Glasgow, G40 1DA
Tel: 0141-554-4452   Fax: 0141-550-3834

Information and Training Project

Who Cares? Scotland is a campaigning organisation continually focused on improving the quality of life in care. It is run by young people for young people. *

Wholesale Grocers' Association of Scotland

30 McDonald Place,
Edinburgh, EH7 4NH
Tel: 0131-556-8753   Fax: 0131-558-1623

Kate Salmon, *Executive Director*

Trade association of wholesalers of food, drink and grocery distribution. e-mail: wgas@cablenet.co.uk. *

Wildfowl and Wetlands Trust – Caerlaverock

Eastpark Farm,
Caerlaverock,
Dumfriesshire, DG1 4RS
Tel: 01387-770200   Fax: 01387-770200

J.B. Doherty, *Centre Manager*

Willing Workers on Organic Farms (Scotland)

Pillars of Hercules,
Falkland,
Cupar, KY15 7AD
Tel: 01337-857749

Mr. Bruce Bennett

Provides contact between volunteers wanting to gain experience of working on organic holdings and farmers needing extra help. *

Women in Publishing Scotland

c/o Larousse plc,
7 Hopetoun Crescent,
Edinburgh, EH7 4AY
Tel: 0131-556-5929   Fax: 0131-556-5313

Ilona Bellos-Morison

Women's Auxiliary to the Baptist Union of Scotland

'Failte',
4 Argyle Street,
Dundee, DD4 7AL
Tel: 01382-43486

Mrs. G. C. Neilson, *Secretary*

Women's Forum Scotland

c/o IPMS,
18 Melville Terrace,
Stirling, FK8 2NQ
Tel: 01786-465999   Fax: 01786-465516

Ms. Helen Stevens, *Secretary*

Women's Health and Family Project

1 Russell Place,
Hilltown,
Dundee, DD3 7RU
Tel: 01382-810230

Ms. Sheena Keeley/Ms. Margaret Brown/
Sue Hunt

Counselling and support service, free pregnancy testing, library resource, drop-in service on health issues, space for meetings, and free workshops. Disabled access, on bus routes with friendly staff and confidentiality assured. A new stress management service has been introduced. *

Women's Legal Defence Fund

12 Picardy Place,
Room 5,
Edinburgh, EH1 3JT
Tel: 0131-557-1018

Ms. Shelley M. Mortimer

Women's Royal Voluntary Service (Scotland)

44 Albany Street,
Edinburgh, EH1 3QR
Tel: 0131-558-8028   Fax: 0131-558-8014

Mrs. Anne Boyd, *Director*

Scotland's largest active volunteering charity carrying out a wide selection of services to the community. *

Woodcraft Folk in Scotland

95 Morrison Street,
Glasgow, G5 8LP
Tel: 0141-429-0952

Woodland Trust

see The Woodland Trust

YLG (Scottish Branch)

Glenwood Library,
Glenwood Centre,
Glenrothes,
Fife, KY6 1PA
Tel: 01592-755866

Ms. Heather Sidney, *Secretary*

Yorkshire Terrier Club of Scotland

34 Kinmundy Drive,
Westhill,
Aberdeenshire, AB32 6SU
Tel: 01224-743034

Ms. S. Arroyo

Young Disabled on Holiday

Flat 4,
62 Stuart Park,
Corstorphine,
Edinburgh, EH12 8YE
Tel: 0131-339-8866

Ms. Alison Walker

The charity organises holidays in the UK and abroad for people aged 18–35 with a physical disability. Helpers are provided by the charity on a 1:1 basis. *

Young Enterprise Scotland

The White Cottage,
Torr Road,
Bridge of Weir, PA11 3BE
Tel: 01505-615200   Fax: 01505-615200

Mr. Owen McGhee, *Chief Executive*

Young Enterprise Scotland is an education/ business partnership with charitable status. We aim to give young people in the 15–19 age group a real business experience by allowing them the opportunity to run their own small business. *

Young Men's Christian Association (Scottish National Council)

James Love House,
11 Rutland Street,
Edinburgh, EH1 2AE
Tel: 0131-228-1464   Fax: 0131-228-5462

Rev. John Knox, *Director*

Young Scots for Independence

6 North Charlotte Street,
Edinburgh, EH2 4JH
Tel: 0131-226-3661

Ms. Ruth Sharp

The YSI is the official youth wing of the SNP and is committed to the establishment of an independent Scottish Republic within the European Union. *

Young Women's Christian Association (YWCA of Great Britain Scottish National Council)

7 Randolph Crescent,
Edinburgh, EH3 7TH
Tel: 0131-225-7592   Fax: 0131-467-7008

Ms. Isabel A. Carr, *Scottish Director*

The YWCA's priorities are young women aged 16–26 in the areas of personal and spiritual development and campaigning on poverty and violence against women. *

Youth Clubs Scotland

Balfour House,
19 Bonnington Grove,
Edinburgh, EH6 4BL
Tel: 0131-554-2561   Fax: 0131-555-5223

Carol Downie, *Chief Executive*

Youth Clubs Scotland is the largest non-uniformed voluntary youth organisation in Scotland providing innovative projects for young people between the ages of 8 and 21 years. *

Youth with a Mission (Scotland)

Stanely House,
14 Stanely Crescent,
Paisley, PA2 9LF
Tel: 0141-884-8844   Fax: 0141-884-3868

Mr. Stephen Mayers, *Director*

An international, interdenominational missionary organisation seeking to mobilise, train and send missionaries into the urban needs of Scotland as well as unreached people groups worldwide. *

YouthLink Scotland

Central Hall,
West Tollcross,
Edinburgh, EH3 9BP
Tel: 0131-229-0339   Fax: 0131-229-0339

Mr. George Johnston, *Chief Executive*

YouthLink Scotland works as the intermediary body to support and promote the work of voluntary youth organisations in Scotland, in the interests of young people. *

Keyword Indexes

The indexes that follow list organisations in one of 32 categories. In many cases organisations will appear in more than one index but it is often the case that some organisations are difficult to place in a particular category. In addition, where no reply has been received from a body, it has not always proven possible to place it in a keyword index. Every effort has been made to render lists that are accurate and useful, but in any event these indexes should provide a helpful starting point in searching for organisations in a certain sphere.

Agricultural and animal husbandry

Aberdeen Angus Cattle Society
Agricultural Education Association
Agricultural Training Board
Association for Veterinary Clinical Pharmacology &
    Therapeutics
Association of Deer Management Groups
Association of Scottish Bacon Curers
Association of Scottish District Salmon Fishery
    Boards

Association of Scottish Shellfish Growers
Association of Veterinary Anaesthetists of GB &
    Ireland
Ayrshire Cattle Society of Great Britain & Ireland
Bee Farmers Association
Blackface Sheep Breeders' Association
Bluefaced Leicester Sheep Breeders' Association
British Deer Society – Scottish Office (BDS)
British Romagnola Cattle Society
British Society of Animal Science
British Veterinary Association (Scottish Branch)
City Farms Scotland
Community Gardening Projects Scotland

Animal interest and welfare

Architecture

Charitable agencies

Children and young people

Education

Scottish Learning Difficulties Association
Scottish Legal Education Trust
Scottish Music Education Forum
Scottish Parent Teacher Council (SPTC)
Scottish Physical Education Association
Scottish Pre-Retirement Council
Scottish Pre-School Play Association (SPPA)
Scottish Prostitutes Education Project (SCOT-PEP)
Scottish Qualifications Authority
Scottish Road Safety Campaign
Scottish School of Forestry
Scottish Schools Ethos Network
Scottish Schools' Equipment Research Centre
Scottish Secondary Teachers' Association
Scottish Society for Northern Studies
Scottish Teacher Researcher Support Network
Scottish Training Advisory Service (STAS)
Scottish Training Foundation
Scottish Traveller Education Programme
Scottish Universities Council on Entrance
Scottish Universities Physical Education Association
Scottish Wider Access Programme (West)
Scottish Women's Rural Institutes
Sino Scottish Institute
Skill: National Bureau for Students with Disabilities, Scottish Branch
Socialist Educational Association
Student Awards Agency for Scotland
Swimming Teachers Association (Scottish Division)
Tangents
The Educational Institute of Scotland
The Prince's Trust – Action in Scotland
The Scottish Agricultural College
The Scottish Farm and Countryside Educational Trust
The Scottish Hotel School
The Scottish Office Education and Industry Department
The Scottish Society for Autistic Children (SSAC)
The Society for the Protection of Unborn Children (SPUC)
Turning Point Scotland
UNICEF in Scotland
Values into Action Scotland (VIA)
WEA Scotland (Workers' Educational Association) Scottish Association

Engineering and technology

Amalgamated Engineering & Electrical Union
Associated Society of Locomotive Engineers & Firemen
Association in Scotland to Research into Astronautics Ltd (ASTRA)
Association of British Solid Fuel Appliance Manufacturers

Association of Consulting Engineers, Scottish Group
Boiler and Radiator Manufacturers' Association Limited
British Ladder Manufacturers' Association
British Metals Federation (Scottish Office)
British Polyolefin Textiles Association
British Wind Energy Association, Scottish Branch
Building Research Establishment – Scottish Laboratory
Chart and Nautical Instrument Trade Association
Colliery Officials & Staff Area NUM
Domestic Heating Council
Electrical Power Engineers Association
Energy Action Scotland
Energy Design Advice Scheme
Engineering Council
Engineering Education Association
European Desalination Society
Federation of Civil Engineering Contractors
H.M. Inspectorate of Mines (Scotland and East England District)
Heating and Ventilating Contractors' Association (Scottish Region)
Industrial Society
Institute of Energy – Scottish Branch
Institute of Hydrology
Institute of Plumbing (Scotland)
Institute of Quarrying (Scotland)
Institution of Engineers & Shipbuilders in Scotland
Institution of Structural Engineers (Scottish Branch)
Iron & Steel Trades Confederation
METCOM Training (National Foundry & Engineering Training Association)
Minerals Engineering Society
Mining Institute of Scotland (formerly Institute of Mining & Metallurgy)
National Association of Colliery Overmen, Deputies and Shotfirers (Scottish Area)
National Metal Trades Federation
National Union of Mineworkers: Scotland Area
Offshore Contractors' Association
Offshore Manufacturers' & Constructors Association
Recycling Advisory Group Scotland (RAGS)
Royal Academy of Engineering
Royal Environmental Health Institute of Scotland
Royal Scottish Society of Arts (Science & Technology)
Scottish Architectural Education Trust
Scottish Association for Building Education & Training
Scottish Association for Metals
Scottish Collaborative Initiative in Optoelectronic Sciences
Scottish Council for Educational Technology (SCET)
Scottish Ecological Design Association
Scottish Electronic Manufacturing Centre
Scottish Employers' Council for the Clay Industries

Environment

Food

Gender issues

Government

Health and medicine

DIRECTORY OF SCOTLAND'S ORGANISATIONS

History

Housing

Abbeyfield Society for Scotland Limited
Chartered Institute of Housing in Scotland
Commissioner for Local Administration in Scotland
(The Ombudsman)
Employers in Voluntary Housing
Housing Association Ombudsman for Scotland
Key Housing Association
Kirk Care Housing Association
Positive Action in Housing Limited
Positive Housing
SHARE
Scottish Association of Care Home Owners
Scottish Christian Alliance Limited
Scottish Churches Housing Agency
Scottish Council for Single Homeless
Scottish Federation of Housing Associations (SFHA)
Scottish Homes
Scottish Housing Associations Charitable Trust
(SHACT)
Scottish National Housing and Town Planning
Council
Scottish Tenants Organisation (STO)
Scottish Veterans' Residences
Scottish Women's Aid (SWA)
Servite Housing (Scotland) Charitable Trust
Shelter Scotland
Sheltered Housing Owners' Confederation of
Scotland
Tenant Participation Advisory Service (TPAS)
Tenants Information Service

Information services and technology

ASLIB, Scottish Branch
ASSIST (Scotland)
Accounts Commission for Scotland
Advice Service Capability Scotland (ASCS)
Arthrogryposis Group
Association of Pension Lawyers – Scottish Group
Biomathematics and Statistics Scotland
Blissymbol Communication UK
British Association of Academic Phoneticians
(BAAP)
British Broadcasting Corporation
Broadcasting for Scotland Campaign
Citizens Advice Scotland
Common Services Agency
Companies House
Disability Information Scotland (Disablement
Information Advice Line)
Disability Scotland
Engender

European Movement (Scottish Council)
Federation of Independent Advice Centres (Scottish
Region)
General Register Office for Scotland
Immigration Advisory Service
Independent Schools Information Service
Institute of Information Scientists (Scottish Branch)
Israel Information Office in Scotland
Land Reform Scotland
Legal Services Agency (LSA)
Market Research Society in Scotland
Meteorological Office
Money Advice Scotland
National Library of Scotland
National Monuments Record of Scotland
National Network of Community Businesses
National Union of Journalists
Network Scotland
Ordnance Survey
Over-Count Drugs Information and Advice Agency
Registry of Friendly Societies
SCRAN (Scottish Cultural Resources Access
Network)
SSC Library
Saltire Society
Scotland's Churches Scheme
Scots Language Resource Centre Association
Scots Language Society
Scottish Advisory Committee on
Telecommunications (SACOT)
Scottish Association of Citizens Advice Bureaux
Scottish Association of Smallscale Broadcasters
Scottish Association of Track Statisticians
Scottish Avalanche Information Service
Scottish Cancer Registry
Scottish Community Care Forum
Scottish Conservation Bureau
Scottish Council for Research in Education
Scottish Criminal Record Office
Scottish Drugs Forum (SDF)
Scottish Human Computer Interaction Centre
Scottish Jewish Archives Centre
Scottish Law Librarians Group
Scottish Library & Information Council
Scottish Library Association
Scottish Local Government Information Unit
Scottish Meteorological Records
Scottish Milk Records Association
Scottish Music Information Centre
Scottish National Dictionary Association
Scottish Natural History Library
Scottish Pet Register
Scottish Poetry Library
Scottish Poisons Information Bureau
Scottish Pre-Retirement Council
Scottish Property Network
Scottish Record Office

Law

Society of Messengers-at-Arms and Sheriff Officers
Society of Solicitors in the Supreme Courts of
    Scotland
Tenant Participation Advisory Service (TPAS)
The Association of Scottish Police Superintendents
The Lawyers Christian Fellowship
The Scottish Assessors' Association
The Scottish Office, Solicitor's Office
The Society of Law Accountants in Scotland
Tranquilliser Addiction Solicitors' Group
United Kingdom Environmental Law Association,
    Scottish Branch
Women's Legal Defence Fund

Leisure and hobbies

Association of British Mountain Guides (Scotland)
Association of Model Railway Societies in Scotland
Association of Scottish Philatelic Societies
Association of Ski Schools in Great Britain
Association of Speakers Clubs
Basset Hound Club of Scotland
Bearded Collie Club of Scotland
Bernese Mountain Dog Club of Scotland
Boston Terrier Club of Scotland
Boys' and Girls' Clubs of Scotland
British & International Golf Greenkeepers
    Association
British Association for Shooting and Conservation
    (BASC)
British Association of Teachers of Dancing
British Disabled Water Ski Association
British Federation of Young Choirs
British Holiday & Home Parks Association
British Marine Industries Federation Scotland
British Numismatic Society
British Show Jumping Association (Scottish Branch)
British Ski and Snowboard Federation
British Sub Aqua Club (Scottish Federation)
British Waterways
British Wheel of Yoga
Bulldog Club of Scotland
Bullmastiff Society of Scotland
CHARM (Amateur Chamber Musicians Register)
Caledonian Bulldog Club
Caledonian Dandie Dinmont Terrier Club
Caledonian Railway Association
Camanachd Association
Camping and Caravanning Club (Scottish Region)
Chihuahua Club of Scotland
Chow Chow Club of Scotland
Clydesdale Horse Society of Great Britain & Ireland
Cocker Spaniel Club of Scotland
Committee for the Promotion of Angling for the
    Disabled
Costume Society of Scotland

Cricket Society of Scotland
Cyclists' Touring Club Scotland
Dalmatian Club of Scotland
Dance School of Scotland
Duke of Edinburgh's Award Scheme
Elkhound Association of Scotland
English Setter Society of Scotland
English Springer Spaniel Club of Scotland
Federation of Scottish Schools Sports Associations
Federation of Scottish Skateboarders
Feisean nan Gaidheal
Fitness Scotland
Flatcoated Retriever Club of Scotland
Fox Terrier Club of Scotland
Golden Retriever Club of Scotland
Gordon Setter Club of Scotland
Grand Lodge of Ancient Free & Accepted Masons
    of Scotland
Griffon Bruxellois Club
Guide Association Scotland
Haggis Hurling Association
Halliwick Association of Swimming Therapy
Handbell Ringers of Great Britain
Institute of Piping
Irish Red & White Setter Club of Scotland
Irish Setter Club of Scotland
Irish Terrier Club of Scotland
Japanese Akita Club of Scotland
KEEP WELL Services
Labrador Club of Scotland
Ladies' Golf Union
Lhasa Apso Club of Scotland
Medau Society of Great Britain & Northern Ireland
Morris Minor Owners' Club (Scotland)
Mountain Bothies Association
Mountain Rescue Committee of Scotland
Mountaineering Council of Scotland
National Baton Twirling Association of Scotland
National Federation of Music Societies (Scotland)
National Playing Fields Association (Scotland)
OYC Scotland (Ocean Youth Club Scotland)
Old English Sheepdog Club of Scotland
Outward Bound Scotland
PHAB Scotland
Papillon Club of Scotland
Pointer Club of Scotland
Poodle Club of Scotland
Pyrenean Mountain Dog Club of Scotland
Railway Society of Scotland
Ramblers' Association (Scotland)
Reality at Work Scotland (RAW)
Rhodesian Ridgeback Club of Scotland
Royal & Ancient Golf Club of St. Andrews
Royal Caledonian Curling Club
Royal Caledonian Horticultural Society
Royal Scottish Automobile Club (Motor Sport)
    Limited

Literature

Scottish Music Education Forum
Scottish Music Hall Society
Scottish Music Industry Association
Scottish Music Information Centre
Scottish Music Therapy Council
Scottish Musical Instrument Retailers' Association
Scottish Musicians' Benevolent Fund
Scottish Opera for All
Scottish Pipers' Association
Sonic Arts Network
The National Youth Orchestra of Scotland
The Royal Scottish Pipe Band Association
The Scottish Society of Composers
Traditional Music and Song Association of Scotland

Politics

Amnesty International
Broadcasting for Scotland Campaign
Business for Scotland
Communist Party of Scotland
Democracy for Scotland
Federation of Student Nationalists
Forthtell
Japan Society of Scotland
Justice and Peace Scotland
Medical Action for Global Security
Representation in Scotland, European Commission
Scotland Against Being Ruled by Europe (SABRE)
Scottish Campaign Against a Federal Europe
Scottish Campaign for Nuclear Disarmament
    (CND)
Scottish Conservative & Unionist Party
Scottish Cuba Defence Campaign
Scottish Educational Trust for United Nations &
    International Affairs
Scottish Friends of Palestine
Scottish Green Party
Scottish Green Student Network
Scottish Italian Association
Scottish Labour Action
Scottish Labour History Society
Scottish Labour Party
Scottish Labour Women's Caucus
Scottish Liberal Democrats
Scottish Militant Labour
Scottish National Party
Scottish Republican Forum
Scottish Republican Socialist Party
Scottish Tory Reform Group
Scottish Trade International
Scottish USSR Society
Scottish Unionist and Conservative Party
Socialist Educational Association
The European Movement (Scottish Council)
The Scottish China Association

The Scottish Patriots
Unit for the Study of Government in Scotland
Young Scots for Independence

Professions and trades

ASLIB, Scottish Branch
Amalgamated Engineering & Electrical Union
Arts Management Training Initiative (Scotland)
Associated Society of Locomotive Engineers &
    Firemen
Association of Chartered Certified Accountants
Association of Chief Architects of Scottish Local
    Authorities
Association of Directors of Education in Scotland
Association of Directors of Social Work
Association of Educational Advisers in Scotland
Association of Head Teachers in Scotland
Association of Installers & Unvented Hot Water
    Systems (Scotland & Ireland)
Association of Paediatric Anaesthetists of GB &
    Ireland
Association of Planning Supervisors Limited
Association of Public Analysts of Scotland
Association of Registrars of Scotland
Association of Scottish Dowsers
Association of Scottish Health Service Librarians
Association of Scottish Shellfish Growers
Association of University Teachers (Scotland)
Association of Veterinary Anaesthetists of GB &
    Ireland
Book Publishers' Representatives' Association -
    Scottish Branch
Booksellers Association: Scottish Branch
British & International Golf Greenkeepers
    Association
British Actors' Equity Association
British Association of Prosthetists and Orthotists
    (BAPO)
British Association of Social Workers (Scotland)
British Association of Teachers of Dancing
British Association of Teachers of the Deaf (Scottish
    Region)
British Dental Association (Scottish Office)
British Hospitality Association (Scotland)
British Medical Association (Scottish Office)
British Polyolefin Textiles Association
British Society of Hearing Therapists
British Union of Social Work Employees (Scottish
    Office)
British Veterinary Association (Scottish Branch)
Broadcasting, Entertainment, Cinematograph &
    Theatre Union (BECTU) (Scottish Office)
COSHEP (Committee of Scottish Higher Education
    Principals)
COSLA (Convention of Scottish Local Authorities)

Royal Pharmaceutical Society of Great Britain, Scottish Executive
Royal Town Planning Institute in Scotland
Royal United Kingdom Beneficent Association
SELECT
Sailors' Orphan Society of Scotland
Scotch Whisky Association
Scottish Artists & Artist Craftsmen
Scottish Association for Educational Management & Administration
Scottish Association of Amenity Supervisory Staff
Scottish Association of Community Education Staff
Scottish Association of Directors of Leisure Services
Scottish Association of Educational Technology Advisers
Scottish Association of Family Conciliation Services
Scottish Association of Geography Teachers
Scottish Association of Local Government Educational Psychologists
Scottish Association of Master Bakers
Scottish Association of Psychoanalytic Psychotherapists
Scottish Association of Publishers' Educational Representatives
Scottish Association of Sign Language Interpreters (SASLI)
Scottish Association of Speech & Drama Adjudicators
Scottish Association of Staff Development Officers
Scottish Association of Track Statisticians
Scottish Association of Volunteers Managers
Scottish Association of Watchmakers & Jewellers
Scottish Association of Writers
Scottish Basketmakers' Circle
Scottish Building Apprenticeship and Training Council
Scottish Building Contract Committee
Scottish Building Contractors' Association
Scottish Building Employers' Federation
Scottish Centre for Journalism Studies
Scottish Centre for Post Qualification Pharmaceutical Education
Scottish Centre for Studies in School Administration
Scottish Chiropodists Association
Scottish Cinematograph Trade Benevolent Fund
Scottish Colportage Society
Scottish Confederation of Trade & Industry
Scottish Consortium of Timber Frame Industries
Scottish Conveyancing & Executry Services Board
Scottish Corn Trade Association
Scottish Crofters Union (SCU)
Scottish Daily Newspaper Society
Scottish Dairy Trade Federation
Scottish Dairymen's Association
Scottish Decorators' Federation
Scottish Egg Trade Association
Scottish Federation of Grocers' & Wine Merchants' Association

Scottish Federation of Housing Associations (SFHA)
Scottish Federation of Meat Traders' Association
Scottish Federation of Merchant Tailors
Scottish Fire Service Training School
Scottish Fish Merchants Federation
Scottish Fisheries Protection Agency
Scottish Fishermen's Federation
Scottish Fishermen's Organisation
Scottish Fishery Group
Scottish Flour Millers Association
Scottish Football Managers & Coaches Association
Scottish Furniture Manufacturers' Association
Scottish Furniture Trades Benevolent Association
Scottish Glass Association
Scottish Glass Society
Scottish Grocers' Federation
Scottish Grocery Trade Employers' Association
Scottish Handmade Cheesemakers Association
Scottish Health Visitors' Association
Scottish House Furnishers' Federation
Scottish House-Builders Association
Scottish Institute of Reflexology
Scottish Joint Consultative Committee for Building
Scottish Joint Industry Board for the Electrical Contracting Industry
Scottish Joint Negotiating Committee for Teaching Staff in Further Education – Management Side
Scottish Joint Negotiating Committee for Teaching Staff in Further Education – Teachers' Side
Scottish Kippers and Herring Fishers Association
Scottish Knitwear Association
Scottish Lace and Window Furnishings Association
Scottish Law Agents' Society
Scottish Leather Producers' Association
Scottish Legal Services Ombudsman
Scottish Licensed Trade Association
Scottish Light Clothing Manufacturers' Association
Scottish Marine Trades' Association
Scottish Master Plasterers' Association
Scottish Master Slaters' & Roof Tilers' Association
Scottish Master Wrights & Builders Association
Scottish Meat Wholesalers Association
Scottish Medical Practices Committee
Scottish Milk Trade Federation
Scottish Mohair Producers Association
Scottish Motor Trade Association
Scottish Mountain Leader Training Board
Scottish Music Industry Association
Scottish Music Therapy Council
Scottish Musical Instrument Retailers' Association
Scottish Musicians' Benevolent Fund
Scottish Newspaper Publishers Association
Scottish Nursery Nurses' Examination Board
Scottish Offshore Training Association Limited
Scottish Parent Teacher Council (SPTC)
Scottish Pelagic Fishermen's Association
Scottish Personnel Services
Scottish Pharmaceutical Federation

Religion

Methodist Church in Scotland
Mission Aviation Fellowship
National Bible Society of Scotland
National Commission for Social Care (Catholic Church)
National Prayer Breakfast for Scotland
National Seminary in Scotland
Prison Fellowship Scotland
Reality at Work Scotland (RAW)
Reformed Presbyterian Church of Scotland
Religious Society of Friends (Quakers)
Roman Catholic Church in Scotland
Royal National Mission to Deep Sea Fishermen
Royal School of Church Music
SSC – A Club for the Youth of Scotland
Salvation Army
Scotland's Churches Scheme
Scottish Association for Church Music
Scottish Baptist College
Scottish Baptist Men's Movement
Scottish Catholic Historical Association
Scottish Catholic International Aid Fund (SCIAF)
Scottish Christian Alliance Limited
Scottish Christian Benevolent Trust
Scottish Church History Society
Scottish Churches Architectural Heritage Trust
Scottish Churches China Group
Scottish Churches Housing Agency
Scottish Churches World Exchange
Scottish Congregational Church
Scottish Congregational College
Scottish Counties Evangelistic Movement
Scottish Crusaders
Scottish Episcopal Church
Scottish Episcopal Renewal Fellowship
Scottish Evangelical Research Trust
Scottish Evangelical Theology Society (SETS)
Scottish Evangelistic Council
Scottish Gospel Outreach
Scottish Joint Committee on Religious and Moral Education
Scottish National Christian Endeavour Union
Scottish National Council of YMCAs
Scottish Prayer Book Society
Scottish Reformation Society
Scottish Reformed Church
Scottish Sunday School Union for Christian Education
Scripture Union Scotland (SU)
Seventh Day Adventist Church (Scottish Mission)
Soldiers' & Airmen's Scripture Readers Association
Synod of the Methodist Church in Scotland
The Boys' Brigade (BB)
The Church of Scotland Guild
The General Assembly of the Church of Scotland
The Girls' Brigade in Scotland
The Lawyers Christian Fellowship

Union of Catholic Mothers (Scottish National Council)
United Free Church of Scotland
Women's Auxiliary to the Baptist Union of Scotland
Young Men's Christian Association (Scottish National Council)
Young Women's Christian Association (YWCA of Great Britain Scottish National Council)
Youth with a Mission (Scotland)

Science

Association in Scotland to Research into Astronautics Ltd (ASTRA)
Association of Basic Science Teachers in Dentistry
Association of Public Analysts of Scotland
Biological Recording in Scotland Campaign (BRISC)
Biomathematics and Statistics Scotland
Botanical Society of Scotland
British Association of Clinical Anatomists
British Geological Survey – Scottish Office (BGS)
British Society for Medical & Dental Hypnosis, Scotland
British Society for the History of Pharmacy
British Society of Animal Science
British Society of Audiology (Scottish Branch)
British Trust for Myelin Project
British Wind Energy Association, Scottish Branch
Centre for Human Ecology
Chartered Institution of Water and Environmental Management (Scottish Branch)
Estuarine & Coastal Sciences Association
Institute of Biology, Scottish Branch
Institute of Energy – Scottish Branch
Institute of Food Science and Technology (Scottish Branch)
Institute of Hydrology
Institute of Information Scientists (Scottish Branch)
Macaulay Land Use Research Institute
Manufacturing, Science & Finance
Meningitis Research Foundation (MRF)
Resource Use Institute Limited
Royal Environmental Health Institute of Scotland
Royal Scottish Geographical Society
Royal Scottish Society of Arts (Science & Technology)
Scottish Association for Marine Science
Scottish Association for Metals
Scottish Biomedical Association
Scottish Biomolecules Group
Scottish Centre for Pollen Studies
Scottish Collaborative Initiative in Optoelectronic Sciences
Scottish Consumers' Association for Natural Food
Scottish Crop Research Institute

Social services

Sport and fitness

Travel and transport

Visual arts

SALVO – The Scottish Arts Network
Scottish Association of Speech & Drama
   Adjudicators
Scottish Ballet
Scottish Broadcast & Film Training Unit
Scottish Cinematograph Trade Benevolent Fund
Scottish Civic Entertainment Association
Scottish Community Drama Association
Scottish Dance Theatre
Scottish Ensemble
Scottish Glass Society
Scottish International Children's Festival
Scottish Mask & Puppet Centre
Scottish Music Hall Society
Scottish National Association of Youth Theatres
Scottish Official Board of Highland Dancing
Scottish Official Highland Dancing Association
Scottish Screen
Scottish Sculpture Trust (SST)
Scottish Sculpture Workshop
Scottish Theatre Marketing
Scottish Youth Dance Festival
Scottish Youth Theatre
The National Youth Theatre of Scotland
The Scottish Traditions of Dance Trust
Wallace Clan Trust for Scotland

Future editions of the Directory

If you would like your organisation to be considered for inclusion in future editions of this directory, please copy this page, complete the details and send the form to the publishers (the address can be found on page ii). Please also use this form if you wish to amend existing information about your organisation.

DIRECTORY OF SCOTLAND'S ORGANISATIONS

Organisation:

Address 1:

Address 2:

Address 3:

Address 4:

Post code:

Telephone: *Fax:*

e-mail:

Contact: *Position:*

Description (about 25 words):